BANGLADESH

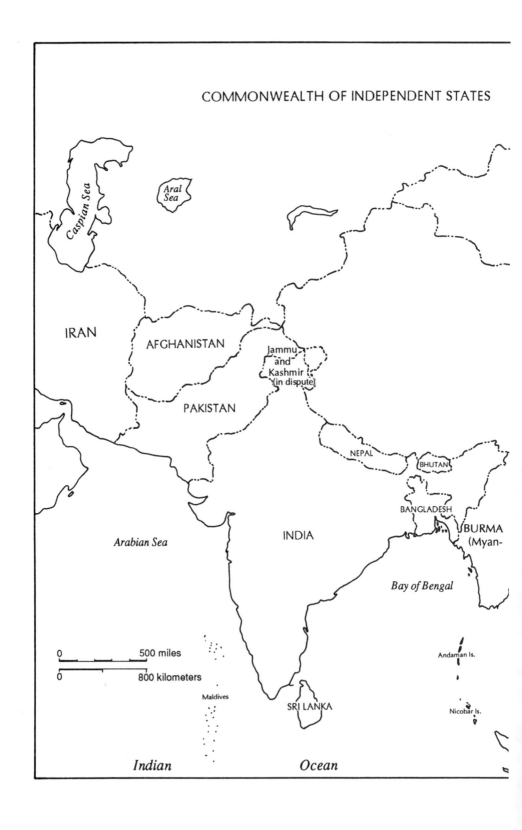

COMMONWEALTH OF INDEPENDENT STATES

Caspian Sea

Aral
Sea

IRAN

AFGHANISTAN

Jammu
and
Kashmir
(in dispute)

PAKISTAN

NEPAL

BHUTAN

BANGLADESH

BURMA
(Myan-

Arabian Sea

INDIA

Bay of Bengal

0   500 miles

0   800 kilometers

Andaman Is.

Maldives

SRI LANKA

Nicobar Is.

Indian   Ocean

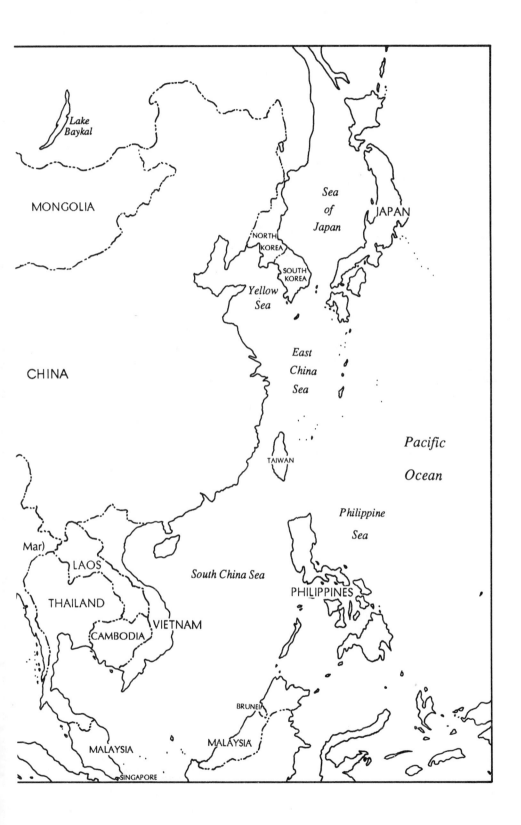

THE ESSENTIAL ASIA SERIES

◆

David I. Steinberg, editor

BANGLADESH

REFLECTIONS ON THE
WATER

James J. Novak

INDIANA UNIVERSITY PRESS
Bloomington • Indianapolis

The paper used in this publication meets the minimum requirements of American National Standard for Information Sciences—Permanence of Paper for Printed Library Materials, ANSI Z39.48-1984.

Manufactured in the United States of America .

Library of Congress Cataloging-in-Publication Data

Novak, James J. (James Jeremiah)
    Bangladesh : reflections on the water / James J. Novak.
        p.   cm.—(The Essential Asia series)
    Includes bibliographical references and index.
    ISBN 0-253-34121-3 (cloth : alk. paper).
    1. Bangladesh.   I. Title.   II. Series.
DS393.4.N68   1993
954.92—dc20   92-41794
            1 2 3 4 5 97 96 95 94 93

For Naomi:
My wife, friend, and partner in writing ✦

CONTENTS

FOREWORD

David I. Steinberg

A DEMOCRACY REQUIRES AN EDUCATED AND INFORMED PUBLIC. This dictum applies
as much to foreign policy as to domestic affairs. Yet the American educational system as a whole has sadly neglected foreign affairs and shown little
interest in peoples of other countries, although recently it has shown some
improvement.

This lack of interest is especially unfortunate in the case of Asia. Asians
comprise more than half the world's population, and live in the fastest growing and most economically dynamic area of the globe. In this century, the
United States has fought a series of wars in Asia the causes and ramifications
of which are still murky to most of the public. Asians have also become a
significant minority in U.S. society. There are thus a variety of urgent reasons for better understanding Asia.

There is little excuse for our neglect of the subject. Asia has extremely
rich written records, sophisticated oral traditions, extensive archaeological
remains, and even a several-centuries'-old tradition of Western scholarship
dealing with many parts of the region. There is no reason why the general,
informed public should not have access to better information on the diverse
societies and cultures of Asia.

Part of the problem is who does the writing. Most works by academicians
are so specialized as to be unapproachable, often abstruse, miasmic, inacces-
sible, and expensive. Those of us in academe and related fields often make
excuses for our own and our colleagues' propensity for using arcane and
specialist language. Through our writing, we intend not only to convey
knowledge precisely, but also to ratify our sense of membership in the particular intellectual clan reflecting our academic disciplines or research interests.
Although in the social sciences we may be inured to these pontifications,
which we assume will assist in our professional advancement and other desid-
erata, to inflict them on the public inhibits rather than fosters the spread of
knowledge and understanding that we had hoped to impart.

Many years ago I was struck by the fact that an intelligent and engag-
ingly written body of literature existed on a number of European societies,
engrossing both the intellect and the emotions and gracefully conveying to
the general reader the complexities of those societies. Such volumes combine

the accuracy of social science research with the charm of literature, two attributes that need not be in conflict. I was particularly impressed by Barzini's *The Italians*. Writing of such caliber is pitifully lacking for Asia.

Occasionally someone has asked me what single volume one might read for insight into a particular Asian society. I have often been hard pressed to respond, suspecting that their reading time would be relegated to the long airplane passage to Asia, punctuated by meals, movies, and mewling infants. Further, many books, however valid, seemed outdated. Recommending, for example, what I considered to be the best work on Burma—published in 1882—did not seem to be the answer. Neither did suggesting a thoughtful but turgid text, useful in a graduate or undergraduate course for its accurate detail but excruciating in its pace. Today there is a pressing need to convey to the educated generalist the sense of Asian societies, or at least their most salient characteristics. To do this requires sensitivity both to the society studied and to the proclivities of each author and his or her vision of such a culture. To construct, even if it were possible, a general formula for a series of volumes on disparate societies that would reflect the idiosyncratic diversity of both the societies and the authors seems undesirable.

With the encouragement of the Indiana University Press, we have therefore stimulated a number of authors to write works that maintain individuality and at the same time explain the society in question. Asia *is* essential now more than ever, and we hope this series will highlight that fact and help English-speaking readers to understand the countries covered.

Bangladesh, insofar as it is in our consciousness, often conjures up images of cyclones, deprivation, famine, and the ultimate calamities. These impressions, as much as they may be correct at any single point in time, are misleading, leaving out a past and present both rich and vibrant. James Novak has balanced these current impressions with a broad historical look at what once was, and is again becoming, a prosperous and important regional center, making us aware that the artificial, modern borders imposed by politics mask an important, culturally diverse regional context that has cried out for explication.

PREFACE

THE CHAPTERS THAT MAKE UP THIS BOOK are the result of a combination of travel and living in Bangladesh, of endless conversations with scholars and actors in Bangladesh history, and of as wide a reading of the sources as a nonscholar can manage. It is not a book of original research so much as an interpretive one based on primary and secondary research sources.

At the outset, let it be said that the author has been making trips to Bangladesh for more than twenty years, having first been attracted to that part of Bengal by a mural he saw as a child of eight on the wall of the main cafeteria at the University of Notre Dame at South Bend when his brother Michael entered the seminary there in 1947. That mural portrays a Bengali jungle scene with missionaries working among the people, who are depicted in native dress seeking health care and education. The missionaries are dressed in white and wear sun helmets; their costume suggests that the painting dates at least to the 1930s. Viewed in the light of today's sensitivities, it is downright *pukka sahib* embarrassing. Nevertheless, the picture was powerful enough to set two young boys wondering. Richard, my next-oldest brother, went to East Pakistan (now Bangladesh) first, many years later, as a Holy Cross missionary; he was followed eventually by this author. In the intervening years, thoughts of Bengal never left my family for long, because the Holy Cross Fathers had a mission there and they mailed us regular appeals for funds; we also received bits of information from visiting missionaries on leave. To this knowledge I added the reading which young persons will do on things that interest them. And as a Notre Dame graduate student, I often sat under that mural, having lunch.

It was upon completion of his first priestly studies in 1955 that Richard made a vow to serve ultimately as a missionary in East Pakistan. When he announced that vow to my father, a strange thing occurred. After we left the Novitiate House in Bennington, Vermont, my father suddenly, and uncharacteristically, pulled our car to the roadside and stopped. Then he cried. Recovering his composure, he told me he had had a vision that had seemed so real: he had seen my brother stabbed. As my father was a man of intuition but not of visions, this demonstration of emotion greatly impressed me. Nearly nine years later, in January 1964, while I was serving in the U.S. Army in Germany, my father called to say that Richard had been murdered in East Pakistan. "By stabbing?" I asked. "How did you know?" my father replied. I reminded him of his vision; he had forgotten. (It is, by the way, to my parents' credit that they pleaded for leniency for the two men convicted of Richard's murder. Their plea was heeded. After serving seven years in jail, they were released in 1971 in a general prisoner amnesty when Bangladesh achieved independence from Pakistan.)

The death of Richard, a person of extreme gentleness and mischievous wit, precipitated my efforts to read as much as possible about Pakistan, both East and West, with the intention of going there some day. Henceforth, books, magazine articles, and conversations with visiting Bengalis became a staple of my life. After I left the army, my employment with Pfizer, a multinational pharmaceutical company, not only brought me into contact with Pakistanis but also in the early 1970s took me to live in Hong Kong, where travel to Bangladesh became part of my job. Thereafter my studies increased as I met more people and had better guidance in my reading. I started visiting Bangladesh nearly every year, and after leaving the business world, I lived there as representative of the Asia Foundation. In that capacity I met many Bangladesh scholars, politicians, and journalists. I also became acquainted with the libraries, especially at the universities. I left Dhaka after suffering a heart attack in 1985, but my annual visits recommenced in 1988, each of them lasting two or more months.

Needless to say, one does not concentrate on a country like this one unless it reflects love. And indeed, more than once I vowed not to write about Bangladesh because I felt that objectivity would escape me. Anyone who reads this book will confirm that it has. For me, Bangladesh is a nation more loved than analyzed. It was with joy that I witnessed the posting (in the summer of 1992) of my son, Joseph, to Bangladesh as a junior U.S. Foreign Service officer, the third family member in two generations to be posted there.

Turning to those who particularly helped make this book a reality, I am especially grateful to Professor Richard Baxter Eaton for many pleasant evenings spent on my terrace in Banani, Dhaka in between his forays into the documents of early East Bengal. Richard is a first-rate scholar whose own book on Bangladesh is in press (University of California Press, 1993) as I write. It was his enthusiasm for the country that helped give me the courage to write about the subject. I also am indebted to Professor Rafiuddin Ahmed of Chittagong and Cornell universities for many discussions, arguments, and incredibly informative seminars in 1982–85 on Islam in Bangladesh and, more recently, for kindly reading the manuscript and making suggestions to eliminate errors, to correct spellings, and to place certain incidents into better perspective.

This book also owes much to the skills and help of the South Asia Library, at the Van Pelt Library, University of Pennsylvania, especially to Kanta Bhatia, a most amazing bibliophile on the subject of South Asia. My thanks also to Dr. Abdul Mommen Choudhury of Dhaka University and the

Dhaka University Library for his help in making books available to me for use in the research room and for his many conversations on books and research information on Bangladesh. I also must thank Fazlul Halim Chowdhury, vice chancellor of Dhaka University, for his introduction to the university's library system and for helping introduce me to research facilities in Bangladesh. Also, Qazi Jalaluddin Ahmed, former secretary of education, proved to be an immense aid in my research, and Professor Kabir Chowdhury of Dhaka University helped me understand the role of poets in the political thought of Bangladesh.

In another vein, I am indebted to my late Uncle Jacob Rock ("Yakoob" in some circles privileged to have known him), chief financial officer of Rock Furniture of New York City, who bequeathed to me his dear friend, Sadri Ispahani, chairman of Ispahani Industries, Ltd., who in recent years has repeatedly and generously provided me with house, home, and close friendship in his family circle in Magh Bazaar, Dhaka. Also, Sadri's best friend and my friend, Humayan Kabir of Pfizer, must be acknowledged for twenty years' assistance in understanding Bangladesh. Likewise deserving of my gratitude is the author and former Bangladeshi minister A. M. A. Muhith, who gave me invaluable insights into Bangladeshi history on many a wintry evening in New York while he suffered through an enforced political exile and I was enmeshed in my research. The book also owes much to the emotion-filled sojourn in New York of Nellie and Mohammad Ikramullah while their son, Shakib ("Rajan"), was treated for leukemia. A bright, beautiful, wonderful child, Rajan died in 1988, aged five years. He too helped inspire this author.

In addition, this book needed the interjection of David Steinberg, Distinguished Professor of Burmese Studies at Georgetown University, who introduced this book's author to its publisher and whose encouragement and assistance proved pivotal in making this book what it is, a work based on research and personal experience and eschewing the jargon of social science. David has proved to be a real friend whose contribution will not be forgotten, coming as it did when the author had given up all hope. Likewise, John Gallman, director of Indiana University Press, proved to be a kind, wise, and positive editor who helped make the manuscript much better. And for the wonderful jacket photograph I am grateful to the esteemed Bangladeshi photographer H. M. Ameer.

Anyone who knows me would guffaw if I failed to acknowledge my wife, Naomi Rock Novak, who not only edits and critiques my works but also makes certain they get done. Without her assistance the book would not have been completed. Much of what is good and human in this work is a result of her inspiration and encouragement.

Needless to say, responsibility for the book, including its weaknesses, is my own, and I make reference to those who have helped only to indicate my thanks for their contributions.

BANGLADESH

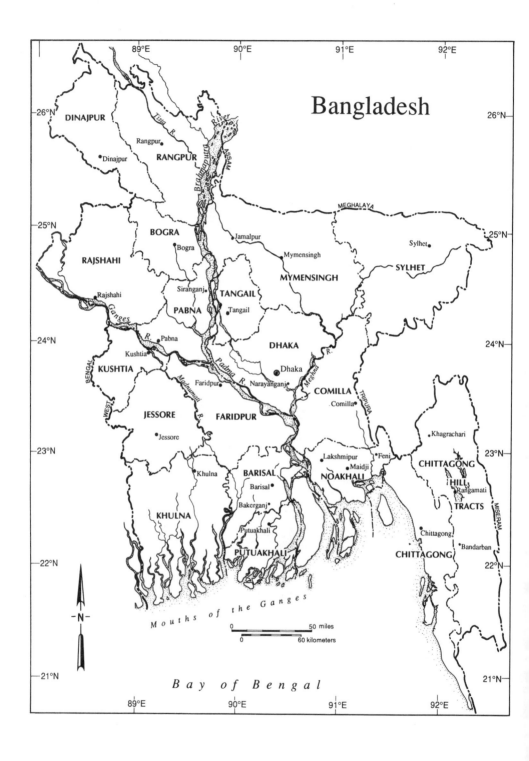

1

The Scene

Every year they come. Usually in winter, indeed most of them in winter. When the weather is nice. They try to avoid the hot and rainy season, which comes in May and the summer. They come in winter because the winters are delightful, like those of Florida and North Africa and because they want to get away from winters in Tokyo, Geneva, or New York. Not tourists you see. But mostly officials. Officials of the World Bank or the International Monetary Fund, officials of such U.N. agencies as UNICEF or UNDP or of the various governmental aid agencies like USAID, UK-ODA, JICA, and Swedish, Canadian, and Australian CIDA. Scattered in among them are the buyers for the retail stores who come to place orders for summer lines, buyers from K Mart or other outlets in the United States and Europe who carry sketchbooks with the latest fashions they want made here. Salesmen come also, to get in on the growing import trade or to place bids on aid-financed projects. Reporters come to do pieces on poverty, on elections, on the most recent flood or disaster. A few scholars come, serious of mien, analytical of eye.

The tide of visitors is not high enough even at peak to overfill the two main hotels in Dhaka, unless, of course, there is a conference. Dhaka (formerly spelled Dacca) does get conferences: meetings of the Non-Aligned Nations, the Least Developed Nations, the Islamic Nations. And from time to time a visitor of great importance descends: the queen of England, the French president, the prime minister of Pakistan, the defense minister of China. The two international hotels cope pretty well with the influx; still, movement is afoot to build a third big hotel.

Few visitors come just to see the country or the people. Most come because Bangladesh is part of their job. Plain old tourists and loving friends rarely come. Rather, nearly everyone has an angle. Most enter with great courtesy, of course, at first; but most have a limited schedule and want what they came for—usually some commitment, some set of facts, some measurement. If they do not get it, the courtesy fades and they may become quite choleric. Even the Japanese sometimes lose their stoic calm.

These are important and determined officials. And they guess rightly that Bangladeshis want to give them what they want. After all, Bangladesh is a developing country, one of the world's poorest, with a per capita income of about $200 annually and a population growth rate of 2.4 percent (which means that the population will double in about twenty-nine years). No Bangladeshi is in a position to tell any foreign official to go to hell. The locals must be nice, and they have become adept at it. So even if the visitors don't come to see Bangladesh or its inhabitants, at least Bangladeshis get to see them and, by osmosis, to learn a few things. Maybe the outsiders learn as well, even if they'd never admit it.

Generically, there are two kinds of visitors these days. (No one since 1947–49 has tried to immigrate, except for the rare spouse of a Bangladeshi. Even these immigrants keep their original passports.) The first kind of visitor is the old-timer who has visited at least once before and always is looking for changes since the last visit. Anyone who has visited before is an expert when he or she returns. The second kind is the first-time visitor, determined to be nice and to like the place. Basically, however, the two are alike: they have come for a purpose and intend to achieve it.

The truth is that all foreigners are visitors. They are not part of the scene. They do not adapt—except for the missionaries, and they are not many. The British, who ruled this land for nearly 190 years, never intended to put down roots. With few exceptions, after a lifetime of work they did not stay on. They always went home to retire. Even the Punjabis between 1947 and 1971, when Bangladesh was part of Pakistan, never stayed except for a few "unfortunates" who married in. And so it is today, forty-five years after the British left and twenty years after the Pakistanis left: the visitors have no intention of staying; indeed, they stay for three or four years, not even the working lifetime of the British, and then go home. They come as and remain visitors, whether they speak the language or not. Even those who come for repeat visits intend to leave.

Most visitors are men, and that is as it has always been, although in recent years many more are women. Many of the women are older, less attractive than the diplomats' wives and certainly less attractive than the screen models viewed here on VCRs. The same is true of the men. Except for some young volunteers with various charitable agencies, most look like officials: a little plump, balding, and knobby of knee. The women, as a rule, dress badly; the men can be divided into suit-and-tie and leisure-suit class, the former usually more important. (Although fashions change, and just a few years ago the safari or leisure suit was the sign of the sophisticated traveler.) Sitting in the hotel lobby one can watch this parade of visitors.

What has changed most over the years is that whereas once most visitors were Westerners, today the mix is about 50 percent from the East. The East Asians now are unquestionably a major factor, with South Koreans, Japanese, and Singaporeans predominating. To supply Bangladesh's military needs, the mainland Chinese have stepped in, along with the British, of course. The Japanese and Chinese are the greatest aid-givers, although the latter give mostly military aid and sell more military hardware than they give, while the South Koreans and Singaporeans are major players on the commercial front, especially in the garment, electronics, auto, and other import industries. As is true throughout the Third World, the presence of East Asians is a sign of the upbeat nature of the economy. The Americans, Russians, and British, once such large factors, are receding from view, with big projects firmly in the hands of the Japanese—the new fertilizer factory in Chittagong, for example, and the new first-time-ever bridge on the Meghna River, opened in 1990. Even the swimming pool at the country's poshest golf club, at Kurmitolah, was built with Japanese government aid.

Perhaps only 10 percent of the visitors ever leave Dhaka to see the rest of the country. Indeed, even among aid agency officials, only a tiny percentage visit the countryside, so few that making reservations at provincial hotels is unnecessary. Except for missionaries and representatives of private voluntary agencies, few visitors, Western or East Asian, ever visit the hinterland, the exceptions being the port city of Chittagong and Ghorasal, where there is a major power station and a noticeable Soviet presence. Otherwise, one may say that the number of foreigners decreases geometrically in direct proportion to the distance arithmetically one is from the hotel and north Dhaka. In fact, most foreign residents live almost within walking distance of the international airport. The same is true with autos: the farther one gets from Dhaka, and the decline begins about ten miles from the city, the fewer the autos, Rangerovers, or Pajeros. The truth is that the absence of autos reflects not only the absence of foreigners but also the absence of Bangladeshis involved with foreigners. Dhaka itself is crammed with traffic, but the vehicles virtually disappear when one reaches Arica, about two hours north. Even Chittagong, the second largest city and the biggest, most active port, has comparatively few cars.

The same could be said of nearly every developing country that has not reached the exalted category of newly industrialized, as have South Korea, Taiwan, Singapore, Malaysia, Hong Kong, and most recently, Thailand— countries which are graduating into the ranks of the Developed World. Others, such as India, Pakistan, Bangladesh, Vietnam, Cambodia, Laos, the

Philippines, and parts of Indonesia, are still in the Third World. They have a large foreign presence not of businessmen but of officials involved in economic development, particularly in dispensing aid. "Aid" is the kind of activity that attracts officials and creates capital cities that cater to them. Nearly everything in Bangladesh is built with aid: even the hotels and the golf courses at Kurmitolah and Chittagong were financed by Food-for-Work wheat. Ninety percent of all development activities are financed by aid.

And Bangladesh is an aid-recipient nation, having absorbed a total of $16 billion since 1972—some $800 million annually for 110 million people, or about $8 per capita. Pledges of aid are far greater than $800 million per year, but only so much can be absorbed. The total is paltry compared to the $3 billion received by Israel with its three million people, or the $2 billion plus that goes to Egypt, or the billions in loans to Latin American countries that are being written off by the world's banks. Nevertheless, Bangladesh's aid is considerable if it is realized that the government collects almost no taxes and that aid finances nearly all the country's development activities. Since the government receives the aid, it controls most of the nation's spending power. And that explains the importance of Dhaka, since Dhaka is the capital. Like the disappearing traffic as one heads away from the capital, everything that is not government is proportionately cash-poor to the degree that it is removed from government.

Because the government is so aid-dependent and will not sufficiently tax its own people, the foreign officials who come for a few weeks or a few years have a disproportionate say in what the government does—or even thinks. A Robert McNamara or some other high banking officials may not make all the guest lists in Washington, but when they visit Dhaka they can make the knees of the nation's most high and serene officials knock. And, by the way, some Bangladeshi males have a mannerism of shaking their knees back and forth when they sit, as if they are cold.

Annual World Bank and International Monetary Fund consortium reports are major political news in Bangladesh, and the heads of finance ministers and civil service secretaries roll when the reports are negative. Indeed, no government could long stand against the combined dislike of all the national and international aid-givers. Not only do these viceroys of charity dictate the country's macroeconomic policy; they also set quotas for minorities in government employ and try to intervene in the most intimate aspects of life by sending out scores of thousands of "motivators" to tell wives to take pills and husbands to wear condoms. They dictate where and when bridges are built, such as the recent debate over the Jamuna Bridge, and they determine the duties to be charged on imports. In short, there is no aspect of life they do not oversee. They even intervene in elections by sending observers to make sure that the government they aid does not cheat—and, some believe, to ensure victory for the party of their choice.

Aid has created a style called Pajero. At one time the style was Land Rover and Toyota Land Cruiser, imitation Jeeps. But now Pajeros are in, providing they have air conditioning, luxury suspension systems, specially designed comfortable seats, and stereo systems: those are the real signs of wealth in Dhaka. The Mercedes and the Toyota Crown, though still fashionable, lack the sense of action and sportiness of the Pajero. Besides, the latter reeks of aid money and government connections, as it connotes someone who, from time to time, must take very important people into the countryside. Not that many Pajeros actually travel to the countryside. Rather, they make travel on some of the bumpier roads more comfortable for the bottoms of people whose careers depend on that part of their anatomy. If one sees a convoy of such vehicles, one knows that the visitor is high-powered; in convoy, the ranking is done by vehicle type: Pajeros are tops, Nissan Patrols are for the middle level, and Land Cruisers or Land Rovers are good enough for the lesser lights.

Vehicle type signals just one of the differentiations between visiting officials and their hired consultants. Officials come to make or convey decisions. They seldom do any real work but are briefed up to speed by lower officials who work for them. Significantly, such officials depend on a lower class, called consultants. It is easy to tell them apart: the first group wears suits and ties; the second sports safari suits.

In the world of aid, almost no real work is done by officials. Aid agencies contract with consulting firms to identify, design, cost out, and implement projects, and these firms in turn provide economists, engineers, socioeconomists, costing estimators, computer experts, and population-control experts. The consultants mostly are a rather dull lot. Often visiting the country only for short periods, they measure, count, analyze, and define some aspect of the aid enterprise, much as physicians gather lab reports on the quivering hunk of flesh that has been referred to them. Consultants go all over the world. Many have worked in fifty or more countries, always staying in first-class hotels just like those in Dhaka and dealing with the same kind of officials. They have seen it all, heard it all, and have dealt with aid-wallahs before. No wonder they're dull. They're often bored.

Before they come, the consultants are well briefed on what is expected of them and what conclusions are being sought. Therefore they spend their time developing reports the officials want to see. They are not naïve; they know that aid officials have certain agendas for their clients. And consultants, who work on daily wages, albeit quite high ones, are not about to lose their friendliness with the aid agencies that hire them. One cannot imagine a Swedish aid agency, for example, recommending a project that did not use Swedish products. The Swedes are no worse than anyone else.

And that, of course, is the problem. For the project often begins with the product, and the aid agency, responding to its political masters, will look for projects that sell the product. If Holland has excess capacity in its machine-tool industry or Britain wants to dispose of used telephone exchanges from Birmingham (two real examples), the aid agency will offer to give these items as aid. The United States donates food aid largely because it is cheaper to give it away than to store it. And God help the USAID director who recommends curtailing food aid. He will face the wrath of the U.S. farm lobby. In worse trouble would be the consultant who recommends any policy that goes against first his country's projects and second any product the officials are pushing. The trouble with aid, then, is that it seldom is given based on the recipient's priorities. And while that is not always bad, in Bangladesh it is serious, as often the country's leaders see other priorities.

As Bangladesh is poor, it cannot refuse any aid, even if a given project goes against its interest. American food, for instance, is given to the government, which sells it on the open market to raise cash to cover its deficit. The first evil arising from this system is that food prices are artificially depressed. That hurts 90 percent of the local farmers, most of whom have very small tracts of land. It also is bad because generous food aid makes it unnecessary for the Bangladesh government to collect taxes. Also, much of the food aid is given in kind: workers on highways are paid in pounds of grain, which they either eat or sell to dealers for cash. It is hard to pay one's rent in grain. Indeed, one UNDP official noted that aid to Bangladesh was enough to cover all development expenditures plus the government's entire budget.

Thus aid often hurts the farmers and manufacturers and corrupts the political processes. For what is the sense of democracy if the people are not required and refuse to pay taxes? One retired minister recently noted that except for excise taxes and tariffs, the cost of collecting the taxes that *are* collected equals the revenue. As for the farmers, who pay no land tax and seldom pay income tax, they often come out net winners. Loans they have taken are forgiven by the aid-financed government, so they don't have to pay, for instance, for that tubewell they bought last year. Businesses often do not pay their government debts, knowing that sooner or later the aid-givers will refinance the banking system and past loans will be written off. Such debt forgiveness and lack of taxation fosters an unhealthy sense of irresponsibility toward scarce capital and an attitude that the aid-givers can afford to absorb the cost. Indeed, the notion that debts do not have to be repaid affects most classes of people, to the detriment of the country.

And lest anyone suspect that the court system is deliberately starved of funds so as to make legal attempts to collect impossible, one incident will be instructive. Not long ago, a minister of industry shouted at a judge for deliberately delaying a court case against a defaulter. So upset was the minister that he had a heart attack that night.

Thus foreign aid is the equivalent of Eve's apple to Bangladeshi elites.

One of the country's noted economists has compared aid to an intravenous injection of addicting narcotics.

All this does not mean that all aid has been wasted. On the contrary, Bangladesh is richer by far today than at any other time in its history. It has been nearly half a century since the last famine and eighteen years since the last serious food scare, when a near-famine occurred. In fact, in 1989 the rice crop for 110 million people was nineteen million tons, compared to eight million tons for seventy-five million people at independence in 1971. Incredibly, then, food output has been growing faster than population. Although the 1989 harvest was abnormally high by about 10 percent, it was enough to provide 1.1 pounds of dry rice daily for every man, woman, and child. Consider how much cooked rice one pound of dry rice produces: the ratio is about four to one.

Furthermore, the electric system built with help from the United States and modeled on its rural electrification schemes, now reaches around the country, so that every district and subdistrict has power, although only 20 percent of the sixty-five thousand villages so far have formed cooperatives and tapped in. Roads too are much improved, and bridges are being built for the first time over the largest rivers—the Meghna, Gumti, Jamuna, and Karnaphuli—thus reducing long waits for crowded ferries. Tubewells are found everywhere, their engines used to power many smaller boats and rice-processing equipment. Also thanks to aid, there are huge fertilizer factories and power-generating plants, fueled by local natural gas. And the railroads have upgraded equipment and the airports are well maintained.

In every way and in every aspect of life the nation is better off than twenty, ten, even five years ago. People live longer, most eat more, and nearly everyone is better dressed and has greater access to modern communications and medicines. Moreover, trains, boats, buses, and airplanes have more connections with other parts of the country and the world. And remember, Bangladeshis don't even tax themselves nor do they intend to. Only aid accounts for much of this change.

There's not a chance that the country is ready to relinquish aid. Far too many people are living on the edge of disaster for that. Furthermore, it is wrong to maintain, as some do, that all aid is a waste or that most of it goes to the rich. Some is wasted. Some goes to the rich. But most of it helps make life easier than at any time since the dreadful famine of 1943 forced the country to its knees. At that time, when the people needed aid, they received little; five million people died. Five million.

And do not doubt, even for a moment, that Bangladeshis who are serious about themselves and their country are anything but grateful for the aid. But more of that later.

Nevertheless, aid is not the only reality. Despite its reputation as the world's poorest nation, Bangladesh has a business sector, which over the years has played a major role in its development.

For many years, jute and tea were the main earners of foreign exchange and therefore the major source of real resources for financing imports of badly needed foreign goods. And for much of the country's recent history, which begins with the British conquest in 1757, tea and jute brought a host of visitors from Threadneedle Street in London, where tea is traded, or from Dundee, Scotland, the world's jute-processing capital. In recent years the British have sold turboprop jets for the domestic air routes.

Given the British influence in these industries, there is a certain gentility to the travelers who come, a certain old-fashioned plantation gentility of well-dressed men and women, of gin and tonic and good Scotch sundowners, of Scottish or English accents, of white flannel trousers and blazers, of high tea, lawn parties, and tennis.

To this day, most such travelers are guests of the old tea and jute families, have dinner at the British High Commission, and travel to Kulaura, Satgaon, Ghazipur, Mirzapur, Narayanganj, Karnaphuli, or Chittagong to stay on the plantations or at the quarters of the processing plants. And there are meetings at the Tea and Jute exchanges as well as at the tea board and jute board. Golf, tennis, croquet. In winter, there's boar hunting in the tea areas, duck hunting on the major rivers. (Though hunting was outlawed recently, if you know the right people it's still possible, especially duck hunting on the rivers.)

For many years, jute was Bangladesh's chief export. Buyers came from around the world to obtain this golden fiber, to be made into sacking for grain or tobacco, or used as carpet backing or in wartime as sacking for sandbags and netting for camouflage. Jute is native to Bangladesh, where it has been cultivated from time immemorial. It became a mass-production item in the nineteenth century when the Dutch, who had a trading station in Chinsura (now in India), began to use it to ship coffee from their colonies in what is now Indonesia. A parallel development of jute production technology in Dundee, Scotland, helped create a worldwide demand for jute, so that at one time all grain sold on the world market and most cotton bales had to be baled in burlap made of jute. In 1854 the first jute factory was built in India, and Dundee gradually became a manufacturing center for jute finishing equipment, while the processing came to India and, after Pakistan separated from India, to what is now Bangladesh. Indeed, the move to processing in the 1950s was the beginning of the first real industry in this country in modern times, although Bangladesh always has been the world's largest jute producer.

For two centuries jute was a major cash crop for farmers. In the nineteenth century it became the "golden crop," not only because of its yellow flower but also because of increasing world demand. Farmers would calculate each year, according to a rule of thumb, how much land they would devote to rice versus jute, depending on the previous year's prices.

Jute is planted in the dry season from April to June and harvested after the end of July, when the water is still deep in the fields but after jute's flower wilts. The monetary wealth created by jute contributed to one of Bangladesh's golden ages, 1890 to 1910. That was during British rule, when this section was one of the most stable, educated, and forward parts of India and provided one-third of the revenues of Britain's Indian Empire.

Jute is not a plantation crop like tea but a small-holder's cash crop. In recent years, shrinking demand and, worse, declining prices due to the emergence of synthetics, have been major factors in the decline of monetary wealth among Bangladesh's farmers. In fact, jute's astoundingly low price on world markets is the primary cause today of poverty in the countryside. No reliable crop has been found to replace it. The decline of jute accounts, too, for the displacement of many small landowners and the movement of many landless families to cities. This jute crisis has reduced the need for cash-paid labor and has formed the backbone of a food-for-labor phenomenon, wherein the poorest women are paid with a few pounds of wheat to do the heaviest, meanest jobs. That is one of the most degrading aspects of the nation's poverty, really a form of aid-financed slavery. For is not payment in kind the hallmark of slavery? The need for the presence of food-for-work is directly related to the fall of jute, due to the cash shortage.

Yet the jute industry struggles on. Huge factories, which no longer produce anything but still employ workers through government subsidies financed by aid, keep the industry in the doldrums. There is too much capacity, too much produced, and too many government-owned mills, again financed by aid, to make profits obtainable. But the government fears the layoffs, and the industry limps on with little spent on research and development to help this natural, biodegradable product compete against environmentally damaging synthetic substitutes. Jute is an industry in need of vigorous leadership, but it is handcuffed by aid-financed subsidies to avoid hard political choices.

Tea, as one might expect, also was developed by the British. It was native to Bengal's hilly countryside, especially along the eastern borders near Assam in India. It is possible that even China got its first tea from Bengal. Discovering tea plants growing wild in the nineteenth century, the British turned them into plantations. Soon the tiny hills were carpeted with tea bushes planted under the cover of widely placed shade trees. Tea gardens are green oases that allow shafts of golden sun to fall upon the women in their bright-colored dresses as they gracefully pluck the leaves from neatly pruned, hedgelike shrubs. Many gardens have processing plants where the leaves are withered, cut, torn, twisted, fermented, dried, and sorted. There are 160 major gardens in Bangladesh and an extensive tea market in Chittagong.

The tea gardens are far from the cities. As a result, tea planters and plantation workers are isolated from Bangladesh's surrounding rice culture. The plantations are feudal fiefs—if *feudal* implies that the owners must provide housing, medical care, some access to education, and cradle-to-grave security for their work crews to offset the isolation and lack of alternative employment.

It is important to know that well into this century the idyllic view of the feudal tea gardens was marred by something one rarely mentions nowadays: the "slave laws," which bound workers to a plantation and provided for severe punishments, including physical beatings, for those who attempted to escape. Today many tea-garden workers, descended from coolies forcibly imported years ago, still speak languages not readily understood in the surrounding areas.

Tea and jute buyers tend to arrive in the rainy season or near its end, when the crops are being harvested and crop size—and therefore prices—can be gauged. Orders are made at the Tea Exchange in Chittagong, where an auction is held for tea that has been graded and tested and where, in a dark room with black walnut painted desks, the auctioneer tries to bid up the price while experienced brokers hold him down.

Another industry has grown up in recent years that attracts a flock of visitors: garments and textiles. Though it has enjoyed a rebirth over the past fifty years, the big boost came only a decade ago when overseas buyers, mainly American, began to order ready-to-wear items. Since then, shipments to the United States, Asia, and Europe have doubled and tripled many times over, so that an entire system of container freight by air and sea has arisen. In turn the garment industry has stimulated local manufacturers to produce buttons, fasteners, zippers, and cloth. To meet demand, local entrepreneurs hired or contracted with South Korean– or Hong Kong–based Chinese to build factories and supply sewing machines and other equipment. South Korea's aid agency and manufacturers played a major role in developing this industry, and now one often encounters East Asians who are helping build it. In addition, tired buyers from mainline clothing marketers, from K Mart to blue-jeans makers, occupy the hotels, as do their production supervisors and quality-control experts, who come to make certain each order is filled with the right product, done the right way at the right time. Bangladesh labels now are found worldwide.

What is ironic about the recent garment and textile industry is that it was pioneered in this part of Bengal and until early in the nineteenth century, Bangladesh had a near monopoly on the production of cotton cloth. For their own reasons (detailed later) the British deliberately destroyed this industry and decimated Dhaka's population by over two-thirds in the mid-nineteenth century. Although weaving skills were not destroyed, the growth of the garment industry in this decade is an instance of déjà vu. Now, throughout the country, yarn spinning, cloth making, and garment manufacturing are under way at every level of technology.

With the growth in the garment industry has come a new business: weaving of cotton and synthetic yarn. Some is used by Bangladesh's garment industry and some is exported, often illegally, to India, where dyeing and finishing techniques are much more sophisticated, though Bangladesh is catching up. The growth of this yarn business, which uses imported cotton, may be laying the groundwork for at least a modest effort to grow cotton locally, especially in western Bangladesh. Among those who know the cotton and garment business, Bangladesh is slowly working itself into being a major player over the next thirty years. Thus along the road to Bogra from Arica is found factory after factory rhythmically thumping and spinning away at a level clearly audible above an auto engine.

In recent years there has been an increase in travel to Chittagong, where a new export zone has been built and industries are producing diverse products, including video players and recorders, radios, light bulbs, and other electronic and plastic products. Television sets are being assembled from imported components, and one company is producing tennis and athletic shoes of world-class looks and quality. Around this zone is growing up a new set of industries that the world has noticed, for the zone is sold out and new zones are being created. They have brought a new kind of buyer—for electronics and mass-consumer goods—to Bangladesh. There is even hope now of attracting more advanced technologies, such as production of television screens and inner parts. While no one yet is talking of a Silicon Valley, the hope is for a slow growth in this business. In the meantime the growth of the electronics sector is bringing Japanese, Chinese, Thai, Indian, and Singaporean businessmen.

Bangladesh also has an iron and steel industry of sorts. It is called ship breaking, an endeavor that takes advantage of hard-working, inexpensive labor. Vessels no longer serviceable are brought from all over the world to be scrapped. They are dry-docked, and the frames are disassembled, sorted, and either sold as scrap on the world market or melted down at steel facilities in Chittagong to be resold as girders or other products.

Another major industry is evident in the country's center, along the main rivers between Barisal and Dhaka, where brick factories, shipbuilding and maintenance factories, steel fabrication, and light industries of all kinds have found a base near to shipping. A new port at Mangla in the southwest has opened but has not yet become an industrial center, as there is no road network linking the port to the rest of the country.

Then there is the leather industry. Although the country has twenty-two million cows and buffaloes and thirteen million goats, the processing of hides into shoes and other leather goods for export is a recent phenomenon.

Before that, leather exports were confined to unprocessed hides, as there was a tax on the export of processed ones. But if one hangs around hotel lobbies, it is hard to miss the fact that this industry, which in the past decade has made enormous strides, is attempting to enter the export side of the business. Buyers and machinery salesmen are seeking local manufacturers who can produce export-quality shoes, bags, coats, and luggage. Already there are signs of a breakthrough in these areas, and the leather wallahs from New York are booking hotel rooms. The leather industry is only in its infancy, but it is one more industry of the future.

In addition to those whose visits are related to jute, tea, garments, and electronics, other visitors come to buy handicrafts, frogs' legs and shrimp—which is plentiful in the Bay of Bengal and in ponds where shrimp are raised through pisiculture.

Finally, there is another export industry, one evident on most airplane flights to and from Dhaka: people. Labor is contracted in Dhaka for employment in the Middle East and elsewhere. Bangladeshis are widely respected as bright, hard-working, and cheerful workers who often have a good grasp of English. Such workers, most with secondary school degrees, can be found in large numbers of countries, working at diverse jobs, from high-technology ones to brute or specialized labor in service industries.

What is important about the country's industries is that they are aimed at exports, and exports are the only way that Bangladesh can earn enough to pay its loans and get off aid. The commercial visitors, unlike the aid officials, are the people of the country's future, who will help it reclaim its place in the world. For no nation in the past hundred years has been able to achieve self-sustained economic growth without being a major competitor in international markets.

The next set of visitors are salesmen who come to sell imports. Most are from Asia, with Japan, China, India, Singapore, and Hong Kong leading the list. The United States, followed by France, Canada, and the United Kingdom, also sells a lot. But the majority of foreign products on the market are of East Asian origin, mainly Japanese. Nearly all cars, electronics, wrist watches, and so on come from the East and are marketed through established import houses. The year-round one sees the East Asians in the hotels—and in government offices, for the government has huge sources of foreign exchange and huge needs, which it can fulfill with aid money. The erstwhile Soviets also come to trade, but mostly on a barter basis and on a government-to-government relationship with the nationalized industries.

The Chinese, British, and, to a lesser extent, the Pakistanis, sell weapons, and there are a number of Bangladeshi arms dealers who front for the army. They hang around the Dhaka, Kurmitolah Golf, and Bogra Officers' clubs. The presence of Chinese in Chittagong is particularly noticeable; they do a lot of business with the Bangladesh Navy. China's chief-of-staff and minister of defense visited Bangladesh not long ago, renewing contacts that go back to the tenth century, when Chinese travelers learned Mahayana Buddhism and wrote lengthy treatises about the region. China always has been interested in the Indian subcontinent, and as China competes with India for mastery of Asia in the twenty-first century, Bangladesh is likely to be a pawn in the game. Bangladesh looks to China to protect it from India, which adjoins it on three sides. And Bangladesh's air force depends on F-8 MIG fighters from China, some willed to it by Pakistan when it moved on to F-16s. The British, as well as the Swedish Bofors firm, supply Bangladesh's military forces with guns, sighting equipment, trucks, and electronic gear. The British never keep less than a brigadier at their High Commission (embassy). And the Swedes, for all their love of peace and neutrality, most of all like a good arms deal. Remarkably, the Americans and erstwhile Soviets sell almost no arms to Bangladesh.

The British, as always, have a deep commercial relationship with Bangladesh. And while their presence in the local marketplace is smaller than it once was, they sell tea and jute equipment and a range of British-made goods, especially tobacco and excellent pharmaceutical products, as well as toiletries, machine tools, and industrial and electronic equipment. Moreover, not long ago they sold Bangladesh medium-range turboprop planes for civilian passenger use.

The Dutch are both good customers and good salesmen, providing two generations of Fokker aircraft for the domestic airline, although American DC-10s were chosen for the growing and profitable international airline, Bangladesh Biman. The Dutch, through their trading ties at Chinsura nearby in India, have long experience in this part of the world, and they help with waterways and dikes.

Tiny Denmark and Belgium also have a long association with Bangladesh, and the latter is an excellent customer for its products. Indeed, the Danes, like the Dutch, had a trading station in India, and the Belgians have a long trade history, no small part of which has been their contribution to the educational system. For many years, many of the country's leaders were educated in Calcutta, at Saint Xavier's College, run by Belgians.

Lest anyone think that the Japanese are only selling cars, they also have built the major highway bridge over the Meghna River on the Dhaka-Comilla-Chittagong road and are working on another bridge over the Gumti—no easy engineering feats. And Japan is the country's largest aid-giver. The Japanese also have a master plan for developing agro and light labor-intensive industries along the Dhaka-Chittagong rail and road corridor, where some of the best farmland and a huge reservoir of inexpensive labor can be found.

One of Bangladesh's biggest aid suppliers as well as trading partners has been the erstwhile Soviet Union. Their ideology aside, the Soviets pioneered power-generation facilities at Ghorasal, assisted the tea and jute trade, and were a constant source of good will and friendship. New links with the successor states of the confederation of the former Soviet Union are being forged.

The Chinese have sold Bangladeshi farmers large numbers of sturdy, low-priced tubewell engines. Wherever one goes this red-and-chrome-colored engine can be heard put-putting in the fields or seen sending out streams of silvery water into the canals along the paddies. These engines also have revolutionized river travel, as they power small launches and country boats—carrying the greatest amount of freight by far, compared with any other form of transport. So plentiful are these engines that they have helped irrigate thousands of acres which, in the dry season, once were neglected. Tubewells irrigated 1.6 million acres in 1983, 2.4 million in 1987, and an estimated 3 million in 1990. Indeed, the north, infamous for dry-season dust storms just two decades ago, today is green as far as the eye can see, thanks to these simple, diesel-fueled engines.

Other important visitors never make it to hotels or appear in statistics. They certainly never attend seminars, even though they know the trade situation better than the economists do. They are smugglers, the heroes of the economy. Bangladesh has a long seacoast as well as a very long border with India and an isolated one with Burma. Looked at one way, these smugglers are continuing an ancient "trading" tradition with India, Burma, the mountain states of Tibet and Nepal, and Southeast Asia. For instance, rice, jute, white polyester cloth, and Western imported goods go across the border to India; cows and manufactured goods return. The best estimates maintain that this trade equals 22 percent of the official trade volume. Everyone who counts is involved in some form of smuggling, even ministers and military people. It's not that difficult, for smuggling is facilitated by the connivance of the Bangladesh Border Constabulary, the Indian Border Defense Forces, and, undoubtedly, higher officials on both sides of the border.

On a far smaller scale are those visitors who come to work with local subsidiaries of multinational companies. Although the situation may change before long if the country remains stable, right now there are hardly any multinationals—a few banks, a few pharmaceutical companies, perhaps not more than a dozen concerns. Usually these visitors are supervisors, auditors, or, from time to time, technical people who come to help introduce new technologies.

In 1990 there were more than forty-nine thousand officially recorded visitors, almost all of whom came for business. Rare are the visitors who want to see the country's ancient monuments, swim at its beautiful beaches, or eat its incredible cuisine. At the Rajshahi Hotel hangs a beautiful poster. Showing bright blue sky and lush green fields, it reads: "Visit Bangladesh

. . . Before Tourists Come." What it means is that Bangladesh is a tourist bargain. For less than $25 a day one can visit the provincial towns and stay at Parjatan Hotels, built and maintained by the National Tourist Board. And there is plenty to see: ancient cities where the Buddha is said to have walked, ancient mosques, tombs of the Muslim saints, Hindu temples that predate the last millennium, and picturesque villages accessible only by riverboat cruise.

Where and What Is Bangladesh?

While the land that is now called Bangladesh is a very old nation, only in 1971 did it escape from foreign domination, which had endured for 190 years. From June 24, 1757, to August 14, 1947, the country was controlled by the British Empire. The people were taught in English and were subject to English law. In fact, in no other part of Asia have so many people been ruled for so long or been so exposed to the West as has been the case in Bangladesh.

During this period, Bangladesh was the eastern part of a larger unit known as Bengal. Because Bengal's western portion is mostly Hindu, when the British left it chose to remain in India, which also is predominantly Hindu; today it is West Bengal State, whose capital is Calcutta. East Bengal, with a largely Muslim population, voted to become part of a newly formed state called Pakistan, whose people were mostly Muslim and whose two halves, West and East, were divided by eleven hundred miles of India.

From August 14, 1947, to March 26, 1971, though Bengalis in East Pakistan were the majority, they were ruled from Pakistan's capital of Islamabad in the West by Pakistanis who, while Muslim, were of different ethnic origins, namely Punjabis, Pathans, Sindhis, and Baluchis. Moreover, the Bengalis were not allowed to use their native Bangla language; they were forced to learn Urdu, the language of the North Indian Muslim elite that had been chosen as Pakistan's state language for its supposed "Islamic" character. The Bengalis viewed this prohibition as a symbol of West Pakistan's disregard for Bengali culture and identity. Partly for this reason, though they had freely decided to join the new nation of Pakistan, which they had helped found when India was partitioned, the Bengalis soon became disenchanted and discovered the hard way that they had thrown off one colonial ruler for another. In the ensuing years the situation became increasingly intolerable, as the West Pakistani Punjabi elite, which has dominated Pakistani politics since independence, arrogated to itself the best jobs and most of the development funds.

When the Bengalis began agitating for greater autonomy and their leader, Sheikh Mujibur Rahman, won an election that would have made him Pakistan's prime minister, the Pakistan Army rolled into action. On the night of March 26, 1971, army tanks suddenly appeared at Dhaka University and elsewhere in the eastern sector and began shooting Bengali intellectuals and politicians. Over the next nine months the West Pakistanis, by their own admission, killed thirty-five thousand Bengali intellectuals, doctors, professors, lawyers, journalists, and artists, including leaders of the Hindu minority. All told, three hundred thousand to one million Bengalis died in this brutal civil war, which ended in December when the Pakistan Army surrendered to an advancing Indian Army assisted by millions of Bangladeshi Freedom Fighters. What had begun as an attempt by the East to gain greater autonomy ended with the birth of a new nation.

The emergence of Bangladesh revealed to the entire world what its people already knew: Bangladesh, one of the most densely populated countries on earth (two to three thousand people per square mile), was one of the least developed nations on earth—a sorry category for what once had been the richest province in the British Empire. What is not widely known is that Bangladesh's wealth had been depleted long before the British left India and what wealth remained had been harmed irreparably by Britain's longstanding policy of fomenting separatist tendencies between East and West Bengal. For the East was an agricultural area, while the West was more industrial. The bifurcation in 1947 had set development back by decades.

Most people know Bangladesh only for its poverty. They know nothing of its culture—that, for instance, it has a neighboring community with which it shares race, ethnicity, language, and history but not religion. Both communities are Bengali, speak Bangla, and have a common ancestry. The only difference is that Bangladeshis are mostly Muslim while their brothers just across the border in Indian West Bengal are mostly Hindu. Moreover, twenty million of Bangladeshis' blood brothers live in the nearby Indian states of Bihar and Orissa. The people of this region, who are called Angas and Oryas, speak a language directly related to Bangla. In antiquity they occasionally were united or at least allied with the Bengalis against foreigners. When the British arrived in Bengal to found Calcutta in 1690, Bihar, Orissa, and Bengal comprised a single state governed by native rulers semi-independent of the Moghul emperors in Delhi. The native rulers' capital was at Murshidabad, now in West Bengal, and before that in Dhaka. The Bengalis also share a common heritage with people who live in the Seven Sisters Indian border states and territories to the east and north that include Assam, Tripura, Meghalaya, and Arunchal Pradesh.

Bangladesh, then, is a political reality where 60 percent of the Bengali people live, while the other 40 percent are its neighbors. So when you arrive, you should keep in mind that you are in the east-central part of a much larger reality within the eastern Indian subcontinent. Look at a map of India. Find the easternmost section. Bounded by the state of Uttar Pradesh in the west and stretching eastward to the foothills of the Himalayas, this area embraces all of Bihar, Orissa, West Bengal, Bangladesh, and India's eastern tribal states with their Bengali people. By climate, geography, landscape, crops, animals, language, and dress, this area is vastly different from western and southern India. In the old days, when the British traveled by train, they tried to pinpoint the precise spot where the tropical outweighs the dry continental climate. They found it in southeastern Uttar Pradesh. Benares, or Varanasi, is the place.

Northwest India, extending from the Punjab and Rajasthan well past Delhi to the eastern fringes of the United Province, or Uttar Pradesh as it is now called, is dry. With little rainfall, it is a wheat and barley area that relies on oxen and humped-back cows for draughts. Houses are of mud brick and flat-topped, trees are all deodars (Indian cedar) and tall oak, and the landscape tends to be khaki, reminiscent of the Middle East. The people are light-skinned, straight-nosed, often nearly European-looking. Women are clad in sarees over short blouses, or *chakras*, and men wear loose-fitting pants with long-sleeved shirts that end somewhere between the lower thighs and knees, called *kurta* and pajama.

East India, in contrast, is semitropical, with palm trees. The people have darker skins, grow rice, and use water buffaloes. Village houses often have bamboo mat walls and sloping thatched roofs. Some older ones have terra cotta roofs. The land is wet, and often flooded; rains are heavy. The world's largest delta areas are found around the mouths of the Ganges, the Meghna, and the Brahmaputra. And while women wear sarees, until recently they seldom wore the *chakra* (short, blouse-like) top. Men wear a sarong-like garment called *dhoti* by the Hindus and *lungi* by the Muslims; while working in the fields, they often wear a breechcloth. The dhoti and lungi are different versions of a similar dress, with the dhoti more like a Roman toga and the lungi more like a sarong. Villages are scattered amid lush, green, wooded areas built on mounds high above the fields as protection against flooding. The ambiance is that of Southeast Asia (which this region borders), even down to the conical hats, or *tokas*, often worn by farmers in the field.

This tropical lushness, which differentiates East from West India, embraces the Angas, Oryas, Banglas, and their tribal cousins in the hills to the east. And it is here in the heart of the river deltas, in this climatic, geographical, riverine, cultural, and linguistic complex, that one finds Bangladesh.

It is one of the pities of politics that this huge climatic and cultural complex is separated politically, one part from the other, and is unified more by smuggling than by official policy. Make no mistake. To a great degree, East India and Bangladesh represent a single culture. For goods, radio and television programs, newspapers, telephones, and gossip ignore borders. Just look around.

Bangladesh's national anthem is based on lyrics by Rabindranath Tagore, a Bangladeshi-born Hindu poet who lived in what is now West Bengal, and on a melody by a revered Bangladeshi bard, Lalan Shah. Tagore also wrote the national anthem of India. Likewise, though the giants of modern Bengali poetry—Tagore, Kazi Nazrul Islam, and Lalan Shah—all hail from Bangladesh, a good part of the culture's poetry and modern literature originated in West Bengal. Now West Bengal watches more Bangladesh television than its own, the two Bengals share their radio and news programs, and many Bangladeshi youths go to school in Calcutta.

This last point is crucial. Ever since it was built by the British in the early eighteenth century, Calcutta has been the cradle of modern Bengali culture. Many of Bangladesh's senior citizens went to school there, and many of its scholars still go there for higher studies. It is from there that Bangladesh's secular politics and love of democracy derives. Most of its political parties have their roots in ideas and movements begun in Calcutta in the first half of the twentieth century. Today, despite religious differences, it is impossible to deny the linkages—personal, scholarly, social, and emotional—that exist between the two parts of what long had been a united Bengal. Each side always will occupy a special place in the heart of the other. How can it be otherwise when many of Calcutta's greatest writers, among them Tagore and Nirad Chaudhuri, and many of its leading families hail from Bangladesh while substantial numbers of Bangladeshi leaders in many fields were educated across the border?

This is not to say that there is any hope of the two Bengals reuniting in the near future. That political idea cannot be accepted now, for too much suspicion lingers from the internecine battles of the 1940s, early 1950s, and 1971.

Many first-time visitors are pleasantly surprised at the modernity and vibrancy of life in Bangladesh, especially in Dhaka. They didn't expect the density of traffic; the modern, clean airport with efficient inspectors and "green" customs lines for those with nothing to declare; the skyscrapers and streets brightly lit at night; the plush first-class hotels; the riksha drivers' exuberance; the beauty of the countryside.

They were expecting poverty, degradation, and hopelessness, as most television news shows and aid agency advertisements focus on the poor, who generally are portrayed as passive victims of floods or worse. But Bangladeshis are anything but passive sufferers. They are doers. Even beggars are active and enterprising, as is quickly apparent just outside the airport. It's not uncommon to hear a first-time visitor say, "This isn't what I was led to expect," or "It really doesn't seem to be as bad as they say." Even if visitors wander into the worst *bustees*, or slums, they are surprised at the people's industriousness and cleanliness. (No matter how poor, Bangladeshis bathe twice daily and wash their clothes before evening.)

What surprises many visitors is that the needs of the poor are so slight, while their ability to help themselves is so much greater than outsiders are led to expect. Consequently, many visitors feel they have been misled by aid lobbies and television networks that play to sensationalism and neglect to mention that without any kind of welfare or support system, Bangladeshis manage to get by.

While Bangladesh is poor compared to the West or to Japan, Taiwan, and South Korea (it is richer than West Bengal), it is not a passive country waiting for a handout. The people work hard, as many investors and some multi-national companies are starting to learn. They have a work ethic that is driven by need but also by pride and a way of life where work is an honor, a challenge, an endeavor to be respected.

Crime, though common, is not as organized or as deadly as most every-where else. Streets are safe before midnight, and the countryside is always safe. Workers are honest, and farmers pay their debts. The government has never had a debt crisis or blocked dividend payments, and it has a record of honest reporting and data preparation. While corruption exists among politi-cians, soldiers, the civil service, and the police, it is no worse than in other countries at a similar stage of development, although in recent years, with the rise of a New Class, it has become more open, cynical, and organized. Foreigners who have done business in other nations are surprised at the accessibility and good manners of Bangladesh's government officers. While they may not be able to accommodate, they are attentive and reasonable, without the haughtiness of the Indian civil servants or the authoritarian manner of the Pakistanis.

And judged by its past, the country is making progress. In one way it doesn't matter that it's still far poorer than most of the rest of Asia. Most Bangladeshis don't know that. They only know how things have changed for them. In this respect the nation has made progress on every front since the British and Pakistani eras. Furthermore, most countries do not really begin developing until they are independent, so Bangladesh's development clock really began ticking only in January 1972. From this perspective there has been progress. As one woman said recently, "There's a sense of well-being for the first time in years."

Not that all is well. Bangladesh is in the throes of economic development and at that stage when many people who can no longer support themselves on the land are migrating to the cities. This migration is not a straightforward one-step process. Rather, people leave the land and try to find work in small villages, doing agricultural processing, road building, or personal service. Some stay there and some migrate to the new subdistrict towns designated as government centers in the past several years. They find work there or drift on to such district towns as Bogra, Rajshahi, Khulna, Comilla, and Sylhet. And finally the overflow converges on Dhaka, where camps of migrants are found around the ever-expanding city. This migration is the most dramatic aspect of the changes under way in Bangladesh, the one the visitor is sure to see almost immediately. It is a process of migration similar to movements seen throughout the developing world, from Seoul to Mexico City. It is a process that took place in Europe and America in the nineteenth and early twentieth centuries. It is a painful process to watch. And yet it is a sign of change that brings hope, for it is a universal first step in the development process. Nonetheless, it gives Dhaka an outward look of poverty that belies the city's growth since 1972, a growth based on positive economic development, which is what draws the migrants. There is no welfare in Dhaka; hope of employment attracts the poor. And this hope is being realized in a city that has grown from a sleepy provincial town of several hundred thousand at independence in 1972 to a capital of world proportions, with a population of more than four million in 1992. The city has grown by scores of square miles in just two decades and is far more stable than it usually is given credit for.

There is also political stability, albeit all too often under military or dictatorial government. This stability can be made uneasy by strikes or demonstrations, for, as in most poor countries, tensions do run high. For years there have been endemic problems at Bangladesh's universities, better known as places of political intrigue than of learning. Yet if the visitor looks at the country as a native does, he or she will see that the essentials remain operating and that more than 88 percent of the people live in the nearly always tranquil villages.

Transport, fertilizer, seeds, oil, gasoline, natural gas, electricity, telephones, roads, and river transport are better than ever. Bridges span rivers hitherto impossible to thus cross. Rail service is regular, safer, and faster, with much new equipment. Food supplies are stable and remain available during floods and other natural catastrophes. Medical care is improving, though not nearly fast enough, while cholera, malaria, and leprosy are not as widespread as they were two decades ago and smallpox has been virtually eliminated. Widespread malnutrition still exists, however, especially among those who no longer are productive on the land but have not yet found security in town and city.

Also on the down side, the jute industry has declined due to a massive drop in world demand; the university system is far worse than ever, with endless closings because of political violence; drugs and alcoholism are major problems in the cities; and population continues to grow, while industrialization is slower than necessary.

But the cities are not representative of the nation. In fact, Dhaka is not even representative of the other cities. In recent years it has become rich and increasingly out of touch with the rest of the country. The elites, especially, have lost their ties to outlying areas and have developed a siege mentality, like that of Washington's Beltway or Tokyo's Tower. One need only drive a few miles out to see that the pressure cooker of Dhaka's cocktail party circuit is irrelevant.

Indeed, one of the pleasures of Bangladesh is to leave Dhaka behind. For then life is quieter; people are calmer, happier, friendlier; the earth is richer; the air is clear and fragrant with flowers; and rivers offer picture-perfect scenes along verdant shores. Only in the countryside can one feel the grandeur, the glory, of the country the Moghuls called the Paradise of Nations.

2

The Seasons

FOR SHEER LOVELINESS, there is no land on earth more beautiful, with a climate more pleasant, than Bangladesh. What water is to the rainy season, the ancient elements of air, fire, and earth are to the dry season, coalescing to produce a land of sunshine and flowers. Yet, as in so many other ways, Bangladesh is different when it comes to seasonal changes, having six overlapping seasons, each part of the nation's story. These seasons and their chief characteristics are *barsa* (June–August), monsoon rains; *sarat* (September–October), jute and rice harvest; *hemanto* (October–November), time to replant; *seet* (November–December), flowers bloom; *basanto* (December–February), cool, time for weddings; and *grisma* (March–May), hot, leaves fall. It is in the rhythm of the seasons that you get to know the real Bangladesh.

Barsa

Of the classical elements—air, water, earth, and fire—only one is symbolic of Bangladesh: water. For Bangladesh is not so much a land upon water as water upon a land. One-third of Bangladesh's physical space of fifty-five thousand square miles is comprised of water in the dry season, while in the rainy season up to 70 percent is submerged. Water is the central reality of Bangladesh, just as its shortage is the central reality of Saudi Arabia. At least 10 percent of the people live in boats, up to 40 percent depend on the sea and rivers for a livelihood, and 100 percent depend on the rain and floods for food. Water is the main source of protein, the major provider of crop fertilizer and transport, and unquestionably the greatest source of wealth. Bangladesh's main crops—rice, jute, and tea—cannot exist without huge amounts of water.

Bangladesh also has both the world's largest delta system and the greatest flow of river water to the sea of any country on earth. It has water from rivers, the sea, rain, wells, tidal waves, floods, dew and humidity, and the melting snows of the Himalaya Mountains; water that is tidal and fresh, sweet and brackish; water that is blue, green, muddy brown, gray—water, the stuff of Bangladesh.

But most visitors never experience this reality. They arrive in the dry season, between November and June, or in the cool months of January and February. (Occupancy in the main hotel is highest and near capacity from December to February and lowest from July to September.) Far too many never know the joy of the monsoon rains or of the wet season's first downpour. They choose to come when the weather is dry, when the rivers are tame, when the sea is calm, and when the sky is blue, bereft of humidity and arid in the northerly Siberian cool winds. If lucky, they will have time for a leisurely boat trip on the Padma, the Jamuna, or the Meghna, or on these rivers' countless tributaries. If not, they will miss the essence, the *dhat*, of Bangladesh, the land of water, the nation of water upon the land. And while they will see a beautiful land in the full glory of springtime, they will not be submerged into its deepest darkness. For the coming of the rains and floods is the real beginning of life here, the time when people go inside more: inside their homes, inside themselves, inside their fields, inside their very souls. How Bangladeshis manage the rainy season and the water is the key to how they manage their lives.

In May and early June the land is dry and rivers are low. Fishing is difficult, as the bigger fish migrate; even the ponds, or tanks (*dighis*), are shallow, and pond-grown fish are scarce. Everywhere, tubewells pant as they try to irrigate stone-dry fields. So oppressive is the sun's heat that women sit before their fires of twigs, dung patties, or rice straw and rice husks barely feeling heat from the hearth. Men move with great deliberation, and even children are subdued. The yellow-beaked white gulls that live along the rivers sound parched, the cow's cud is dry. The noonday sun bears down in microwaves of blue, red, and black heat, while the earth bounces the heat back. Dust blows around the stubble of khaki-colored fields, which were lush green not long ago. Water buffalo dash to the river, where they submerge themselves, leaving only their eyes and horns above water. The small, brown seven brothers, birds so common in Bangladesh, flock languidly in the shade of the pipal tree.

Into this inferno come the rains. For weeks their arrival has been presaged by disturbances in the skies as the monsoon winds blew up the Bay of Bengal toward Bangladesh, forcing back the warm winds from the continental landmass. So violent are these atmospheric upheavals that small cyclones form and tremendous bursts of thunder and lightning rend the air. Airplanes often are caught in terrifying downdrafts and bounce over the bay like matchboxes on a sea. Yet after the storms and cyclones pass, the heat and stillness return; the crows and magpies begin crying out, their calls mawkish and rude. This period is one of dry birth, dry labor, dry heaving before the water of the womb breaks and life appears. With the coming of the rains begins the heat and cool of the year's most majestic period. Like the *jalal faqirs* who dance as dervishes before the majestic beauty of Allah, so does the Bangladeshi come back to life.

The first drops are best. One watches the rain fall in a heavy downpour. But so parched is the land that the dust absorbs it, the hard earth is not even stained at first, and the water vaporizes. Suddenly the earth begins changing color, the shafts of rain beat down like millions of tiny plows, and an earthy, super-sweet smell arises. Within the first thirty minutes, runnels begin to form and gurgle, and a rising crescendo is heard which sounds like a tinkling bell. It is the sound of rain pellets striking thatched and tin roofs, mingled with a gurgle as it runs with increasing speed through the canals and fields, as it creates a rushing sound in streams and a roaring in rivers. Meanwhile, overhead, dark gray and brown clouds have obliterated the mighty sun, which just days ago seemed so unconquerable. Remarkably, the rains always arrive at just about the time of the sun's annual apex, on June 24, after which the days grow shorter. So total is this conquest of the sun that it seems unlikely that the sun god, Surya, still exists. Instead it is the time of the Hindu gods Vishnu and Varuna, of the Muslim Pir Badr and of Panch Pirs of the sea; it is the time of darkness and unfathomable depths.

From mid-June to the end of October is the time of the river. Not only are the rivers full to bursting, but the rains pour down so relentlessly and the clouds are so close to village roofs that all the earth smells damp and mildewed, and green and yellow moss creeps up every wall and tree. The rivers keep rising, at first running in muddy brown torrents and eventually appearing like swollen, ancient beasts that wash across the land on their relentless, sullen, menacing march to the sea. As the rains continue, the fields fill up, first the lower parts and gradually the higher, until the village mound, the *dibi*, is an island and the river bank merges with the land. Soon all the earth is covered with water: fast-moving and swirling or silt-laden and sluggish. The earth itself becomes a water mass, brown and soupy, an earth seemingly devoid of a solid base, an earth of ever-changing shape and texture. Minutes are measured in the rise of the water, hours in the length of the rain shower, and days in terms of the shadows' brightness and darkness. Cattle and goats become aquatic, chickens are placed in baskets on roofs, and boats are loaded with valuables and tied to houses. Cooking fires are impossible, even if dry rice husks, hay, or extremely scarce wood were available. So the staples become precooked rice, a dry lentil called *dal,* and jackfruit, a large, smelly melon that ripens on trees during this season. As is the case the year-round, most people cannot afford meat or much fish, even if they could cook it. Vegetables, which are not widely eaten anyway, are unavailable. In many houses, even those away from flood plains, beds often are constructed on legs three to five feet high, reached via ladders.

Because most villages are built on artificial mounds raised above the fields, as the floods rise villages become tiny islands, accessible only by boat. In this world the village community becomes the entire universe, a self-sustaining outpost cut off from civilization and hence from such essentials as medical care for most of three months of the year—every year. The rain waters rise right into the village, right up to the doors of the huts; often the waters separate one part of the farmer's compound from another, so that the cooking hut can be reached only by walking on boards that connect like bridges. The cooking hut often is more elevated or uses bricks to rise above the water.

The rain also fills the night. There is a delicious cool in the evenings that seems to instill the heat-baked body with new life. The sound of rain—the patter on a tin roof, the soft soaking sound on the thatch, the gentle stream on the bamboo corner post, the gurgle in the runnels along the path outside, the swish of the wet leaves in the trees, the bell-like tinkle of water running through the rice paddies from one level to another, the distant rumble of the flooding river—is associated with night. The noise of the rain brings privacy to each corner of the hut where a family crowded together enjoys that peace of silence. Lovers lie on the mat listening to the rain's rushing.

To the first-time visitor, the rivers' rise seems to be tied to the rains. Yet this is but partly so. The rise of the rivers everywhere in the northern part of the Indian subcontinent is related to the melting snow well beyond Bangladesh, high in the Himalayas where the summer sun at last has unlocked the flow of the glaciers, so that by the time the rains begin the rivers already are rising. To the uninitiated, cause and effect—rain and rising rivers—seem to be so clear-cut that the amount of rain (from sixty inches in the west to 144 inches in the eastern hills annually) appears to be the sole variable. What is critical, however, is how much snow accumulated during the winter high up on the world's largest mountain range and the amount of sunlight-induced melting that occurred in spring and summer. While the rain is significant, it is the flood itself, the massive movement of water down the southern divide of the mountains, that is the determining factor.

That is true, too, of the Ganges—or the Padma, as it is known here—which journeys ever so far from the Karakorams in northwest India, as well as of the many tributaries of the Gangetic skirt that feed into it from the north. The Padma flows more than eighteen hundred miles, filling more slowly than the Brahmaputra, but filling with certainty and majesty as it makes its way across the plains to Bangladesh, carrying the silt of India and the ashes of millions of Hindus who are burned each year at the funeral ghats along the Jamuna and Ganges, especially at Benares. Probably no river on earth is the repository of so much human ash as is the Ganges; and it is these human ashes, borne by torrents of water, that are carried beyond the Farraka barrage and India into the plains of Varendra, Bang, Samatata, Radha, Nadia, Maldah, Tipperah, and Kamrup, the names of the ancient kingdoms that make up modern Bangladesh. The Ganges-Padma is not just a river but the last resting place, the mother's breast, the flowing course of Indian history. This mighty river, which changed its course in the fifteenth and sixteenth centuries to its present location, is the main artery of the Indian subcontinent, the path along which came the people who represent the present culture of Bangladesh, who left the old culture high and dry to the west, where the old main path remains evident around Calcutta.

Yet the Padma is not Bangladesh's chief river. That honor goes to the Brahmaputra (called the Jamuna by Bangladeshis), the principal river of the eastern Himalayas, which cuts its way through a stone gorge into the plains of Assam before thrusting its pointed ends into the Shillong Hills of Meghalaya and passing down to the plains of Bangladesh. For Bangladesh has no mountains or even real hills. Basically it is a flood plain delta comprised of soft silt built up over the eons at the confluence of the Padma and Jamuna. The confluence of these two mighty waters long ago was given erotic overtones by the Baul boatmen of Bengal whose songs are the backbone of the poetry and notions of life that still haunt Bengal. No mightier river exists than the Jamuna, the father of rivers, the mate of the mother of rivers. It is the Brahmaputra, the Jamuna, that divides Bangladesh into western and eastern sections.

Finally, there's the Meghna, which joins the Padma and Jamuna at their confluence and then flows southeast to the sea. Called the Mighty Meghna, it is not as long or nearly as large in volume as its brother and sister. Rising in the western slopes of the Assam hills in Sylhet in northern Bangladesh, it meets the two larger rivers about eighty miles before they flow into the sea. The place where the three rivers meet forms an inland sea in the heart of Bangladesh, a sea that often is so wide one cannot see the banks even from midstream. Like the others, the Meghna has tributaries and feeder streams, which form an intricate network and help link Bangladesh's waters. The Meghna is the third river of the delta, the one that gives a clue to the meaning of the tantric *tribeni* or *triveni* of the Baul boatmen, a word laden with erotic meaning relating to sexual restraint and love.

Beyond the Meghna the land rises to the east. In the southeast, other rivers, the Feni, the Karnaphuli, and the Naf, emerge from the mountains of Arakan of eastern India and Burma. While not of the same scale or system as their mighty compatriots, they too play a role in the tale of Bangladesh and its culture. They irrigate some of the most beautiful land on earth, especially the Gomai field along the Karnaphuli and part of the lush Tipperah plain.

The reality of the rivers and their deltas is the reality of Bangladesh, just as the rain and the humidity are part of that reality.

From June to October the rains rule. Indeed, from July to September the flood rules. Noah in his worst days would not have wanted to sail in Bangladesh, where the rains last longer than the biblical forty days and forty nights and where the rains prompted raiding warriors from Delhi to dub Bangladesh that "hellish paradise," hellish to men who like to have their feet on solid ground, hellish to those who like a green more muted than the royal emerald of Bengal. One need only look at the dark green of the Bangladesh flag compared, say, to the green of the flags of Eire or Pakistan to see that Bangladesh's green is not simply green but a very pit of greenness. A landsman is not at home in Bangladesh; only a sailor, marine, or riverman is. Everyone in this land is amphibious by nature. Everyone and everything is ruled by water; all life depends on the coming of the rain.

It is the rain that drenches the fields and covers the rice and jute plants. It is the rain that fills the canals, the ponds, the water cisterns, and the *beels*, the low areas where water gathers. The rain and the river, for in a delta the main waters all coalesce, call forth a very special time of year. The rain brings coolness back to the land. And with the rich soil now besotted, fertility returns, both to the land and to its inhabitants. In the cool air of an evening, lovers turn to each other for warmth. The rains are a time of love and fertility and of a womblike wetness and security. With the roads flooded and travel somewhat risky, village families live close together in their huts in an extended sabbath until the waters recede. Water is everywhere. It fills the eyes with seeing, the ears with hearing, the touch with moisture, the nose with fresh and earthly scents, the palate with cleanness.

The rains fill the ponds and streams, and the daily baths, difficult and warm in the hot season, suddenly are cool and refreshing. Children leap nude into the ponds. Women swim in their sarees, dunking their streaming black hair. Men dive in wearing their skirtlike sarongs or *lungis*, relaxing before they lather. The rains, having turned stagnant water fresh, make bathing a pleasure again. And as no one bathes as often as Bangladeshis, at least no one in north India except their brothers in West Bengal, the bath is one of the pleasures, the true luxuries of their lives—enhanced by a good bar of soap, a toothbrush of some sort, and a comb. But the bath is more than that; it is a cleansing, a purification, a way of beginning and ending each day. The bath, in river or pond, is the time to wash one's saree or lungi under the water, modestly, and to emerge in clean clothes, waiting for them to dry between downpours or by virtue of body heat. No bath in a Western bathroom, no matter how ornate, ever can equal in intensity the satisfaction that a Bangladeshi farmer, his wife, and his children can garner in their nearby water, where together they bathe and talk, mother and father, sister and brother. And it is at the bath that the day's gossip is exchanged, men to men, women to women.

This daily immersion is the baptism, morning and night, of Bangladesh, the nearly sacramental rite that arises from the water and is done so naturally and unconsciously that it is rarely remarked on. The thirst for cleanliness, for freshness in body and clothes, is probably the country's most unremarked natural activity. (Compare it to many parts of England and Europe, where the weekly bath, summer and winter, in one's own dirty water remains the norm.) This emphasis on bodily cleanliness passes into every part of life in the village compounds, where the small houses and utility buildings are always kept rigorously clean. One wonders what other diseases would exist in Bangladesh were it not for this emphasis on cleanliness. More to the point, one wonders what artistry would be lost from the communal nature of the bath and the restrained sensuousness it imparts to life. Hollywood certainly would turn the bath of the Bangladeshi into pornography, but the Bangladeshi turns it into a dance, a folk art, part of the scenery. It is one of the most erotic aspects of life in the country, but not a sexy one; it is a modest art of great joy and dignity.

Water is not only the font of life in Bangladesh. It is the means. Boatmen ply the rivers, and the nation is filled with pilots, or *sarengs*, who intimately know the shoals and sandbars, the tricks of the currents and the dangerous floods. The waterways here are like the earth in other countries. Watch a European not accustomed to the sea get on a boat. Then watch the light movements of a Bangladeshi woman—a pregnant one in swollen green saree—as she steps on and stands gracefully like a ballet dancer as the oarsman drives his dhow across the water. The pilot and the oarsman are to water travelers what the guru and pir are to spiritual seekers. They lead the initiate through the waters from shore to shore, from here to eternity, with a certainty and dexterity that is breathtaking. From the fast packet boats, which each evening leave Dhaka for Khulna, one after another at full throttle, to small dinghies driven by engines meant for tubewells, to old country boats powered by four oars and steered from the rear by a helmsman holding a fan-shaped bamboo tiller, to the pastel sails of boats moving upstream on the monsoon winds, to the boats of the men who run along the banks towing heavy-laden vessels against the current, boats and boatmen are symbols of Bangladesh. Boatmen are the navigators of the second floor of the nation, the guides through the darkness to the light. The helmsman is the inner guide of the country's soul, the pure heart of man: free, disciplined, and completely in tune with his environment. Off he goes into the torrent singing his prayer. "Panch pir, panch pir, pir badr," in honor of a mythical Sufi saint who is the patron of all sailors, of all at sea.

Beneath the water are the fish, the *mach*, the symbol of Jesus and Vishnu, of the soul trapped in a body, the *ruh*, or soul, of the water swimming beneath the sea, where the fisherman, like Father Time, sinks his line to catch his prize, to raise it to the light. With hook or net, by the millions these fishermen ply the waters day and night to fetch the chief source of protein, the oil of life, the symbol of aphrodisia. The rivers, massive and fertile, never cease to yield up new souls for the fishermen to savor. Like gods, they know what is in the dark and the deep. Fine mesh nets slung on bamboo poles jut from the shores; small dhows, with dull kerosene lamps lighting their bows, drift in the evening mist, often dragging a net in the blackened wake.

Also intricately bound up with water is jute, Bangladesh's main cash crop, which begins to ripen and to be harvested during the floods. Developed as a modern industry in the nineteenth century, Bangladesh jute is sown before the rains, wherever the flood waters will be deepest along the canals and river banks. During the rains, when some of the crop is several feet high, farmers dive down, sometimes eight or nine feet, using the stalks as their guides, to cut the root and harvest the fibrous plants. The wet stalks are placed on bridges, roads, or roofs to dry. Those who dive for the pearls of jute are some of the world's most intrepid farmers and finest swimmers.

Fishermen, boatmen, bathers, jute divers—the heart of this nation—owe much of their poetry, their art, their song to their aquatic land. For instance, Lalan Shah, the Baul poet and songster who influenced Tagore and whose tune is used for Bangladesh's national anthem, was inspired by the plain speech of this land's boatmen and fishermen. As with Lalan Shah, nearly all that is sensuous and innocent, sweet and gentle, in Bangladesh is related to the never-changing, always moving rivers, to the contemplation of time and the river, to the beginning and the end, to the unvarying sequence of the seasons reflected on the rivers' mirrored surfaces, and to the flow of life to the sea, where all the rivers merge into oneness. All the greenness of the fields, all the pink of the lotus, all the yellow of ripened rice, all the white of the winter flowers emerges from the water; all the songs and folk dances, all the rhythms of the country singers owe their birth to the water—to its deep, undulating melody. And all that is contemplative, reminiscent of the Buddha, whose presence once blessed this country, arises as it did for Siddhartha, the Buddha, as he contemplated the presence of the river's face and ever-changing flow.

The river also is the source of forgiveness. For there, when the moon is full of an evening, rites are held for bathers—a declining minority today—to cleanse themselves of their sins. The full moons of January and March mark two special times when the waters are holy. The moon of the eighth day of Chait, in the dry season—about April, Bangladesh's first month—marks one of the most powerful evenings of the year for some people. On that night all sins are forgiven and millions, from all faiths, can be seen partaking of the ritual, quietly out in the river, standing with hands joined in the light of the moon and praying to be washed of their sins.

And yet, beautiful and sacred as they are, the rivers also are a source of terror, terror that comes of an effulgent stream tearing away at a riverbank and carrying a village with it; of a river changing course and plowing a new furrow two miles wide through fields that have stood for a century. A Bangladesh river has its own will and the power to do as it likes, when it likes. It cannot be placated, bribed, even addressed, as it neither hears nor sees. And thus, as many a Bangladeshi will relate, rivers are pure will, uncaring of life around them. To love a river is to truly know unrequited love.

Then there's the sea, which in Bangladesh is another formidable reality. For Bangladesh is a delta where not only do the rivers flow into the sea but the sea, via the tides, also flows into the rivers. Indeed, a fascinating phenomenon is that rivers more than a hundred miles from the sea change directions with the tides, so that the same river may flow south in the morning and north at night. Thus one must contemplate tide and river, time and tide, river and eternity in this land where fresh and salt water mix, where fishes of the sea and the mountains meet, where turtles of the sea and the jungle and alligators and trout all come together. There are no absolutes here—in water, land, crops, or pisiculture. Indeed, this mingling of rivers and sea, rivers and rain, water and earth, ashes of men and soil of the Himalayas, this cocktail of bathers, boatmen, and fishers of the sea, this land where rice and jute grow only in deep water, this land of rain, melted snow, and the sea is a land of water, a roiling, smiling, frothing, sweating, spitting, washing, and wetting substance.

The mixing of the currents of the rivers and of the salt and the fresh is much like the culture, comprised as it is of the rivers of Hindu, Buddhist, Muslim, and animist civilizations, each of which has flooded the nation in its time. And as with all floods, silt has been left that nourishes the present population.

Moreover, the rivers are much like this nation's politics: a source of never-ending interest, a rich alluvial stream, and a treacherous current and tidal storm that kills. Intrigue, envy, vengeance, greed drive the politics of any nation. But in Bangladesh, violence arises in paroxysms of bloodshed, like cyclones upon a previously passive river or tidal bores that crash violently up a river's course. Cyclones killed half a million people in 1970 and nearly two hundred thousand in 1991. Tidal bores killed tens of thousands at Urirchar in southern Bangladesh along the Bay of Bengal in 1985 and at Sandwhip Island in southeast Bangladesh, as well as in Chittagong and nearby islands in 1991.

It is this fluidity, this never-ending change brought by and symbolized by its waters, that makes the nation rich or poor, happy or sad, healthy or sick, strong or weak. The water and the rainy season set the tone. Too much or too little; too much silt or not enough. What can one be certain of in a nation of silt, where the soil turns to fluid, where the silt long since has covered the stone to a depth of several hundred feet over the centuries so that not a single stone is to be found in the riverbeds, on the shore, or near the surface in most of the country? What is solid, dependable, reliable from year to year? Is it the soil, so rich that it enables Bangladesh to produce a little over one pound of dry rice daily for every man, woman and child, to produce tons of vegetables and millions of ducks and fish? Is it the climate, so mild that buildings of the lightest materials provide adequate shelter the year-round? The answer is that what is solid and reliable is the rain and the need for rain. That is what the country is about.

The rain and the river, the sea and the river, the water. That is the first lesson of Bangladesh. Too much water and Bangladesh starves. Too little and it starves. One loves the water or not. But to love Bangladesh is to love a nation built upon a foundation of river and sea, with a roof that lets in the rain.

But what of the floods? Unfortunately, they represent one of Bangladesh's most misreported aspects. For they are not the unmitigated calamities which annually ignite a panic in the international media, especially in the silly season of August when the press is particularly subject to melancholia, at least that segment that has not scheduled its annual holiday. It almost has become a rite of passage that each year reporters with nothing better to do, often the newest of novices it seems, are dispatched to cover Bangladesh's annual "tragedy," to report as though the floods were a preventable occurrence, an unmitigated disaster. Few foreign reporters or editors know or care to learn how vital the floods are. Few will ever understand that the floods are a repository of the rich silt that accounts for the nation's fertility, that they are essential for the growth of rice, jute, and other crops, not to mention for the replenishment of the underground water table. Few understand that drought is a far greater danger.

Thus, in 1769–70, drought killed one-third of Bengal's people. In 1943, five million died during a drought. And in recent years India's neighboring West Bengal state has suffered from the fact that in the seventeenth century the Ganges shifted its course to modern-day Bangladesh. Consequently, in the early 1980s, India dammed the Ganges to divert much of the water, forcing it to flow into West Bengal (part of India) instead of into East Bengal (Bangladesh). This dam is a far greater danger to Bangladesh than any flood. Already this diversion has begun to dry up once-fertile plains in western portions of this land. And today Bangladesh faces still another fear: were India also to divert the waters of the Brahmaputra (Jamuna), which flows into northern Bangladesh, as it has planned, Bangladesh's long-term viability would be endangered.

Likewise, few foreign reporters bother to learn that in the past decade deaths from flooding have dropped annually, thanks to government actions, which have brought food and drugs into affected areas, and to precautions taken by local people themselves, including the purchase of more boats. Thus the worst flood in two centuries, in 1988, reportedly killed fewer than two thousand people, whereas the massive flood of 1787, when the Brahmaputra changed its course, wiped out one-third of the populace.

Nor do many foreign reporters visit northwest Bangladesh, the Rangpur-Dinajpur-Rajshahi Division, where the land is part of the old delta and is so elevated in what is called the Barind Tract that there is comparatively little flooding and rainfall is less than half that in the eastern areas around the main delta. Needed there are barrages, irrigation, and canals, not dikes and levees. Reporters also fail to visit the hill tracts in the north and east, where water levels are twice those on the plain. There, as the monsoon winds sweep vast amounts of water over the tree-covered hills, floods from swollen streams in narrow defiles often kill far more than in the flooded wide plains below.

Obviously, flood control is important in this water-logged land. It may well be that one day systems of dikes and embankments, coupled with better dredging of the rivers, will be able to reduce the flooding without harming agricultural output or disturbing the delta's natural drainage. Such schemes would have to be carefully examined before implementation, however, to protect this nation's natural heritage, lest the deluge be replaced by drought.

For the moment it is important to note that the annual frenetic reporting of the floods, along with heart-rending appeals for aid from the Bangladesh government and the world's private aid agencies, should be viewed with skepticism. Bangladesh's floods are not natural disasters but an essential part of the ecosystem with which the country is coping quite well. Similarly, cyclones (called hurricanes in the United States and typhoons in China) are as much a part of the ecosystem in Bangladesh as they are in Florida and the entire U.S. East Coast, in the Philippines, and on China's southern coast.

This is not to deny that there are serious water-related ferry boat sinkings, rail accidents, tidal waves, cyclones, and tornadoes. Tidal waves are especially deadly owing to the population density in low-lying areas near the Bay of Bengal on the country's southeast coast. These areas are really silt sandbars, or chars, that rise from the river and are only two or three feet above high tide. In 1985 at Urichar, a tidal wave killed ten thousand people who lived on a fertile char island. And in 1991, near Bangladesh's popular resort area of Cox's Bazaar, a cyclone wiped out an estimated one hundred thousand people, though the true numbers never will be known because not only are the reporting systems geared to exaggeration so as to garner aid, but whole villages that have never been recorded in the census may have been obliterated.

It is virtually impossible to protect these char lands; only a system of better weather forecasting and more adequate evacuation could help. Perhaps the day will come of Dutch dikes and reclaiming land from the sea. (Some such dikes were built after the tidal wave of 1970.) But until then the situation will remain unchanged: a calculated risk that sometimes is massively fatal. No government program will succeed in discouraging people from living on the char lands because the land is very fertile, made up as it is of pure silt. And given the scarcity of land in Bangladesh, the urge to cling to one's own land, even at the risk of cyclone, is overpowering. Even the most exposed char island, Sandwhip, whose rajah always was one of the country's richest leaders, has been populated for centuries.

With the deluge also comes sickness and death. For while the rains and the floods bring so much to the land, they also carry away so many. At no other time of the year are there are many *janazas*, the Muslim prayers for the dead. For the rainy season spawns colds and respiratory infections; it is a time of greatest danger to those who harbor tuberculosis cysts in their lungs. (Five million Bangladeshis suffer from active tuberculosis and many more millions carry the TB bacterium, which, in the face of bad weather and/or inadequate diet, often flares into the rust-red sputum of active disease.)

The rainy season, as well as its aftermath, is a time of massive deaths from other infectious diseases, especially typhoid and a host of diarrheal diseases, led by cholera, which swiftly drains the body of essential fluids, so that people who hours earlier were shivering in the damp suddenly are dying swiftly, as dry as victims of thirst in a desert. Most vulnerable are the very young and the elderly, those of weak constitution, of tired, malnourished bodies, who succumb to the damp and the chill as they wrap themselves in wet shawls or lie in a rocking boat with sides open to the wind, as family members comfort them helplessly. Yet here too there is improvement and hope. In 1971, in the midst of the civil war that led to Bangladesh's independence, a simple rehydration solution, consisting of a pinch of salt and a fistful of sugar in a jug of water, was developed in this country by researchers at what is now called the International Centre for Diarrhoeal Diseases Research, Bangladesh (ICDDR, B). This solution, which poor people in Bangladesh and worldwide are being taught to make at home and/or which is being distributed in millions of packets annually, is saving millions. Heralded as a miracle drug, it is the basis for such products as Gatorade, widely used by athletes in the United States.

As for the floods themselves, they have become less devastating. Flood-caused famine, which occurred as recently as 1974, is unheard of today. And while malnutrition remains a serious problem in the rainy season, it too has decreased in magnitude. The government-run food distribution system, begun in 1972 and completed only recently, has dramatically alleviated flood-related starvation thanks to a nationwide network of warehouses, some refrigerated. Thus, while in 1787 more than one-third of the populace died in a flood in then-British Bengal, in 1988, during one of the worst floods in two centuries, barely two thousand members of a populace five times larger lost their lives. Likewise, in the much-publicized cyclone of 1991, the problem was not food supplies but helicopters to distribute it. The solution was to use military units to supplement the food distribution system. Significantly, despite the destruction and loss of life, only 1 percent of the nation's total food production was destroyed.

As for the rainy season, ultimately, it ends by degrees. The rains become lighter, then less frequent; finally the gray-brown of the sky gives way to patches of blue. The sun of September and October warms the bones, and the recessional of the waters occurs in a more hopeful atmosphere. By November, cranes and Siberian ducks begin hovering overhead, as winter descends in the north. At night the air is cooler and drier. By December the air is very dry, as are clothes and blankets. Days are warm, skies are blue, nights are clear. And best of all, as the harvest begins, flowers bloom and jute plants turn gold—the real gold of Sonar Bengal, Golden Bengal.

Sarat

As September begins, skies are blue and an occasional cool, northerly autumn wind sweeps down from the distant Siberian plains. By month's end the sky is a sea of aquamarine, vast expanses of bright green rice shoots dominate the landscape, and drying jute's musty, sawdustlike smell permeates the air. Singers reach for their *echtars* and *dotars*, as once again the sound of music enlivens ferry boats and village squares. Flowers are blooming, the rice and the remaining jute crop is coming in, and the harvest is beginning. Most spectacular are fields upon fields of golden stalks—the ripening jute, the essence of Sonar Bengal.

Throughout the land, long stalks of jute lie drying on bridge railings, embankments, roofs, and roadsides. For as the jute flowers fade, harvesters dive down into the still, deep water to cut the plants at their roots, emerging with thick, brownish-black, water-logged stalks six to fifteen feet long. Allowed to wither until their leaves fall off, the stalks are retted for a week or more in water where bacteria help separate the rich fiber from the bark. Next, jute farmers complete the process by taking the stalks, white or gold depending on the strain, and stripping off the fibers, which are about two millimeters wide. The fibers then are graded for quality, sorted, and baled by middlemen, who do the first grading in *kutcha* (temporary) facilities before transferring the crop to *pucca* (solid or permanent) buildings for final sorting and grading by professional dealers. From there the jute is either exported or processed for use in burlap bags, curtain fiber, or carpet backing. (In the meantime, the rice harvest has begun, and drying rice replaces jute throughout the fields and byways.)

It is in the manufacturing process that jute fills the nostrils with its wood-like smell. First it is softened with water and oil, then "carded" when the fibres are ground into "hackle" (slivers free of vegetable matter), and then, in a process involving drafting, roving, and spinning, the fibers are rolled and drawn into a threadlike substance akin to heavy rope. Jute then emits the characteristic odor of burlap, a smell that permeates Bangladesh during sarat, along with the humid scent of mud and rice straw and the dry smell of rice polished in the harvest.

Native here, jute has been the main cash crop for farmers in the wetlands since the 1700s. Starting in the 1960s it became increasingly replaced by synthetic fibers, which are not necessarily cheaper but are easier to work with, stronger, and more versatile. As a result, the price has fallen and jute farming has declined dramatically. Two major consequences have been increased poverty in the countryside and larger numbers of landless laborers, because jute farming is highly labor intensive. Unfortunately, the human aspect of jute's decline has not been examined adequately by government, academia, the press, or commentators on Bangladesh. For jute is a difficult crop to replace. After all, what other crop needs a hundred inches of rain?

During sarat, as the jute harvest proceeds, the flood waters recede under a cerulean sky, which is reflected throughout the jade green, water-logged rice fields, whose delicate shoots undulate in the languid sun. Blue, gold, and green, the colors of sarat: blue sky, golden sun, and jute, green vegetation, a profusion of greens, from emerald to jade, pea to lime, shamrock to sea-green, personified by palm, mango, mehndi, banana, and plane trees, by ordinary grass and elephant grass, by mustard, rice, and chili plants, by bamboo shoots and sugar stalks, by tobacco leaves and tea bushes, by pulses and water lilies. The verdancy, the verdure of all greens imaginable burst forth under the sunlit sky. During the rainy season, under brown and slate-gray skies, these greens often appear to be black or olive drab; but under the newly awakened sun, these soothing, peaceful greens complement the golden jute, emitting wave after wave of relaxing visual vibrations.

Into the midst of this green descend snowy white Siberian cranes, which stand bandy-legged in the paddies among the native egrets, while brown-and-black ducks appear in such numbers that their arrival casts a shadow over square miles of river surfaces and sometimes appears to darken the sun. Humid though the air remains, it emits a sweet, comforting warmth with just the slightest sense of chill late at night.

While in northern climes autumn means dying flowers and cooler weather, in Bangladesh autumn brings cooler weather, but also flowers. For flowers grow in the cool season, and leaves fall before the hot season in March and April. It is during sarat that Bangladesh becomes a paradise. In this period, there is no equal in all of Asia to this country's warmth and beauty.

Sarat's weather is remarkable because it is so unexpected. Located on the Tropic of Cancer like Texas and much of China, Bangladesh is protected from winter by the Himalayan Mountains, which screen out the harsh Siberian winds and retain the langorous warmth of the South Sea monsoon winds. In the west of the Indian subcontinent, this effect creates deserts; but in Bangladesh the rivers and the heavy rains create a damp, warm, protective air cover. Even the British, who fled the heat and rain, came back to Bangladesh in winter for the air, the flowers, the sparkling nights. Calcutta and Dhaka in British days were fashionable places to be in the dry season, for horse racing, for parties, for the lovely way of life.

Comes sarat, the clouds disperse and that glorious Bangladesh sky returns with its depth of air, so that every star stands out starkly and the stars appear to be at different distances. The sky is not marbled with bright stars or the hazy glow of the Milky Way but is deep and blue-black like the sea beyond the tidewater. The sky has a depth of light and an ether, a tremulous, vaporous, rarified atmosphere that appears to bring the sunset and the moon, the stars and the comets down to earth, where people in their dark villages can gaze up and feel the sky's ethereal presence. Whether at the beach at Cox's Bazaar or alone on the deck of a river steamer, one senses this effect: as though someone were standing up against the sky, head and shoulders among the stellar worlds. So clear is the astral light that one can see a loved one's eyes reflect the night sky.

Hemanto

For the first time since the rains, from the end of September to the middle of November, the land emerges. During the rains, water covers over 80 percent of Bangladesh's land. Only the nipple tops of villages above their breastlike mounds remain visible. And in most parts of the country, only roads built nineteen or more feet above sea level are not submerged beneath the flood of over two hundred inches of water that falls during the rainy season. If in addition to the rains an unusual amount of snow melted in the faraway Himalayas the previous spring, then even high roads and villages will be flooded. For instance, in 1988 Dhaka was under several feet of water, though it is sixty feet above sea level and 150 miles away from the sea.

However, as noted earlier, most of Bangladesh is barely above sea level. Indeed, except for the hills along its northern and eastern borders, the land in no way resembles that of most other countries. For its "land" consists merely of the accumulated silt of the rivers Jamuna, Padma, and Meghna, as well as sand, and soil dragged down over the millennia from the mountains where the rivers are fed. This soil is deposited year after year on the floor of the beach. Thus Bangladesh's land was formed. Or is forming.

For Bangladesh occupies a new or active delta where the rivers are still forming land. In the dry season, new islands, peninsulas, or even entire counties suddenly appear each year in the midst of rivers or in their wide mouths near the sea. These char lands, consisting of soil deposited during the last rainy season, may grow or be washed away the following year. In fact, no part of Bangladesh is not liable to be reformed or to disappear over the course of the coming century. Bangladesh is thus unique: the rivers are always changing course, and the topography is forever being altered.

While West Bengal State in adjacent India occupies part of the old and stagnant delta, which is unlikely to change in the foreseeable future, Bangladesh is subject to revision and indeed prospers because it is bathed by annual floods with their gift of silt. It is the newness of the delta that gives Bangladesh both its haggard look after floods and its vibrant fertility, miraculously clean air, and natural liveliness.

To put into perspective the magnitude of the annual deposit of silt in the delta formed by the Meghna, the Padma, and the Jamuna, one must know that the river moves an estimated four hundred million tons, or fifty million cubic feet, of earth each year. The delta covers sixty-five thousand square miles and is over five hundred feet deep. It takes about forty-five years to raise the delta one foot and has taken more than thirteen thousand years to achieve its current dimensions. From the beginning of the delta at the north, the river drops only five inches per mile, dropping to less than one inch per mile at the sea. As the river's decline lessens, its speed decreases and its ability to hold silt diminishes—so that it begins depositing soil first on the flooded fields, then along its own banks, and finally, right in the center of its flow, forming char land. One such char island encompasses 441 square miles in the center of the river's mouth. And the delta of the rivers where the three rivers merge covers an area the size of the Netherlands and Belgium combined.

Thus Bangladesh is a self-made, ever-growing land conceived in the Himalayas and born simultaneously at the three places its major rivers enter the country: near Rajshahi in the west, near the Garo hills to the north, and in the Khasia hills of Sylhet to the northeast. The delta formed by these three rivers forms an enormous blue parallelogram in southcentral Bangladesh, a patch of land that annually grows taller and wider as it stretches toward the sea.

One can see and feel this wealth of new soil by wading out into the fields after the flood recedes and after the harvest, just before the *aus* crop is planted in November, when the soil is so soft that in many areas new rice shoots conceivably could be planted without ploughing. Moreover, the soil is so rich in nutrients that combined with today's fast-growing crop varieties, it is super-productive. For the rains bring silt, the country's largest source of fertilizer and the envy of Bangladesh's neighbors.

During this season, the land is at its most pulsing, luscious best. Throughout the country, festivals flourish to hail the harvest, the end of the floods, the coming of new soil, the wonder of the rivers, and the *melas*, which celebrate the advent of the new season. Carnival equipment moves from the drier northwest to the wetter southeast, from the plains of the Dhaka Division to the Meghalaya plateaus and the Khasia hills. It's the time of the Durga Puja and the Juggernaut festival, when the Hindu community enjoys the year's most joyous celebration, accompanied by dancing and outdoor plays. It's the time when students and villagers stage *jatras*, or plays, of various legends of their areas or folk tales of the river or place.

And although Bangladesh is a relatively flat land, it's not a dull one. On the contrary, as a retired friend, Qazi Jalaluddin Ahmed, who has lived in all parts of the country in government service, put it, "Bangladesh is a small country of large distances." He means this two ways: practically speaking, Bangladesh often is a difficult place to travel, but poetically it is a country that is incredibly diverse. Thus, largely owing to the rainy season, which makes all forms of communication difficult, there are far more differences in architecture, crops, dialect, ethnicity, and customs in each hundred miles of Bangladesh than in three times as much land area of Japan or Germany or even in a thousand miles of the United States.

For example, in the hilly frontier areas in the north and east live many different tribal peoples, including the Garos, the Khasis, and the Koch (originally thought to be related to the White Huns) in the north, and the Chakmas and the Marma, or Lusias, in the south. Some of these tribes, such as the Garos, are Christian; some, such as the Chakmas, are Hindu or Buddhist, and some, such as the Rohinga, are Muslim. Some, who slaughter cows each December as offerings to the moon, are animist; some are Buddhist. All are of Mongolian origin and are related to such tribes as the Hmong who live in Southeast Asia south of Bangladesh's southeastern Chittagong District and in neighboring Burma. These tribal peoples often are badly treated by ethnic Bengalis, who are by far the majority. Moreover, they nurse a grievance stemming from the fact that in the days of the Kingdom of Kamrup, in about the thirteenth century, they dominated most of eastern and central Bangladesh, until they were forced into the frontier hillocks. Although the government strives to satisfy these tribes' demands, the Bengali majority treats them the way the Aryan invaders, who conquered the area three thousand years ago, treated the native Bengalis: they take their land and ignore their culture, always forcing them out of the mainstream. There are more than six hundred thousand of these tribal people whose culture is on the fringe. Some, probably helped by the Indian Army across the border, for several years have been able to tie down two Bangladesh Army divisions in a sporadic but demonically effective uprising. Sadly, if they were treated well, these tribal groups would be among Bangladesh's most loyal citizens, for that is their nature.

These same hilly regions, on the fringes of the jungle, are home to a variety of animals, including boar and deer, and thus are popular hunting grounds, especially for the country's upper middle class and rich. At the beginning of this century, Bangladesh abounded in wildlife, including the famed Bengal tiger and elephants that have since disappeared. As late as the 1930s, rhinos, tigers, and plentiful deer could be found within a few miles of the cities. Finally, these hilly regions are also where tea, oranges, and other crops requiring a cooler climate are grown.

Interestingly, living and working on the tea plantations (tea being Bangladesh's second most important export after jute) are a tribal people brought here from different parts of India by the British in the eighteenth century who speak dialects not easily understood by the surrounding society. Also in these highlands are traders, some would say smugglers, who for centuries have brought products from the mountainous areas of eastern India—especially drugs, wood, cattle, spices, and dyes—to the far eastern plains in exchange for rice and pulses. And in Chittagong in the southeast, near Burma's Arakan region, live the Rohingas, Muslim tribals with roots in Burma, and the Maghs, a Buddhist group also originally from Burma, once renowned for producing the most feared pirates and seamen in the Bay of Bengal. Indeed, during the late Moghul period, around the seventeenth century, the Portuguese, no mean seamen and pirates themselves, teamed up with the Maghs and terrorized the seacoast as well as communities far up the river channels of what is now Bangladesh. The Maghs were great merchants, and today a Dhaka market bears their name. In fact, Dhaka long ago became a major city partly because both the Moghul rulers and their Afghan allies were able to defend it from Magh raids. And Lalbagh Fort, Dhaka's medieval fortress on the Burraganga River, and the walls of the fort at Narayanganj, about fifteen miles to Dhaka's south, were built as defenses against Magh raids.

As for Dhaka, capital of this "small country of large distances," it is, like Washington, D.C., inhabited by people who mostly either grew up in or retain strong ties to outlying districts, such as Rajshahi, Rangpur, Sylhet, Mymensingh, Barisal, Kulna, and Noakhali. Bangladesh has 21 districts, 492 subdistricts, and 65,000 villages. So great are the "distances" in this small country that one is unlikely to encounter anyone, save an intrepid politician at election time, who has visited every district in the past decade, nor anyone who has ever visited all the subdistricts (even though these are the main political and economic divisions), much less more than a smattering of the villages.

But these districts are important. When a man says he's from Noakhali, he probably has a temper as hot as the chilies produced in his area; if he's from Sylhet, he's a sharp businessman, probably descended from pirates (*Saleti* is still the word used in the Gulf of Siam for pirates); if from Srimongal, he's probably involved in tea; or if he's from Mymensingh, he's most likely a jute wallah. Northwest Bengal and such towns as Dinajpur, Rangpur, Jessore, Bogra, and Kushtia, which do not have as much rain or flooding as the rest of the country, consequently grow more sugar cane, silk, and mangoes, crops for which the area is famous, as well as bananas, tobacco, wheat, and corn. The rich delta islands of the Sunderbans, which retain the country's best jungle, have tigers, excellent wood, and a life very remote from the Mercedes and the video shops of Dhaka.

Thus this seemingly tiny nation contains a mix of people in terms of crop, dialect, and sense of regional identity. For example, everyone believes that the people of Kushtia and Jessore speak the best Bangla; thus believed the country's poet laureate, Tagore, and its other great poet Lalan Shah, both of whom came from there. The Bauls, the country's troubadours, are found everywhere, dressed in varicolored rags, singing their country songs for donations. They are the nation's *buskers*, or minstrels, versed in romance and sometimes high on *bhang*, or hashish, but always alive, alert, happy, ready to look you in the eye and talk. Carrying their dotars and echtars, they create a fresh, vibrant mood that matches the season's green fields, blue sky, and fresh waters.

Such is the land and the people that come to life in the hemanto season—when the earth rises from the water and, like a ship's bow, shakes off its drenching burden. And as the land rises, flowers bloom: jasmine, water lily, rose, magnolia, hibiscus, bougainvillea, and a hundred others.

By hemanto's end, the air is no longer humid. In the villages, the land is cool with fresh scents that replace the dry jute smell of sarat. The air is fragrant with crops, flowers, and burning rice stalks, as thatched roofs are repaired, mud courtyards grow solid in the dry air, calves are born, goats prance, buffalo low contentedly, cranes land in the fields, and geese and ducks swim in the streams.

Hemanto also marks the start of the wedding season, enlivened by red, blue, green, or white *shamianas*, tentlike structures lit by gay garlands of lights under which receptions are held first for the groom's family and then for the bride's. The Bangladeshi wedding is a seven-to-ten-day affair. In some families the ceremonies begin when the eldest male blesses the bride and groom. At the second event, the two are bathed in turmeric for purity and the bride wears *mehendi* (a red dye) on her hands and feet. The groom's family then delivers a large array of gifts, usually such practical things as sheets, bedding, cooking utensils, and accessories, as well as sweets. The bride's family then entertains the groom's family *en famille*. At the main reception, held by the bride's people, the contract is signed and the marriage notarized. Then the bride goes to the groom's house, where she is greeted with hoots from the women and good-natured joshing. Her feet are painted vermillion, which she tracks into the house before serving food to her husband's family. Finally the groom's family holds its reception. Often, weddings among the small Hindu minority contain other variations, such as the blowing of conch shells at each stage.

Whatever the religion (Christian and Buddhist, too) wedding celebrations are intense, joyous, boisterous, emotionally wrenching, not to mention expensive affairs that must uphold a family's "standards," real or pretended. For Bangladeshis are an emotional people with an intense family life whose ceremonies and rituals are invested with enormous importance. Moreover, it's difficult to make the necessary compromises and to give up or gain a daughter or absorb a son into the Bengali's complex extended family.

Marriages here are perhaps one of the society's aspects most misunderstood by Westerners—for nearly all (except for a small but growing number today among those rich and educated abroad) are carefully arranged. Despite what many foreigners believe, most are successful. There are many reasons. First, in this relatively small society, the couple come from similar backgrounds and usually either know each other or have friends or family in common. Second, many want to marry each other or at least have no strong objection. Moreover, they are raised, knowing they're expected to learn to love each other and to be faithful, among parents, uncles, aunts, and older siblings and cousins who set examples and coach them as to what is expected and how to behave. Finally, the parents, who at least initially choose the mate, are as concerned with their children's happiness as parents anywhere, and choose accordingly. Consequently, Bangladesh probably has as many happy marriages as elsewhere and more long-lasting ones, despite the laxness of Muslim divorce laws compared to Western ones.

As to Westerners' frequent complaint about the expense, it is true that weddings are very costly. But they are planned from the day a child is born, and the event is much more than a marriage. It is a vast family reunion, a vital social occasion for the community of friends, a chance to repay invitations and favors, and, of utmost importance, a statement of family love for the child and respect for marriage. As one father related half in jest, "After six months of planning, three weeks of intense preparation, and two weeks of ceremony, who would want to get married again? No one has the strength for two weddings." For a foreigner interested in the country and lucky enough to get invited, weddings are the best source of gossip, not to mention social, political, and cultural commentary. To miss the wedding is to miss the buzz.

As everyone at a given level of society is related, weddings are the quickest initiation into crucial or just plain interesting genealogy data. Last names, for instance, usually offer no clues. Families often don't retain last names, married women often are called by their first names preceded by *Begum* (literally, "Mrs."), and the relative handful of last names are used repeatedly. Thus the uninitiated is unlikely to suspect that Zia al Huq is Humayun Kabir's first cousin (on his father's side), that Begum Tahmina and Begum

Rehka are sisters, or that your best friend's tennis partner is married to the minister of industries. For Bangladesh is the land of the original tar babies: touch one and you're likely to find yourself enmeshed in a web of family connections filled with *chachas:* uncles, cousins, sisters, brothers, uncles-in-law, all of whom are somehow related to everyone else you know in Dhaka, not to mention to families in the districts, subdistrict towns, and villages.

Seet

From mid-November to early January, the weather continually becomes more arid, less humid. The earth dries and a dust forms, but so little dust that the dew, which still falls, dampens it well into the day. Open-air activities multiply. In the evening, the elderly don pullovers and cardigans, while the young visit the squash court, football field, cricket pitch, tennis court, or golf course, soaking up the sunlight. Seet also is the season when people return to their roots, to their "ancestral" or village homes to renew their ties.

Expatriates worldwide tend to engage in a competition of sorts: they brag about getting to know the countryside where the "real" people live. This is especially true in Bangladesh, because more than 80 percent of the populace lives in rural areas. Unfortunately, by and large Bangladesh's expatriates tend to view the villagers as noble savages, poor victims, innocent, sweet and beyond reproach. All too often these "natives" are contrasted with the urban elites, who are despised as *nouveau riche* climbers getting rich by stealing the aid donated by wealthy nations. Aside from the fact that most expatriates themselves are leeches on the aid budget, this semi-Marxist comparison contradicts what Marx himself thought of the mind-numbing backwardness of the Bengal countryside he loathed. But Marx, too, was wrong. If it is culture, not noble savages, one is seeking, it exists in the countryside, not in the cities.

Unlike West Bengal, whose capital, Calcutta, is filthy, smelly, run down, and depressingly poor (but rapidly rehabilitating itself in recent years) yet as intellectually and culturally vibrant as London, Taipei, or Paris, East Bengal's major cities are relatively clean, efficient, well maintained—and deadly dull. For instance, though it has genteel people, Dhaka is not a genteel place. It is Manchester not Edinburgh, Dallas not Boston, Nagoya not Kyoto. Especially in Dhaka, the elites are steeped in criticism and cynicism, as they dwell on politics or other people's money. Dhaka is foremost a city of politicians, merchants, and bureaucrats, as artificial as Washington, D.C. The countryside is different. There exist the foundations of Bengali culture.

As Bangladesh is a small country of large distances, any journey can mean a major undertaking. Thus, although the new Japanese-financed bridge over the Meghna has cut the trip by an hour, it still can take seven hours to drive 150 miles from Dhaka to Chittagong, depending on the ferries and the traffic and whether construction crews have blocked a lane here and there. Bogra from Dhaka takes six hours owing to the long wait for the ferry. Ditto for Sylhet and Khulna, both about a hundred miles. Trains can be faster, but they're late, although they have vastly improved in twenty years. Airplane travel is also slow and relatively expensive. For example, the fastest way to visit a friend's village sixteen miles from Dhaka is a three-hour boat ride, as there are no paved roads. Let me take you to Shamsuddin Ahmed's village, Nawabganj, which is typical of many.

We wake before dawn in the gray nautical light to the serenade of birds (reminiscent of a Tarzan film soundtrack) offering morning's first greeting to the sun, as the roosters (yes, you hear them in Dhaka) laugh at the morning star when the mighty sun begins to humble that one-eyed devil, and the *muzzein*, in his quavering but austerely disciplined way, sings the first prayer from the mosque. Under a sky turning peaches-and-cream, we drive through a sleeping city to the *sadarghat* (pier) in Old Dhaka. Parking the car, we stroll through the ancient station and board the *Posia*, a motorized ferry that holds about a hundred people. The boat is vibrant with activity, as passengers settle in or buy snacks from little boy peddlers who sweetly call out, "Ayedelee, aydelo." In the early morning mist, the boat pulls out into the main brown current of the Burriganga, heading south.

The old city along the bank, an endless, topsy-turvy architectural spectrum of minarets and houses, no two alike, piled one atop the other, contrasts favorably with ship skeletons on the shore opposite waiting for wreckers to finish. Scattered haphazardly, early bathers stand in the shallows of the gray water doing their morning ablutions. One wades in, hands extended to touch the tide. Another swims gently in the cool flow. Another soaps himself. Meanwhile, in the ferry's main cabin, a Baul singer, in a crazy-quilt suit of clothes, plays an agonizingly sweet song on his two-stringed dotar, a tale of the land's beauty when the flowers bloom.

South of Narayanganj Fort, whose red stones shine with morning dew in the bright early light, the ferry turns north up the Dhaleswari River to Nawabganj, under a vibrant blue sky that bedazzles the fields and villages of the countryside west of Dhaka. Swishing up the channel, it passes other ferries, country boats with rounded cabriolet tops of bamboo matting and large trailing black rudders, and long, narrow racing vessels powered by small red-and-silver tubewell engines—engines that have revolutionized river transport in the last five years, since they are locally adapted to the boats and not subject to import tariffs. Dipping and swaying, the ferry floats under a vibrant blue sky that is reflected in patches of water amid the light green rice fields encroaching upon the river's edge.

Traveling thus, it is the Bangladesh village that captures one's imagination—perched atop a mound, a clump of palm, mango, and bamboo trees interspersed with grassy family compounds of mud-walled, thatch-roofed huts. As one of the first Englishmen to travel here, two centuries ago, wrote, "No country which is dead level and unadorned by elegant arts can be more beautiful than that through which I have today come. It is one continuous field yielding the richest crops, from all the stiffness of regular fences, only interrupted by the natives' cottages concealed in groves of fruit trees, that are variegated with all the irregularity of luxurious nature."

Square miles of verdant rice fields are spread out as far as the eye can see, punctuated only rarely by village mounds of trees. These tree-blanketed oases are the key to an ecological work of genius. For the village provides height above the flood, trees to cool the huts, silvery springs or ponds from which to drink or in which to grow fish and to bathe, all enclosed and private from other villages, with grass commons for schools or for the grazing of bullocks, buffalo, and goats.

Entering Nawabganj, you instantly feel the temperature difference; it is up to ten degrees cooler than the open fields and so shady that you must adjust your eyes. The village is alive with trees: palm, banana, coconut, jackfruit, mango, bamboo, banyan, mehndi (from whose leaves come vermillion), plane, deodar, and others that were unfamiliar.

Tucked among the greenery and open spaces are family compounds. Each consists of a flat-mud, scrupulously clean, grassless courtyard, about twelve feet square, polished daily with mud to give it a hard, smooth finish. Around it are placed huts—for cooking, sleeping, guests. With walls of mud or bamboo mat, with roofs of tin, thatch, or matting, and with roof timbers of bamboo staves, some have doorways across which hang large, wide banana leaves used to maintain privacy, as women here live in modest *purda* (seclusion). However, unlike the women in such strict Muslim societies as that of Saudi Arabia or even parts of Pakistan, Bangladeshi women rarely wear the *chador* to cover their faces.

No two family compounds abut. Almost always a modest patch of greenery and trees ensures some privacy. Chickens and ducks scurry hither and yon, and cows, tied to trees or stakes in the ground, munch grass along the ambling paths that lead from house to house. As the village mounds are not level, the paths meander, often around large ponds, where women can be seen bathing modestly in water up to their shoulders among water lilies or lotus.

As for the family compound, it is an austere rectangle, devoid of decoration, containing several huts belonging to a family related through the males. Everything is functional, clean, and well maintained. The family's few possessions have their place: clothes on pegs, tools in their own hut. The cooking area can be fairly crude, consisting sometimes only of bricks raised above the black cow-chip coals. Yet the adjacent soil is scrupulously clean, to prevent contamination from rotting foods.

In one compound, the *pater familias*, a wiry, gray-haired, leather-faced old peasant, provides a tour of his family's thatched "drawing room" hut, about six by four feet, which contains simple unpainted wooden furniture: several chairs around a table. The sole decoration is a faded picture of the late President Zia Rahman, who was assassinated in 1981 and whose wife is now prime minister. The room is as superclean and severe as that of a Yankee Puritan. It exudes an air of dignity, hard work, and practicality. Next door is the young men's sleeping hut and opposite a hut for unmarried girls. Married couples have their own huts.

While most villagers live in such kutcha mud and bamboo huts, here and there is found a pucca concrete building. The homes of rich men, some of these buildings are quite imposing, with high ceilings, pillared fronts, and yellow plaster walls. Styled after and sometimes dating to British times, such abodes usually have a center room and two bedrooms at either end. Moreover, as many villages boast young men who work as contract labor for two or three years in the Middle East, it is not unusual to see more modern houses replete with television and other appliances.

Like all Bangladesh villages, Nawabganj is starkly clean and litter free. There is no waste paper, tins, bottles, or other debris that makes up the garbage of the West. Nor is there the filth and rotting poverty found in Western cities, or raw sewage (as the raised mounds absorb and process the waste), stagnant pools of water, or unneeded ditches. There is, however, the pervading, sickly sweet odor of burning cow-chips (cow dung mixed with straw and dried until crisp in the sun), a smell that, mingled with the damp, musky odor of the animals themselves, offsets the acrid fumes from dry rice straw and rice husks burned as cooking fuel.

In a way, this odor reinforces the incredible intimacy that exists here between man and beast, an intimacy reflected, for example, by children tending the goats who talk to their charges, while the wise guy-eyed, bearded beasts often seem to reply. Reflecting on the peacefulness and naturalness of such a scene, one cannot help but think how much we city people lose by separating ourselves from the animal world.

In Nawabganj and other villages, dress is less formal than in the cities. Children wear only shorts; women are clad in simple red, blue, or green cotton sarees; men wrap themselves in their lungis. Nearly everyone is barefooted or at most wears rubber flip-flops. And this lightness of dress emphasizes the villagers' intimacy with nature. Like their mud walls and bamboo mats, their light clothing allows the fresh village air of sunlight and shade to refresh the body. And at night very little is needed to warm the body, as the trees block the vapors that rise from the wet fields.

While most villages sport a small mosque and graveyard, many have no store or market of any kind; inhabitants often have to go far for supplies. As for electricity, only one-fifth of this nation's villages have it. The rest use candles, kerosene lanterns, or battery-powered flashlights.

Immediately beyond the village are the rice fields, a patchwork of paddies that are unmarked but leave no doubt as to who owns or rents what. Around each patch of field is a low mud wall that separates one field from the next.

Farming is a family affair: up early, plough in the morning, plant, weed, or harvest in the afternoon. The men, shirtless from dawn to dusk under an often blistering sun, are the backbone of this nation, descendants of the people whom the British viceroy Warren Hastings praised as the world's best farmers. For not an inch of land is unutilized the year-round, except for periods when it simply must be allowed to rest.

It is virtually impossible to exaggerate the relationship that exists between the farm family and its land. Early in the morning, after the dawn prayer, they are in the field, up to their calves in water in the sowing season, squatting on haunches to weed later, bent down with a small scythe in the harvest, carrying stalks on their heads, burning the field in the dry season, digging with feet in the mud, planting vegetables, rigging sticks to support the bitter gourd, walking behind the oxen to plow. That stretch of land is his and hers, their wealth, their love, their life. They know how it looks at every hour of the day, in every season. They know its smells, its tempers, its needs. It is at once their mother and their child, their brother and their sister. And as they work in the silence of the fields, they can hear it murmur to them, as they murmur back.

Few foreigners visit the villages, some because they would not deign to, some because they feel uncomfortable being stared at and followed (mostly by curious children), and some because they understand the burden their presence mandates. For Bangladeshi villagers are among the world's most gracious hosts, whether or not they can afford it. Any visitor merits the best: the best goat or chicken, the most fragrant rice, the finest sweets. Compared to Western informality, such generosity appears impetuous at best, and most foreigners, if at all sensitive, feel that too much is being made of them.

For my first meal at Nawabganj I am offered a whole five-pound fish, a *ruhi*, curried mutton, chicken in Marsala sauce, saffron rice pilau, cucumber and tomato salad, and a bowl of rice-cake sweets in honey, topped off with tea boiled in fresh cream with sugar. Successive meals are equally grand. As for my young "admirers" who faithfully follow me around, after a day the novelty wears off and privacy is restored.

Looking back now, my strongest memory is of my hosts' simple generosity, uncomplicated openness, and willingness to talk about their lives, beliefs, and habits without self-consciousness or show. Far from being fawning rustics, Bangladeshi villagers, at Nawabganj and elsewhere, have a self-confidence born of knowing who they are and where they fit into the scheme of things. They are not noble savages but ordinary people who have the same vices as others. Their manners and way of life can be enticing to a jaded Westerner. After two days in a village such as Nawabganj, one can be sorely tempted to stay on and adopt its way of life, grounded as it is in essential things, simply achieved. These people have such a natural, intimate relationship with their fields, water, trees, and animals that life outside the village womb seems empty. Such thoughts are easy, perhaps, for one such as me who has tasted modernity and often finds it lacking. But the truth is that the winds of change are wafting through these villages and stirring up the young, as increasing education and the advent of electricity, radios, television, and videos, not to mention overseas contract work, make the outside world both enticing and accessible. Also applying pressure is the growing landlessness, which is forcing more and more villagers to seek work in towns and cities.

It is wonderful in the dry season to visit the villages where 80 percent of the people live—to gaze from the rice paddies at the tufted clouds, to see the sun or stars reflecting from the pool of water in a *beel* (a permanent depression in the land that allows water to collect and lush plants to grow), to commune with the stars, to experience the essence of Bangladesh: the harmony of man, beast, land, water, and air that makes the countryside so integral to the nation's very being.

The more one travels in this small country of great distances, the more one begins to understand and love it. For here people are handsomer, the land is more beautiful, the sky is more alive. And here people sing, about the moon, the flowers, the cow, the orange-red sunset over emerald fields, and love. Meanwhile, in the shadows beyond the lanterns, girls in sarees begin dancing in a lovely, flowing way that bespeaks not sex or showiness but tradition that is thousands of years old and as sweet as yellow flowers blowing in a breeze.

Basanto

The coolest days are from mid-December through February, when days are golden with light and flowers and nights and early mornings are chilly, requiring blankets and sweaters. While Westerners love this weather, Bangladeshis find it extremely cold. Many, especially the *chowkidars* and *darwans* (night guards) and *ansars,* or military police, wrap themselves in shawls and blankets and wear scarves and hats pulled down over their ears. This is the season for lung infections and for tubercular flareups among a poor populace where the disease is widespread. Many a night one is kept awake by a chowkidar's almost incessant coughing in the chill, misty air. Some nights are so crisp and cold that the stars seem to be made of ice in a wondrous sky.

Thus, Nirad Chaudhuri, the great and aging Bengali writer who was born and grew up in this land and lives in Oxford, England, wrote of the Bangladesh sky:

> Our sky was a soft infinity rising from the earth to the unknown and the
> unknowable in equally soft steps. Nearest to us were the clouds, never resting,
> never in one place, never of one color, never of one tone. At sunrise and
> sunset our minds could soar up through their pile on pile, and layer on layer,
> of yellow, gold, orange, red, pink, and grey to the blue spaces beyond, and our
> child mind did go up. The blue, too, was of the softest, not even K'ang-Hsi
> blue was softer—and it seemed to be the color of space condensed into mist.
> At night, we could see stereoscopic distances and depths within it, regions
> after regions of the planets, of the galactic stars, of the star clouds of extra-
> galactic systems, without end from galaxy to galaxy, and never offering any
> friction to the mind in its ascent to the stellar universe. The wonder with
> which all of us were born could never die under that sky.

During basanto, the countryside hums with fairs, parades, and commemorations. There are country fairs, especially at the tombs of saints, and city fairs, such as Dhaka's book fair, the Bangladesh New Year festival of the arts, and the industrial fair. In a more serious vein, Martyr's Day and Independence Day are celebrated at the Shaheed Minar memorial at Savar, about twenty miles from Dhaka, in memory of those killed by the Pakistanis during the 1971 war.

The arts festival is perhaps the most festive of the events, as it celebrates painting and handicrafts, poetry and music, dance and drama. It's a time when everyone—young and old, city or country folk, rich or poor, educated or not, Bangladeshi or foreign—can share this nation's culture. Specially enthralling are Bangladesh's painters, such as Jahangir, Samad, the exuberant Sultan, and Rehka Kabir, whose works exude power and originality in a tradition that stretches back at least two thousand years. Equally strong are the poets, poetry being the national art, enriched with diverse traditions, and immortalized by the likes of Nobel prize winner Tagore, Kazi Nazrul Islam, and Jasmiuddin. There also are plays, dance programs, and concerts, which address universal themes and provide subtle insights into this land and its people.

The chief entertainment, however, is of quite another variety during basanto in Dhaka. For it is the start of the social season, heralded by a frantic whirl of invitations—to weddings, each more beautiful than the last (but all seemingly with the same caterer); to lavish diplomatic dinners in opulent drawing rooms or large, perfumed gardens sparkling with candles or gaslight lanterns; to parties thrown in the honor of visiting VIPs who always schedule their trips at this time of the year; to official dinners at the government's guest house in Ramna, near the Civil Lines of the British era, where judges and high civil servants have their official homes; to various affairs connected with visiting heads of state, when Dhaka decorates its buildings with colored lights and traffic is diverted as caravans of Mercedes speed down the main roads; and to "national days" celebrated by diverse foreign embassies to honor their countries while taking advantage of the weather.

Moreover, every weekend there's a tournament at the posh and private Kurmitolah Golf Course, where winners are presented with the Ispahani Cup, the President's Cup, or cups sponsored by various ambassadors. The frenzy at these events is as astonishing as is the false bonhomie and the desire to be seen. It takes a discerning eye to know who really counts and to pick out the "Ershad golfers," named for the ex-military ruler, an avid and, some say, very good golfer who during his tenure in power (1982–90) favored those who made sure to be seen at the club. Strutting and pretentious so many of them are, instead of being ashamed that their club was financed, according to some accounts, by wheat from the U.S.-sponsored Food-for-Work program and by aid from the Japanese. (There is a plaque to Japanese aid alongside the swimming pool—living proof that aid often amounts to not much more than an income transfer from poor people in rich countries to rich people in poor ones.) Some members of the club made generous contributions from their own funds to make the club a success, but much of the club is the result of government expenditures financed ultimately by aid.

Downtown, tennis and squash, not golf, are played at the slightly shabby and far more egalitarian Dhaka Club, whose members belong for the camaraderie, instead of professional reasons masked as a good time. The atmosphere would be quite a shock to Lancelot Hare, British lieutenant governor of India's East Bengal and Assam provinces, who, when he dedicated the building in 1911 as a watering hole for the ruling elite, dreamt of prolonging Britannia's rule and adhered to the prevailing view that Dhaka (not Calcutta) would be the capital of a divided Bengal. Instead, the club today is the best gossip mill in town. It is there, on Thursday evenings, that the rumors begin circulating, planted by the government's secret police or by the ever-present opposition, then embroidered according to the bibulousness of the teller or listener. Reporters and arms merchants, bureaucrats and businessmen, politicians and lawyers, academicians and snooker players, diplomats and spies—all somehow related by blood, marriage, business, or school ties— gather on Thursdays to learn the latest, sip a Black Dog, smoke a cigar, and enjoy the specialties of what can be, when it tries, one of the best kitchens in town: smoked hilsa fish on toast, masala lamb roast, and rice pilau.

Also during basanto, football (soccer) gets under way at the National Stadium in the city's Motijheel section. Men in sweaters and white flannels begin their annual cricket matches on the *maidan* (green) and at the pitch in Dhanmondi, and hunting season starts in the provinces, mainly for duck on the Meghna, and for deer and boar north of Sylhet in the hills beyond Hobiganj (despite the fact that in a burst of Anglophilic environmentalism, hunting was outlawed in 1989).

Basanto's cool also has a perverse side: it sparks the onset of the nation's eccentricity, its silly season, called politics. To a Bangladeshi, politics is what alcohol or sports are to most of the rest of the world. For Bangladeshis not only watch politics the way Americans watch the Superbowl; they imbibe it. It is the race for power that fascinates—perhaps because it's a contest that truly draws blood, as scores of candidates, supporters, students, and others are murdered each year in political or quasi-political battles in the cities, in the countryside, and on the university campuses.

Bangladesh's political rivalries are as fierce as those of Scottish clans; the attendant violence reaches Mafia levels, and the depth of passion matches that of religious battles. And for some inexplicable reason, most major battles occur during the nicest time of year. Thus in 1971 during basanto, the political fever rose so high that Pakistan's eastern half called for independence and its western half sent tanks to Dhaka University to kill intellectuals, resulting in the nine-month civil war that sparked the birth of Bangladesh.

The rivalries continue. Bangladeshis do not disagree with one another; they hate. They do not debate, for that would assume common premises. They are not interested in the will of the masses, for a tiny elite believes it has a monopoly on intellect. And, as elsewhere, those with money and power pull the strings, often manipulating the disenchanted, be they university students who form gangs armed with guns and Molotov cocktails or village youths who patrol the polls on Kawasaki motor scooters, watching voters from behind sunglasses as they prepare to raid the polling center to stuff ballot boxes.

Political corruption is a way of life. Everyone partakes. At the last contested parliamentary election, in 1986, the political parties agreed on the outcome and then spent three days adjusting the results at the election commission.

Not surprisingly, the political silly season is a tension-ridden time, when the universities often are closed, with good reason. For instance, in 1990, Molotov cocktails were thrown at Dhaka University library, causing panic-stricken researchers to dive under tables. A few weeks later, the library was closed indefinitely after a student was killed when two armed groups clashed. So severe were the tensions and battles in the 1970s, 1980s, and 1990s that the university was closed up to half the school year, forcing families that could afford it to send their children overseas.

What makes Bangladesh unique in this regard is that no other Asian country, including India, permits its so-called political leaders to radicalize and then hide behind its university youth the way this nation's major political parties do: the Awami League, the Bangladesh Nationalist Party, the Jamat-i-Islami, and the Jatiya Party.

Significantly, 1991's basanto election was very peaceful and well regulated, because after the 1990 shooting death other students rebelled against adults using them for political ends and called for a major change in campus politics. Their example spread, and in October countless thousands of citizens took to Dhaka's streets, defying the soldiers and calling for a neutral government to hold elections. The result, in early 1991, was the first genuinely free, competitive election in the nation's twenty-year history where one party did not control the election mechanism. But student politics became more violent, and the cycle began again. Only one major politician, Syed Ishtiaque Ahmed, has courageously called for the return of the campuses to education and the banning of political parties from campus activities.

As for basanto, just as the whirl of events—social, artistic, economic, and political—seems to reach a peak of frenzy, the season fades from the scene. There are two sure signs of its passing: leaves begin falling to allow new shoots to replace them, and vultures from the north descend on the fields for their annual visit.

Grisma

Throughout the cold season of basanto the weather warms a bit each day until the first of March, when the heat begins mounting more quickly. If water is the element of barsa and earth and air are the elements of sarat, the dry season, then fire, in the form of heat and lightning, is the element of the hot season, stretching from mid-March until the rains come in mid-June. The rains are preceded by massive thunderstorms that rend the air in April and May— storms sometimes punctuated by hail, that fling fist-sized pieces of ice that dent car roofs. Ships at sea flounder in heavy winds, and airplanes encounter severe, often dangerous downdrafts and turbulence, as the arid air retreats to the north and the monsoon winds drive up the Bay of Bengal from the south.

Whereas the soil had been brown, by March it turns a dusty khaki and then almost white. The streambeds become shallow, and river craft must take care to follow the main channels, watching for reefs and shoals. With water levels low, old sand boats meander downstream to dig in river bottoms. Dropping anchor, their crew shoves four poles down on each side into the sand as workers straddle running boards, one to each pole. Then, bucket in hand, each dives to the bottom, using the pole for guidance, and drags up a container of sand which is dumped into the ship's hold. Again and again they dive, until the ship is full. For just as there are no stones, so there is no sand in Bangladesh, except at river bottoms. This sand is essential, for it is the basis of cement, the country's building block.

Grisma is the time when Bangladesh's leading industry, in terms of labor and total tons of output, is working at capacity: the brick industry. Nationwide, but especially near Dhaka, bricks are produced from a laterite clay found just ten feet beneath the earth's surface. Mixed with red stain and carbon, it produces a solid, long-lasting brick. In the ancient cities of Gaur,

Mahastangar, and Mainamati stand brick buildings that have endured more than a millennium, even after their mortar crumbled. Indeed, brick-making has been a skill in this land since well before the Christian era.

Bricks also are critical substitutes for stone and gravel. After being fired in a kiln, they are pounded to gravel size for use on roadways and other construction. They also are pummeled into a powder, which is turned into a hard clay used as a roof glaze on fancy houses in Dhaka's posh areas, Gulshan and Banani. Brick work is almost the exclusive province of women, who produce the bricks, shatter them with hammers, and rhythmically pestle them. This is the country's most fascinating and ubiquitous construction art form, evident almost everywhere in the form of smokestack kilns fired by coal or, increasingly, by natural gas, and of women bent over their backbreaking tasks, under a merciless sun.

As rivulets of sweat pour down the skin of construction crews working at tar pits to finish their contracts before the rainy season starts, grisma's scorching heat ignites large fissures in mud-walled huts and in the fields, as farmers don their tokas, or conical, broad-brimmed hats. Meanwhile, tubewells pant as they seek to nourish one more crop from fields that only a few years ago lay fallow during grisma, fields on whose surfaces eddies of dust once collected and often became storms when caught up in drafts of wind that swirl at this time of year.

In the cities, the glare of glass and the sun's refracted heat from buildings and sidewalks is so suffocating that by late afternoon, when the earth seemingly can bear no more, the skies darken and rain falls in a fearful thundershower that can last an evening or, worse, and can blow by without cooling you. So fierce are these storms that they seem to rend the sky with electric blue or fiery red-white streaks of lightning that has the same incandescence with which Bangladesh's atmosphere endows all heavenly phenomena. The lightning is fearfully close and tangible, while the thunder, rolling across the rivers and plains of the delta, surrounds and finally deafens all in its path. By dawn, though the air is clearer, it is already hot and humid.

And still the heat does not abate. Beneath scorched grass the soil cracks open, while silt that had been soft becomes rock hard; flowers wilt, starved of dew and moisture as thunderheads grow less frequent; magpies emit their raucous laugh, crows cough and caw, and gulls along the Ganges shriek dryly. Ducks, Siberian cranes, and vultures flee northward, leaving harried teams of tiny brown seven brothers to roam the parched earth. In the cities, heat and rough humidity, laden with dust, brick grit, and auto fumes, lay heavy upon the land.

Even in the countryside, where some respite exists beneath shady palm and bamboo trees, cows groan and low in the pastures. And water buffalo, having no sweat glands and a body heat that rises quickly, plunge into streams and rivers, leaving only eyes and nose above water.

By now the sun is a round red lamp like the one on Bangladesh's flag. Relentlessly, mercilessly bearing down, it discourages any urge to move, during daytimes that grow longer, interspersed with shorter nights. On and on the heat buzzes, roasts, toasts, bakes, fries, boils, sautés, and broils, until all hope is lost that the rains will ever come.

In Bangladesh, the seasons are reversed from those elsewhere in the Northern hemisphere. The cool or winter season is the time to be outdoors, while summer and the rainy season are best spent inside. This year, with its backward seasons, is one of infinite variety and change, day to day, week to week. It is a year of gradually increasing or decreasing heat, humidity, or rain, a time of flowers, a time of crops: rice, jute, tea, chilies, mustard, mangoes, papaya, watermelon, cantaloupe, lichi, jackfruit, tomatoes, cucumbers, onions, tobacco, silk, cotton, and many more. It is a year of life and death, of sun and moon, of clouds and ethereal clear skies. It is a full year, a year that husband and wife can take pride in having been a part of and having survived.

The Year-Round Season

No description of Bangladesh's seasons is complete without reference to a very special month-long season whose place on the calendar changes annually because it is tied to the lunar calendar of Islam. This is the month of *Ramzan*, or *Ramadan*, the holiest month for Muslims, when no one over age ten is expected to eat or drink anything from sunup to sundown, when human life slows down in the face of the eternal. There is something awesome about the month of Ramadan, which, for penance, sacrifice, and rigor, is far stronger than is the Day of Atonement among Jews or Lent and Good Friday among Christians. As the month proceeds, adult faces become increasingly drawn, due partly to the fast and partly to lack of sleep, as old stories about the Prophet Muhammad are told and retold for children and grandchildren, and as the fasters rise before dawn to take some rice and water to hold them through the day. Come sundown, a siren wails announcing *iftar*, when, in cities and countryside alike, people simultaneously break the fast with essentially the same things: water followed by cooked lentils, beans, and rice. Shortly thereafter, the family shares a large ceremonial dinner. As the month drags on, faces grow slimmer and tempers shorter, and a certain pall settles over life until busy modern man finds himself forced, from time to time, to contemplate the eternal. Ramadan concludes with a night of festivities called *Eid ul Fitr*.

Two months and ten days after the end of Eid ul Fitr, livestock are readied for *Eid ul Azha*, the Feast of the Sacrifice, when the new moon is about to be aspected by Venus. Cattle, goats, and sheep are decorated with ribbons and their faces are painted. They then are sold, one to each household that can afford it or one to two or more families. As the fast ends, on an evening when millions of eyes turn heavenward to glimpse the new moon, a scene from the Old Testament, the Torah, is reenacted—only this time instead of God testing Abraham's faith by asking him to sacrifice his son Isaac, Muslims the world over sacrifice a cow, an oxen, a goat, or a sheep, which they then cook and eat according to Islamic law. This Eid feast is a high point of the year, no matter in what season it is celebrated.

Finally, in this very Muslim nation, every day of the year, rain or shine, five times a day, the muzzein mount the tower in the mosque and call the prayers. Five times a day the devout pray. Five times a day they acknowledge the gifts of Allah. There is no more dignified and awesome call to prayer than the daily marking of the hours of the mosque. No one who hears the call, no matter how secular in orientation, can listen to the stentorian song of the mullah without asking what experience of reality inspires such a powerful and heartfelt cry.

3

Pride and Poverty

W<small>ALKING THROUGH THE BANGLADESH MUSEUM</small> in Dhaka one is struck by the amount of space given to Zainul Abedin, a painter who portrays powerfully the nadir year in the history of Bengal. For in that year a terrible famine killed three to five million people (the exact total is unknown because many deaths went unreported). It was 1943, a time recent enough for many people to recall, recent enough to have a psychological impact not only on the generation that experienced the famine but also on their descendants. And the reason so much space is given to Zainul Abedin, over and above the artistic merit of his paintings, is that many people feel that much of Bangladesh today was shaped by the events of 1942–43, when what had been the richest province in all of India and a cultural pacesetter for centuries, a place that had been the capital of British India, had absorbed blows for two centuries, and still carried more than its fair share, paying for a high percentage of the Empire, at last collapsed and to a large extent lost its confidence.

The Bangladesh of today, the nation of aid and poverty, really was created in 1943, the year of its crushing humiliation, the year Bengal fell from its place of leadership in the Indian subcontinent to a position of abject poverty. It is one thing to stumble and fall; it is another to fall and be bruised; it is still another to fall, be bruised, and not have the strength to recover, to be so beaten down that one begs for food and at last loses all dignity in the begging. It is even worse to have to beg when the world's media watch you and your family in such a shameful position.

Zainul Abedin portrays a world where the crows of Dhaka are fat and

sleek, where the vultures who visit in the dry season are strong and powerful, but where in the heat of drought and wartime, Bangladeshis lay down to
die or were driven by heat and hunger, naked and without hope under a
blinding sun, to wander the roads followed by the scavenging birds.

Anwarul Huq, who shows the author around, is a curator of the museum
and creator of another painting hanging nearby that portrays the heat of the
summer of 1943 in the form of a nuclear explosion. This painting captures
both the horror of war and the scorching heat of that drought whose burns
have scarred the souls of his countrymen.

It is not that Bangladesh had no previous famines. It was that this one
was the final straw. For during the previous two centuries the area most of
which is now Bangladesh had suffered two crushing blows: between 1757
and 1912 a major part of its manufacturing industry had been deliberately
destroyed by the British, and in 1912 its wealth had been transferred to New
Delhi when the British viceroy, as a long-term result of the opening of the
Suez Canal and the consequent shift of Britain's interest to the northwest,
spitefully moved his capital from Calcutta, where it had been for 155 years.
The loss of the capital in Bengal and the drain of cash to the new, faraway
capital created the long-range decline of Calcutta.

While these blows had been borne and absorbed, the final one of 1943
proved to be the watershed. For British India was at war, the Japanese occupied Burma on Bengal's border, scarce food was being exported to help the
war effort while well-fed British troops occupied the country, and all boats
had been smashed to prevent capture by the Japanese, thus preventing the
transportation to the marketplace of rice grown in the countryside. Then
came the drought and suffering—all this within sight of the world press.
How much could one people take?

Thousands fled to the cities. Indeed, it was in 1943 that Calcutta became
overcrowded and that Bengal, the rich and mighty, became in the world's
eyes a place of hunger, skeletal people, desperation, and despair. Between
1905 and 1911 the Bengali people had defied the British Empire when it had
attempted to divide Bengal. In 1943 they were unable to defy anyone. What
was had been destroyed, and Bengalis found themselves mired in despair. It
was in 1943 that Bengal first acquired the image of the "basket case." It was
in that ignominious year that the old image of Golden Bengal, with Calcutta
as the "second city of Empire" under the British, second to London itself,
was erased forever. How long it seems since anyone has thought of Bengal
as prosperous.

Anyone who has contemplated Zainul Abedin's paintings will readily
understand why the summer of 1943 haunts not only the Bangladesh Museum's permanent exhibit but the entire country. For droughts, famines,
floods, and other natural disasters are ever on the horizon, and the legacy of
1943 endures. Thus as late as 1985, 57,000 people were employed in a food

distribution system established as a result of the famine. (In fact, so good has this system proved to be that in 1974 it saved the country from major starvation when the crops failed and food shipments from the United States were delayed by the Watergate crisis. And in 1987 and 1988, this same food distribution system again prevented disaster in the face of massive floods.) Today this enduring distribution system and memories of 1974 are but outward signs of deeper scars inflicted by the wound of 1943. Indeed, much of what now is called the "aid mentality" is a result of this fear of famine, a fear not unlike that of Americans who survived the Great Depression of the 1930s. For in 1943 a still very proud Bengal was forced to its knees, a position from which it has yet to recover. In the ensuing nearly half-century, Bengal never again has felt able to stand on its own, much less to attain the pinnacle it once enjoyed. For until the famine of 1943 Bengal led the Indian independence movement, in both peaceful and terrorist ways.

Thus it is that today Bangladeshis suffer from both lost pride and lost life. It has been so long since they held themselves proud that even they must strain to remember that it wasn't always like this. Once, within memory, their country was a grand and enviable area—the granary of all of east and north India, whose wealth supported the Moghul Empire and later provided the surplus that allowed the British to finance their expansion in India. If Bengalis ever are to reclaim their heritage, they must never forget that by 1757 they were producing over one-third of all cotton textiles used in Europe and had developed almost all the weaves of cotton and silk textiles known today. Indeed, in the sixteenth century, Bengal was called the Paradise of Nations, the land of wealth, renowned for its agricultural surplus and manufacturing wealth. Then, Dhaka, not Manchester, was the home of cotton and silk textiles, and Dhaka was able to dictate terms of trade when the Dutch, Portuguese, British, and French came. As Bengalis had little need for European goods but the Europeans wanted products from Bengal, the foreigners had to pay cash. In fact, well into this century Bengal had a positive balance of trade with the world, just as Britain had in the nineteenth century, the United States had just a generation ago, and Japan and Germany have today.

But in 1943 that glorious past dissolved. You can see its traces in the families walking the narrow roads that straddle khaki-colored barren fields under a dusty, dark, grim sky in Zainul Abedin's paintings. You can see it in his skeletonlike people, who resemble the European concentration camp survivors of the same decade except that they are sitting on a roadside while crows, fattened by feeding on cadavers, wait patiently for the starving children to die. Despite a pleasing use of color, the paintings are bleak, devoid of ideology, offering no hint of Bengal's previous glory. The medium does not alter the message but portrays a people's unvarnished suffering.

Having listened to the old men recall those days and having watched the horror reflected in their eyes, having heard them say "Go, see Zainul Abedin," having witnessed a similar disaster in 1974 when countless thousands starved to death, desperate orphans roamed Dhaka's streets, and only the rich did not go hungry, one still can only begin to imagine the devastation of 1943 that Zainul Abedin portrays so starkly, without melodrama.

Studying his paintings, it's hard to imagine that never before 1943 in its 2,300 years of recorded history had the land that is today Bangladesh been so poor and reduced to begging for such an extended period.

Ancient Bengal

Sitting on the brick ramparts of the ancient city of Mahasthan near the district town of Bogra in northern Bangladesh, a city where the Buddha is believed to have walked, a city whose age predates even the great Brahman past, one can see Bangladesh's former power and prosperity. For Mahasthan is Bangladesh's oldest known city, with the oldest ruins. Its grandeur is marked by a five-kilometer wall encircling the inner city where there exist the remains of ancient Brahmanic, Buddhist, and Muslim temples and mosques. The surrounding land is dotted with ruins of ancient Buddhist monasteries and stupas, especially two huge monasteries located to the wall's northwest and southwest. The Karatoa River, sacred to the Hindus, flows beneath the city's eastern ramparts, and devoted worshipers still bathe in it, particularly in April during the full moon, the time of Bangladesh's New Year. Every twelfth year the bathing is especially sacred, as it coincides with the Narayani Yoga, a special conjunction of planets that usually occurs in December. To the north is a temple to Govinda, the Hindu god, with steps leading down to a bathing ghat.

The Karatoa, a feeder stream of the sacred Ganges, itself is a sacred landmark, a shimmering black mass that reflects the golden moon or a glistening blue one under a radiant sun. The Karatoa is an intimate part of this country's conscious history, which stretches back at least to the second millennium before Christ.

About 2,500 years before Christ, 1,900 years before the Buddha, and 3,100 years before the Prophet Muhammad, there lived on the Indian subcontinent a people of Mongoloid, Austric, or Dravidian descent. As attested to by archaeological digs in the west near the Indus River at Mohenjo-Daro and Harappa in Pakistan, this civilization had developed arts, agricultural wealth, and trade, and was at least as advanced as concurrent civilizations in the West or the Orient. The discovery of this ancient civilization provided the first clue as to what India was before it suffered its first great invasion. Because archaeologists have barely begun to decipher the clues left by these people, relatively little is known about them, except that they offer the best insight yet found into who inhabited India before the great Aryan invasions of 1500 to 2000 B.C., which comprise the seminal historical event in this part of the world. Their remains include buildings and implements equal to those of the Egyptian culture that existed at the same time, except for the pyramids and other distinctively Egyptian monumental works. This ancient culture was overrun by the Aryans in an invasion that marks the watershed of cultural development for the Indian subcontinent.

The Aryan invasion brought to India a language, Sanskrit, a religion, Vedic Hinduism, and a social organization, caste, that have influenced that nation ever since. It was the marriage of the Aryan culture and the local culture as represented at Mohenjo-Daro and Harappa that produced the broad cultural outlines that one day would give rise to Buddhism and grasp Islam to its bosom and ultimately spawn the complex society of modern India, Bangladesh, Pakistan, Sri Lanka, and Burma.

The amalgamation of the Aryan and the native cultures took centuries. The earliest scriptures of the Aryans (ca. 1300 or 1400 B.C.) speak of *dasayus*, or Namasudras, the non-Aryan people of color who lived outside the pale of society but were descendants of the original settlers. Probably 80 percent of the people who live on the subcontinent today are outsiders and "untouchables" and therefore of native stock, while only a few belong to the castes of the Aryan invaders. According to some historians, the Namasudras are the ancestors of today's Bangladeshis. And not even the most authoritative books deny the aboriginal, non-Aryan beginnings of the people, most of whose customs predate the Aryan invasion. As Majumdar, a historian of Bengal, put it, "We may, therefore, legitimately draw the inference that the primitive people of Bengal were different in race or culture, and perhaps in both, from the people who compiled the Vedic literature." This ethnic difference led to a distinctly Bangladeshi culture that has persisted to this day within the nations of South Asia, a difference in look, customs, language, written script, religious outlook, and temperament, all within a geographically unified part of the subcontinent's northeastern corner.

Gradually, however, the people of the lower Ganges were absorbed into Aryan society, with the upper castes called Brahmans and the lower Sudras, "feet." In general, Aryans were upper caste and the lower castes were made up of natives, Namasudras. As caste was and is based on *varna*, color, the darker-skinned natives were on the bottom. Today the same distinctions are made between the *ashraf*, the upper classes, and the *atraf*, the lower ones. *Ashraf* and *atraf* are Persian words that indicate a blood difference. The Bangla equivalent is *uchla sreni* and *nimna sreni*. Other terms that divide the classes but are not blood-based are *bhadralok, chotolok,* and *itarjan,* which refer to the urban professional, lower-middle, and working classes. Thus throughout Bangladesh, mostly lighter-skinned people make up the old upper classes—especially intellectuals, the higher levels of the civil service, the professions, and the business community. Darker-skinned people predominate among the lower-middle class and the villagers, although in the 1980s class barriers seemed to be breaking down, even if caste had not.

By 600 B.C. the people of modern Bangladesh were part of the Aryan culture, though many still lived in the frontier areas of the eastern deltas formed by the rivers. As W. W. Hunter, a senior British civil servant who worked in India, wrote, "The Brahman of the present day are the result of probably 3,000 years of hereditary education and self-restraint; and they have evolved a type of mankind quite distinct from the surrounding population. . . . [They are] tall and slim, with finely modeled nose and lips, fair complexion, high forehead, and somewhat coconut-shaped skull—the man of self-centered refinement." Hunter's description readily fits today's upper-class Bangladeshi Muslims and Hindus, and he was intuitive to have stressed this.

For the influence of generations of such "breeding" is especially evident in a certain refinement, gentleness, and grace that distinguishes Bangladesh's upper classes. It is a breeding born of the ancient Hindu ethic. Thus a Greek ambassador, Megasthenes, who visited Bengal in the third century B.C., described the four stages of a male Brahman's life: the age of learning, when as a youth he studies the Brahmanical texts; the stage of householder, when after a long education he marries; the postretirement period, when he lives as a recluse and has an opportunity to meditate on life's experiences and meanings; and the final stage, when he leaves home to wander as a mendicant holy man, begging bowl in hand. Megasthenes reported seeing this ethic carried out. And while no one believes that all men were like this or that anyone lived this way all the time, it is clear that the ideals of study, duty to family, meditation and reflection, and liberation into the spiritual world always have been an essential part of life in Bengal and still are respected today by people of all faiths. Indeed, there is among Bangladesh's older families a certain reaction against not only crass materialism but also love of wealth.

As for the vast majority of the people, who mostly are poor and live in rather primitive villages, their character perhaps is best summed up by what Warren Hastings, Britain's first governor of Bengal (1771–84), said to Parliament while on trial in 1787 for alleged oppression, cruelty, bribery, and fraud. Asked if he found the Bangladeshis to be "morally corrupt" as others had reported, he replied, though it would have helped him to agree with the leading question, that "I affirm by the oath I've taken that this description is untrue and wholly unfounded. . . . They are gentle, benevolent, more susceptible of gratitude for kindness shown them than prompted to vengeance for wrongs inflicted, and as exempt from the worst properties of human passion as any people on the face of the earth." Hastings's description stands the test of time. Bangladeshi villagers are not nice because of their poverty, as many romantics imagine, but because of the culture they inherited.

While more than 90 percent of Bangladeshis today are Muslim, they are descended from an ancient Hindu tradition that spread across the Indian subcontinent from west to east, from the mountains that connect Central Asia to Iran (named for "Aryan"), to Afghanistan, and on to Pakistan, until this tradition became the way of life not only along the Indus River in the west but also along the Ganges, which runs from Kashmir in the northwest to Bangladesh in the southeast.

And though the Hindu Aryans imposed their culture on the natives, it is likely that many previous beliefs were incorporated into the conquering religion. Thus modern research shows that certain Hindu beliefs—love of the Great Mother, faith in the power of the moon on river water to cleanse the soul, a sense of gentle piety—originated with the Namasudras, so much so that the Hinduism that exists in this land today is close to the Namasudra's beliefs before the Aryan conquest. For instance, one often sees floating on the river little candles mounted on triangular rafts launched by women as votive lights to the gods.

Even as Vedic Hinduism matured and prospered, the first Western invasion of India began, when Alexander the Great of Macedon and Greece conquered Persia and then modern Afghanistan before crossing the Indus and the Jhelum and heading for the heart of India. Alerted to the danger, troops from the lower Ganges in eastern India were rallied under the leadership of a non-Aryan Nanda native king. In 327 B.C. this force, consisting of a huge army of infantry backed by horses and elephants, stopped Alexander's advance on the banks of the Beas River. Worn down by the oppressive heat and bereft of supplies, Alexander's troops begged him not to fight these Gangaridae, these people of the lower Ganges, who according to Ptolemy lived at the delta of the Ganges in what is now Bangladesh. Retreating without giving battle to this superior force, Alexander left India never to return, although traces of Greek civilization remain in the northern area of what is now Pakistan.

Thus ended the first phase of Bangladesh's history. It is from this period that the first known written work in the Bangla language survives on stone. Small terra cotta figurines from it have been found at Mahasthan. Since systematic archaeological digs have not yet been undertaken, it is possible that relics of an even earlier period some day may be found. What is important is that Bangladesh entered Western history as a victor.

The Buddhist Era

Shortly thereafter, a strong government emerged in Bihar, a province just west of Bengal, then called Magadha. It was led by Chandra Gupta, an Aryan warrior who had been Alexander's ally but had broken with him and then ousted the Nanda dynasty. A few years later his grandson, Asoka, after winning many battles, was converted to Buddhism and established the religion throughout his northeastern Indian kingdom of Magadha (of which Mahasthan was a part). A benevolent ruler, Asoka set aside funds for hospitals for men and animals, some of which endured into the early twentieth century, and established monasteries throughout his kingdom. Today Asoka is one of the Indian subcontinent's most revered kings, and the first fragment of preserved Bangla script is believed to be an order from him to use stored grain to relieve a local famine in Mahasthan, also called Pundranagar.

Over the next couple of hundred years, until the time of Christ, the Magadhan Empire declined. About the fourth century another empire, a Hindu one, gained prominence. The Gupta Empire incorporated northern Bangladesh and the cities of Gaud and Pundranagar, but by no means did the empire ever rule completely in north Bangladesh. The Gupta Empire, too, declined. After a period of anarchy, an independent kingdom arose.

For the land that was destined to become Bangladesh the Buddhist period was one of the most fruitful in its history. Most people did not like the Brahmans' alien caste system but found the Buddha's peaceful philosophy congenial to their way of life. For they were simple, gentle farmers who, working astride the dangerous waters of the Ganges delta, were subject to the vagaries of drought and flood.

Though their descendants long since have been converted to Islam, the people who lived in Bengal during the time of Asoka and Christ bequeathed a heritage which today accounts for the pacifist, mild manner characteristic of Bangladeshi villagers. Thus scholars maintain that the Buddhist legacy is evident in the breeding of modern-day Bangladeshi villagers, Muslim, Hindu, or Christian, in their belief in brotherhood, in their treatment of women, especially widows and outcasts, and in their gentleness and charity to all people—a way of life which makes organized state welfare unnecessary. This is something the British conquerors learned. For example, so gentle were the people of this area that when the British recruited for their famed Bengal Army in the nineteenth century, they chose soldiers from elsewhere on the subcontinent. Bengalis were considered a nonmartial race. They were the farmers of whom Hastings wrote: "They were willing to suffer much in order to maintain their links to the land. . . . Therefore they did suffer much."

As to Mahasthan (Pundranagar), it remained wealthy and renowned until relatively modern times, as attested to by the reminiscences of ancient Greek and Chinese travelers, by a visit to its museum, or by a stroll past the remains of its high walls and splendid temples.

Moreover, about fifty miles away is another city, Gaud, Gaur, or Gauda, in which a similar culture thrived. Probably older than Mahasthan, it once stretched more than ten miles along a now-dry branch of the Ganges. Often pronounced Gaura and for many years the name of Bengal, Gaud was an early center of silk sericulture, cotton weaving, sugar, and other agricultural products. Today its ruins mostly are in the neighboring Indian state of West Bengal. Both Mahasthan and Gaud were abandoned when the Ganges and the Karatoa changed course (a phenomenon which periodically occurs in every delta region), because this denied the populace their chief source of water for their daily needs and for transport.

Yet Mahasthan and Gaud bequeathed a lasting legacy because they were not far from the birthplace of the Gautama Buddha. The son of a king of the warrior class, he was born in the sixth century B.C. just a few hundred miles north and west of Mahasthan. At age twenty-nine he sought enlightenment by abandoning his beautiful wife and his father's wealthy kingdom for the life of a *sannyasi*, or mendicant. With begging bowl in hand, seeking to transcend the world of pain and suffering, he subjected himself to great austeries and listened to all who claimed to be wise. After six years and on the verge of despair, he attained enlightenment when he awoke under a bo tree at Gaya in Magadha. He declared the existence of a new casteless world in which correct thought and deeds could lead to the bliss of *nirvana*, or release from pain and suffering. Only by blending oneself into the eternal all where one's personality is extinguished, he said, can the illusion of pain and suffering be overcome. Then, like a drop of perfume, the soul will disappear into the air leaving only a pleasing fragrance. The Buddha attracted disciples (monks) in a brotherhood, or *sangstha*. (*Sangthsa* today means a voluntary organization.) Wandering as mendicants, they began teaching and sending missionaries as far as the Middle East, where there remains a belief that the Buddha's influence will change Christianity and certainly some of the later-day gnostic heresies.

As for the Buddha's influence on Bangladesh, it is believed that he may have visited Mahasthan or Gaud, as they were readily accessible down the Ganges from Bihar. (*Bihar*, a local spelling of *vihara*, which means "Buddhist monastery," derives from the establishment of monasteries by Asoka and his followers in what is now the Indian state of Bihar). Whether or not the Buddha made such a voyage, it is evident that his teachings had basic conflicts with the beliefs and practices of the caste-conscious, polytheistic, fair-skinned Vedic Hindus who lived nearby and subjugated the far more numerous darker-skinned natives. Ironically, this fact probably helps explain Buddhism's swift and powerful ascension in this region. For, over time, Buddhism both absorbed the native groups as equals and attracted many Brahman converts.

Moreover, Buddhist culture tolerated the Brahman Vedic one with its worship of the old Aryan gods, who resembled those of Greece, Rome, and other Aryan areas. Thus the Brahmans, who were the religious and philosophic leaders, controlled everyday life, including the activities of the military leaders, or *Kshatriyas*; of the farmers and merchants, or *Vaisayas*; and of the Sudras, the lowest of the four Hindu classes, one despised by the upper classes. (The "untouchables," or Namasudras, are in effect a fifth class, outside the caste system.) That these two faiths coexisted in relative harmony is evident at the Mahasthan Museum, which has a treasure of Buddhist and Hindu art from this period.

From A.D. 300 to 1000, while the Vedic Brahmans held their own, Buddhism grew increasingly powerful in Bengal, which was part of a vast Buddhist culture that stretched from Afghanistan in the west to Burma, Thailand, and Cambodia in the east, and from Nepal in the north to Sri Lanka in the south. During the height of its power on the subcontinent, Buddhism unified the culture and created a sense of solidarity. Thus at Mahasthan were found coins and statues from the Kingdom of Buddhists who lived about A.D. 200 in Gandhara (northwest Pakistan) almost two thousand miles away. This unity endured until the Muslim invasion led by Mahmud of Ghazni in the eleventh century.

But Buddhism did more than unify the natives and Aryans. It also helped incorporate into the region new invaders, the White Huns, or Scythians, who arrived from the north in the eight hundred years between the Buddha's birth and the second century B.C. W. W. Hunter, a careful historian, believes that Buddha may have been a Scythian, which partially might account for the relatively swift success of his doctrine. The Scythians' descendants lived in Cooch Bihar, just north of Mahasthan, and their descendants, called Kochis, still exist nearby in Bangladesh's district town of Rangpur.

It also is possible that many of Buddhism's tantric practices (occult sexual rituals) came from the Scythians or even from the Greeks. For the Seleucids, a Bactrian Greek dynasty, also influenced northern areas of current Pakistan. Thus Taxila, capital of Gandhara, had a Greek temple dedicated to Athena that was an imitation of the Parthenon in Athens. And according to legend, Thomas, Jesus' doubting apostle, visited Taxila in the first century.

Another milestone was the conversion to Buddhism of a king of the Kushans named Kanishka, who probably was part of a northern White Hun tribe that conquered Gandhara in the first or second century. Discovering that Buddhism had many sects, Kanishka convened a grand council of leaders from around the Buddhist world to compile their beliefs. The result was Mahayana Buddhism, the form that converted China and Tibet and evolved into the Zen Buddhism practiced in Japan. It was this Buddhism that entered Bangladesh, which became a center of learning for pilgrims from the east, closely aligned to other Buddhist countries. About the seventh century, a Chinese Buddhist named Huien Tsang recorded his impressions of Bengal. The documents somehow ended up in Japan in ancient times and were returned to Bengal early in the twentieth century.

As to Buddhism's tangible legacy in Bangladesh, the ruins of three major monasteries remain. The first, Vasu Bihar at Mahasthan, was called Po-shi-po by Huien Tsang. Overlooking verdant fields and picturesque thatched hut villages are two buildings that were part of the monastery where six hundred monks lived, as well as a raised-earth, cruciform mound divided into monastic cells. Despite the power lines and the put-put of tubewell engines that today mar the scenery and serenity, the air of a rural retreat for monks built on a grand scale still endures.

About thirty-five miles away is Paharpur, the largest Buddhist temple remains on the subcontinent. It dates to the Pala Dynasty, which gained power in Gaud in the seventh century, two hundred years before Charlemagne ascended in the West and about the time the Sun God rose in Japan. Paharpur, it is believed, was a major center that exerted enormous influence on Tibet, China, and the entire Buddhist world. Of red brick and terra cotta, like Vasu Bihar, it is built out of a mound seventy feet high (roughly the height of a seven-story building) with cruciform arms more than nine hundred feet long. This stately structure and the artifacts in its museum make Paharpur one of the more beautiful monuments to the grandeur of that distant age.

Nearly eighty miles to the east as the crow flies, in modern Mainamati, are the most impressive ruins of all, dating to the Pala era. Dominating the scene is a three-dome stupa dedicated to the Buddhist trinity: *Buddha* (enlightenment), *dharma* (the path), and *sangha* (congregation or brotherhood). There also are massive brick monasteries, as well as an entire city, with palaces and other buildings.

According to the *Tibetan Chronicles*, a fourth major Buddhist site, Pandit Vihara, existed in modern Chittagong, about two hundred miles to the southeast. However, either it was totally destroyed or a Muslim mosque or Hindu temple was incorporated into and obscures it.

Today the three surviving major monuments to Buddhism, plus smaller ones in Dhaka and Dinajpur, are reminders that long ago, while Europe was mired in the Dark Ages, Bangladesh spawned splendid civilizations, renowned for their intellectual pursuits and other accomplishments.

Thus in this period river trade carried products from the region throughout the Bay of Bengal to Southeast Asia and as far southeast as Indonesia. Moreover, cotton grown in central and western India went to Bengal for weaving, and silks produced in Malda near Gaud and Mahasthan were famed throughout the subcontinent. The region was still a frontier for the new Aryan-Bengali culture, and much of its land was jungle, haunted by tigers and elephants. Still, as more and more land was cleared, there emerged a growing rice surplus that was transported throughout the subcontinent and for which the area became renowned. Indeed, until 1943, Bangladesh remained a rice exporter.

The Return of Hinduism

Throughout the era of Buddhist dominance, Vedic Hinduism, as well as a pre-Buddhist pacifist sect, Jainism, were greatly overshadowed. However, by the eleventh century Brahmanism had ascended again, largely because it had become more appealing as it began integrating into its Aryan Vedic doctrine many aspects of both Buddhism and native beliefs.

The original Hindu doctrine was brought to the subcontinent by the Aryans, the Central Asian tribal people who were related to the Aryans who settled Europe about the same time. Their language and numerical system were close to those of ancient Greek and Rome; their gods resembled Jupiter, Zeus, Apollo, and the Greeks' unknown god; their disciplined scholar caste was reminiscent of the wise men of the Greek academies; and their soldier castes were akin to those of Rome or Sparta. (Indeed, the people of ancient India are similar to those of Homer's time. Moreover, until he died a few years ago, there lived in Calcutta a Belgian Jesuit, Father Antoine, who, desiring an accurate French translation of the Bhagavad Gita, translated it first from its original Sanskrit into classical Greek, as the two languages are close and translation from Greek to Latin or French is well developed.) Also like the Greeks, the Aryan invaders were not racists, though they made distinctions based on caste—that is, on color. Finding a people whose race, language, customs, and values were different, they intermarried to a great degree, while clinging to their own ways. Brahmans, Kshatiyras, and Vaisayas all were "twice born." However, since *caste* means "color," they considered the natives "once born," the feet of the social being. In other realms, they treated women well and limited animal sacrifice to the bull and the horse. Moreover, the Brahmans fostered learning, science, the arts, and the law, and the caste system provided a social order among people of different trades and professions. The Aryans did not offer human sacrifice. Nor did they engage in either *sati* (widow burning) when a husband died or in some of the bizarre occult sexual activities that later developed.

The Hindus have four core beliefs. The first, which many Muslim and some Buddhist Bangladeshis share, is the sacredness of rivers. The second, unique to Hinduism, is the sacredness of cows. The third is caste based on color. The fourth is that the four Vedas, or holy books, are of divine origin.

While the Aryans were not particularly nonviolent, even the Buddha, in renouncing the world and use of force, was within the Brahman tradition. Thus his search for life's true meaning and his belief that all men are equal before God was an expression of the inherent Hindu beliefs that the Jains already were enunciating. To this day the Jains are a peaceful sect whose ethic of nonviolence influenced Mahatma Gandhi and through him Martin Luther King, Jr.

Given this side of Hinduism and given the fact that Buddhism was open to diverse ideas and converts and, as Suniti Bhushan Qanungo, a contemporary Bangladeshi scholar, suggests, offered its monasteries as forums for discussions, it is not surprising that Hinduism began flourishing again as Buddhism's fervor waned. For as Buddhism began declining in the ninth, tenth, and eleventh centuries, there arose in southern India a Hindu reform movement. It was based on a trinity of gods—Brahma the creator, Shiva the destroyer and reproducer, and Vishnu the preserver—within a doctrine that reintroduced a personal god, a concept that had thrived in the Vedic era before the Buddha. Because Buddhism had de-emphasized the personal aspect of God, this new doctrine had a chance to succeed.

While strengthening belief in the trinity, this new Hinduism was split into two doctrinal schools which still exist. Shivaite, named for the god Shiva and based on *shakti* (power), today is the religion of the rich and the poor. Vaishnavite, named for Vishnu, is a more pacifist, Buddhist-inspired doctrine of the middle classes, based on *bhakti* (innocent, joyful devotion). Essential to both was the teaching of Shankara, a ninth-century scholar. He developed the Vedanta school of gnostic thought, which defined an abstract god as the basis for all reality in the universe and saw man in a microcosm bearing in his soul a spark of god's reality.

In south India a Brahman named Ramanujan, a Shankara disciple, converted many Buddhist monasteries to Vaishnavite belief. Later, about the fifth teacher in this line, Ramanand, brought the doctrine to Benares. From there his disciple Kabir spread the doctrine to Bengal. In general the Vaishnavite doctrine taught that the Buddha may have been the ninth incarnation of Vishnu, the preserver. Also, it strongly opposed the taking of life and extreme caste-consciousness. This movement led to the incorporation of many Buddhist rites into Vaishnavite Hindu ones. For instance, women were treated with greater respect by the Vaishnavites than by the Shivaites, which explains why, to this day, women in Bengal, Hindu and Muslim alike, enjoy more freedom than do their religious sisters elsewhere.

These new Hindu strains also had an underside, having picked up accretions of tantric practices, especially connections with the cult of Kali, the evil, frightening portrayal of Shiva's wife. Kali, still the most frightening goddess of Bengal, is portrayed as black-faced, with tongue sticking out in a wanton, shameful manner. Standing on a dead Shiva, she wears a necklace of skulls and appeals to those who need to see their gods, Shiva and Kali, as powerful. To this day, blood sacrifices often are made at her temple, and some of the tantric rituals that surround her are related to blood, sexual arousal, and drugs. The underside of the religious revival of the new Hinduism opened a new chapter in the growth of that religion in Bangladesh.

Tantric exercises were not the only stream that emphasized the doctrines of love. The Vaishnavite school did too, not merely with sexual ritual but with a real understanding of the total relationship between man and God and man and nature. Moreover, the Vaishnavite school had a branch that concentrated on romance, that of Krishna, who as a young man was involved in a pastoral love with the *gopis* (milkmaids). The innocent, pastoral aspects of the Krishna myth opened the poetic eyes of the people to the love of the land and the ways of the farmer.

At the same time, the new emphasis on Vedanta, Shankara's philosophy, opened a new chapter in the outlook of Bengal. For schools of Hindu thought called *tols* began emerging. One at Nadia, along the Bagaritha River in West Bengal, became a renowned seat of learning.

The new teachings, including the Mahabharata and the Ramayana, two ancient Hindu classics, began featuring the god Krishna, Hinduism's version of the gentle Buddha, and brought out two sides of Hinduism: *jnana* and *bhakti*. The first, referring to religion's philosophical or intellectual side, appeals to understanding and enlightenment. The second refers to religion's devotional or emotional side. Shankara and his early disciples founded the first; Kabir and Chaitanya, who lived in the fifteenth century and whose influence on Bengal is as permanent as the Buddha's, developed the second. Ultimately, Chaitanya converted the Buddhist rites that had arisen in Puri, a town in West Bengal south of Bangladesh, to what are today's Hindu rites of Jaganath, one of the most spectacular of all Hindu celebrations, which occurs in Puri. It is the bhakti cult of devotion and peacefulness that gives the Bengali middle classes their gentility and grace. For it is associated with the Vaishnavite cult, which reflects the gentle side of the Buddhist heritage. The Shivaite cult also has a devotional side, called Durga Puja. It was during this period that Durga, the good manifestation of Shiva's wife, also became a center of devotion, as in the Durga Puja festival still held annually by a prominent Hindu family living at Mirzapur near Dhaka.

It should be noted that the new Shankaran Hinduism, like the new Vaishnavism, lacked a sense of heaven or of human spiritual progress, except in terms of either an endless rebirth or, like the Buddha, an annihilation of self into all, the absorption of the self into the sea of reality. Release from the cycle of life and pain remained the goal, and release meant the extinction of self.

Both the Vaishnavite and Shivaite Hindu schools reached Bangladesh around the end of the eleventh century, about the time that the Senas, a Hindu dynasty originating in south India, conquered the Palas in Gaud. Over the next two hundred years, faced not only by withdrawal of royal Pala support but by cruel Hindu Sena persecution, Buddhism in north Bangladesh began withering, though it endured in the country's central and southeastern parts until the Muslims came in 1300. Chittagong, in southeastern Bangladesh, still has a significant Buddhist minority, as that is where the Buddhists fled when their centers of learning were destroyed. One such Buddhist remnant is Yugis Nath, a tantric sect now more or less in the Vaishnavite camp. The Hinduism practiced by the Senas grew and prospered. Most of modern Hinduism derives from the Hindu reformation of the twelfth and thirteenth centuries.

In the Senas' time, what is now Bangladesh was not an entity in the modern sense. Although ethnically, linguistically, and religiously linked, the region was divided into mini-dukedoms, or rajadoms. In the northwest along the Ganges was an area called Varendra that included Malda, Mahasthan, and Gaud and stretched north to the hills of Shillong. To the south, along the Bagaritha River valley, then the main branch of the Ganges, was Radha, which included Burdwan, Nadia, and the area around present-day Calcutta all the way to Puri. South of Varendra and east of Radha was Vanga, which stretched all the way to the Brahmaputra River. Across the river to the north lay Harikela, while to the south was Samatata, a kingdom around Chittagong and Mainamati. To the southeast, between Samatata and Vanga, lay Tipperah, which now encompasses Noakhali and Comilla. To the north and east was the kingdom of Kamrup, now in India's Assam State, and to the south of Samatata was Arakan in Burma or Mayanar as it now is called.

This division endured even while the Senas ruled Radha, Vanga, Varendra, and Samatata. Nevertheless, by that time there had arisen a consciousness of the Bangala, the people who live on mounds. *Bang* was the name of the tribe; *ail* means "divider." Even then the annual rains and floods of the delta made it essential to live on elevated mounds.

There also was a sense of solidarity with the Angas, the people of Bihar; the Oryas, those in Orissa way to the south; and the Vangas. For there already existed a sense of what in modern times came to be called Purbodesh. This concept of a "Greater Bangladesh," consisting of a central core of Radha, Varendra, Vanga, Harikela, Samatata, and Tipperah, as well as Bihar and Orissa, blossomed later, under the Muslims, Moghuls, and British. Ultimately, however, Britain destroyed this unity in 1912 when it divided Bengal. And when the British left India in 1947, their policies led to an even further division of Bengal, when Maldah, Nadia, and Calcutta became part of India.

Under the Senas, all of India's northeastern corner lay under one rule from Gaud: it stretched from Benares and Patna in Bihar to Tipperah and Chittagong in the east; from the foothills of the Himalayas at Darjeeling and Shillong to the hills of Orissa. The Senas' domain embraced East India's rice-growing tropical areas, rich with palm trees, ploughed by water buffalo, and irrigated by the Ganges, Brahmaputra, Meghna, and Karnaphuli rivers. The area was renowned for textiles, silk and cotton garments, fruit, rice surplus, spices, saltpeter, lead, coal, jute, boats, seamen, banks, and trading. With the major cities of Dhaka, Gaud, Benares, and Patna, it had seaports at Chittagong and Orissa and river commerce with Assam, Cooch Bihar, Nepal, and, via the Ganges, all of northern India. Marco Polo heard of the Golden City of the Bangala and its wealth, and described it in his notes on his visit to the East. (It was Ptolemy, the Greek geographer, who called Gaud the Golden City of the Bangala, the city of the kings.)

In the time of the Senas, Gaud, once the capital of the Buddhist Pala kings, flourished as the center of intellectual life and trade for all Bengal. Gaud was home to the most highly developed silk industry of its age, producing a strand so fine that according to a mid-nineteenth-century British observer, it could not be duplicated, as the skill had been lost. It is believed that the city is named for the extensive nearby cultivation of sugar cane, or *gur*. (Also dating from this time are Bengali sweets, which still set the standard across India. Indeed, there is no bazaar without a Bengali sweet store or a city without a Bengali market.)

Likewise reaching the epitome of its glory in this era was Varendra, in the northwest corner, where, under regional *zamindars* (tax collectors), a taxation system was established that lasted into the twentieth century. Today in Rajshahi one finds the Varendra Museum, which evokes memories of the Hindu revival that occurred under the Senas. Rajshahi is thirty to forty miles from the ruins of Gaud, which begin in Bangladesh and stretch nearly twelve miles into India's West Bengal State. Surrounding this ancient city are many square miles of mango plantations that emit an aura of mystery and a lovely fragrance. (The beauty of the territory around Rajshahi and Gaud cannot be exaggerated. The road from Rajshahi to Natore to Bogra presents a lush vista of rice, sugar, and tobacco. From Natore to Bogra to Rangpur the land is flat and verdant with air permanently moistened by the irrigated fields. Years ago such fields were parched in the dry season. Now spouts of silvery water, emanating from a tubewell housed in a bamboo hut, flow over emerald green rice paddies under a robin's egg blue winter sky.)

The rise of the zamindars, believed to have begun at this time, resulted in creation of an architectural heritage in Bengal of massive mansions or castles, *manzils*, found all over Bangladesh. The most impressive, Rani Bhavani, is near Gaud in Natore. With a beautiful home and gardens, it was a presidential retreat until it was converted recently into a tourist hotel. Other manjils exist in Bogra, Nawabari, Narayanganj, Nawabganj, and elsewhere. Most zamindars were Hindu, and the elegance of their estates owes much to the ideals of beauty that arose in the Sena period. Few Bangladeshi villages are not within walking distance of one of these estates.

Such was the legacy of the Sena period. By the beginning of the thirteenth century, however, Sena glory was destined for oblivion. A new force was heading for Bengal's wealth: Muslim warriors from the northwest.

An Army in Search of a People

About the time Europe was awakening from the Dark Ages and starting to unify to form the Crusades, Muslim warriors, commanded by Mahmud of Ghazni from Central Asia, began raiding, following the routes of the Aryans, Alexander the Great, and the White Huns. In about 1020, Mahmud entered the subcontinent via the Khyber Pass and pushed across the Indus into India proper. Along the way he amassed vast wealth and set the stage for others to follow, not as marauders but as settlers and proselytizers for Islam, just as their brother Muslims had done in the Middle East, North Africa, Spain, and Persia.

With Mahmud was a Central Asian scientist-scholar named Alberuni, whose writings still are considered scientific in method and result. Incredibly, that early, he believed the world to be round and computed a remarkably accurate circumference of the globe. Alberuni studied the Hindus' language, becoming proficient enough to learn their religion, astronomy, mathematics, and knowledge of agriculture and industry. His book, translated as *Alberuni's India*, is a classic insight, for it details a complex, structured society. It helped later expeditions because it was comprehensive and accurate and, more important, taught the Muslims to respect Hindu culture more than Mahmud had. Alberuni said that Mahmud's warlike methods had so antagonized the people that Islam had little chance of being accepted. Also, while Alberuni did not believe the Hindus to be as scientific as the Greeks, he found among them an admiration for scientific thinking and a well-developed philosophic mindset that made possible communication between Muslims and Hindus. In short, he created a human link between the best men of Islam and Hinduism, taken in their state of grace.

This link is important because there is a significant difference between the Aryan migration and Islam's spread over the Indian subcontinent. The former entailed the large-scale movement of a horde of invaders and the conquest of local people. In the latter there was no comparable migration. Islam's soldiers came as an army, not as a tribe, and they had to conquer and govern through local citizens. As elsewhere, the Muslims' only hope of permanent settlement depended on converting the natives. To do so they had to create conditions wherein conversion was viewed as both advantageous and admirable. They had to appeal to both good and bad aspects of the inhabitants' natures. Alberuni provided the conquerors with the first intelligent study of the people, including details of their religious history and manners. (A few centuries later, Spanish priests in the Americas did similar studies, with comparable results.) In short, in converting large numbers of people to Islam, the conquerors used techniques of rhetoric common to all proselytizers: sympathy, empathy, incentives, praise, a sense of belonging, a settling of grievances. Thus it was not by the sword alone that Islam progressed.

Islam spread for more than a century before reaching Bangladesh around 1200. Then, Baktiar captured the Sena Empire's capital, Gaud, almost without a fight and found warm food on the table of the fleeing government—whose astrologers had predicted the coming of a Turkish conqueror with extremely long arms. So uncannily specific was this description that one wonders if Baktiar had not influenced the seers, using knowledge Alberuni had garnered about Hindu astrologers.

With Baktiar came a band of Muslim scholars and teachers (or mullahs) who over time converted scores of millions of people to Islam throughout the subcontinent. There are only theories as to why so many people converted, how they were converted, and which groups did so. One thing is certain. The advantage Islam had over Hinduism and Buddhism was its promise of conscious survival into a blissful afterlife if one obeyed Islamic tenets. Such a belief was virtually unknown on the subcontinent except among a handful of Christians in the south. Needless to say, once this promise is made, as in Pascal's wager, merely denying it for lack of evidence is useless. For the chance of eternal life is not easily dismissed. Even more important, such a belief does not lead to passivity and acceptance but calls for worldly action and confidence in the here and now, as life takes on new meaning. One need not fear life's trials, for they are the testing, not the result. One can live, study, have a family, build, and create while having the promise of life eternal, all within a protective Muslim society. On the other hand, there is little evidence that, for instance, people of the subcontinent followed kingly example, as happened with converts to Christianity in Europe and to Islam in the Middle East and Persia. Yet this probably occurred, as there were relatively few "preachers," poor transport, and vast distances.

However it was accomplished, there clearly were vast numbers of conversions, creating what Nirad Chaudhuri, perhaps this century's most profound Bangladeshi-born thinker, called a "new ethnic group of people, born of the same race and language and in geographical contiguity, but who do not look the same, dress the same, or have the same beliefs as others so born." It also is clear that more than two-thirds of the converts came from two areas: the Indus River valley and the valley of the Brahmaputra and Ganges delta—one thousand two hundred miles apart, one in modern Pakistan, the other in Bangladesh. The rest were in central India, around Delhi and other major cities, but not in the Ganges valley countryside. When India gained independence in 1947, what are now Bangladesh and Pakistan still contained majority Muslim populations of 60 to 70 percent, while Delhi, which had been the seat of Moghul power for five hundred years, was only 18 percent Muslim. Remarkably, Muslim majorities had endured in the two riverine areas that had been the richest parts of both the Moghul and British empires. Why this occurred is a major mystery. Another is why people who spoke different languages and settled in river valleys at opposite ends of the subcontinent converted, while those who lived near the seat of Muslim power in Delhi did not.

One theory is that only the Sudras converted. To this is added a Marxist patina based on class envy. There probably is some truth to this, especially in Bangladesh, where the people were initially Namasudras, outsiders to Aryan culture, and where class, caste, and primitive national feelings are intermixed. This theory is supported by the fact that Islam spread among farmers, while landlords and merchants tended to be Hindu. Indeed, earlier in this century the distinction between Hindu and Muslim houses was that the latter used traditional thatch while the former used corrugated metal. But this theory overlooks the fact that nobles and rajas also converted, some for practical reasons and some because they were attracted to the religion. Moreover, if Hunter is right about the breeding of Brahmans, then significant numbers converted. For Bangladesh's upper classes look and act like Brahmans. They also maintain close ties to Hindu Brahmans elsewhere on the subcontinent. Finally, conversions certainly occurred among many other groups, as most of Bangladesh's ashraf (upper-class) families are Muslims descended from Afghans, Moghul Turks, Iranian businessmen, and raja and zamindari clans. Today these groups are as separate from the masses as were their ancestors, and it is fashionable to invent a non-Bengali genealogy. Thus family names ending in Khan point to an Afghan heritage, while Majlis suggests Persian roots.

Another explanation for the vast numbers of conversions is Islam's intrinsic appeal and relation to Buddhism. For there is in Islam's austere discipline, inner harmony, and majestic call to prayer five times a day a certain throwback to Buddhist monastic discipline. Given this, coupled with its belief in equality before God and in a personal God, as well as its promise of life eternal, Islam may have appealed to large numbers of villagers who had an unconscious family memory of the Buddha and his quest for release from this world of pain.

More important in the long run, Islam may have appealed to members of the Hindu warrior class who resented Brahman domination and sought a more straightforward soldierly religion—one that offered the intellectual rigor of Sankaran thought and the soldierly qualities of Rajput princes. This conflict between warrior and Brahman is quite old, and mimics a current one between scholarly bureaucrats and the military. This point is relevant today, because in 1947 when greater India was divided into Muslim Pakistan (including what was to become Bangladesh in 1971) and Hindu India, Pakistan's military caste played a disproportionately large role in government compared to India, where the Brahmans clearly ruled over the *kshatriyas* (military). The difference was that military rule was built into the religion during Islam's golden age, when power was separated, so that the Muslim-led military ruled while administrative matters were handled mainly by Hindus. This pattern was reinforced by the British, who divided power between the military in its cantonment (headquarters) and the administrative or civil lines. This division still exists in Bangladesh.

Lastly, Islam also may have had mass appeal to women. For it condemned the Hindus' widow-burning practices and was more lenient to women than was Hinduism. Much of this may have been due to a melding of Islam, Vaishnavite Hinduism, and Buddhist beliefs—which today is evident as Bangladeshi women play a much more active, open role in society than do their Muslim sisters in Pakistan or the Middle East. In addition, Islam provides for daughters to inherit and places a high value on women in society, compared to Hinduism, with its rites of child exposure of females and burning of widows on their husbands' funeral pyres.

But why was Islam's appeal so strong in Bangladesh? Circumstances suggest three possible reasons. First, Islam's greatest inroads were in East Bengal, in Vanga, Varendra, Samatata, and Harikela, which were on the frontier of the Hindu civilization, while it had little impact in Radha and Malda, where Hinduism predominated. For instance, Radha, along the Bagaritha River, had an entrenched Aryan culture, including the great *tol* at Nadia, which taught the Nyaya form of Hindu philosophy. But East Bengal was largely jungle. Its people may not have been Aryanized and may still have worshiped animist trees and other gods. Second, in the centuries immediately after the Muslim advance, the Ganges' main flow shifted from its Bagaritha to its new Padma branch. It thus flowed more eastward, for the first time meeting the Brahmaputra. This opened the eastern frontier to commerce and gave the Ganges access to the sea via the Brahmaputra and the Meghna. In fact, a U.S. scholar, Richard Baxter Eaton, theorizes that this Ganges shift allowed the Muslims to convert primitive, animist villagers by offering them grants of land newly suitable for rice culture. Finally, eastern Bengal had ports along the Bay of Bengal where Arab merchants, as well as prominent Muslims, are known to have paved the way for the final advance. Thus there is a legend in Chittagong that Pir Badr, a mythical Muslim Sufi saint, visited Bengal in the ninth century while the Buddhists still reigned.

Scholars agree that the original teachers, the Sufi saints of Bengal (who in actuality may not have been esoteric Sufi mystics, but holy Sunni Muslims), whose tombs remain renowned places for pilgrimage, festivals, and fairs, played a large role in the conversion process. For they provided not only education but also a sympathetic and empathetic philosophical approach that blended Shankaran concepts of the ultimate oneness and reality of God and the Sufi gnostic belief that each man has within him a spark of the divine reality. By blending these ideas with the natives' folk beliefs (as Saint Boniface, for instance, incorporated the Christmas tree into Christianity), these saints created a syncretistic approach to conversion. They also added the need for a *pir* (or *guru*, as in Hinduism, or teacher, as in Buddhism), maintaining that one needs a guide to find the ultimate truths.

Let us return briefly to the second possible reason why Islam became predominant in East Bengal: the shift of the Ganges River, an event which was to have enormous, enduring consequences. The shift created two Bengali ethnic groups, a division that, in the centuries to come, would divide the society religiously and geographically, so that there emerged in East Bengal a huge Muslim majority, along the new pathway of the Ganges (Brahmaputra), the Jamuna, and east beyond the Meghna, and in West Bengal a vast Hindu majority, along the Bhagirathi, the Ganges' old pathway. By the time of partition in 1947, the Muslims were an absolute majority in all of Bengal, but especially in the East. When Britain divided India, Bengal was split in half. The Muslims of West Bengal fled east and, with the Muslims already there, joined Muslims of the Punjab and Sind to form Pakistan, a state divided by 1,100 miles of Indian territory. Simultaneously, East Bengal's Hindus fled into West Bengal, which became part of Aryanized India. Today West Bengal's Hindu majority calls itself Bengali, while East Bengal's Muslim majority (which broke with Pakistan in 1971) calls itself Bangladeshi. *Desh* means "country"; Bangladesh is the country of the Bengali people.

However, during the five-and-a-half centuries that the Muslims ruled Bengal (from A.D. 1200 to June 24, 1757, when, at the battle of Plassey, the British statesman-soldier Clive defeated the Muslim army), Hindus and Muslims lived in a united province that included the states of Bihar and Orissa, now in India. The groups mingled and intermarried, and the Muslims depended on Hindu bankers, advisers, and administrators. Many Hindus continued their zamindari existence, living as rural nobility, often lording it over Muslim peasants. Moreover, many Hindus were of the merchant and money-lending class that served the more agricultural Muslim farmers.

In the seventeenth and eighteenth centuries there existed various mystic fraternities in which Muslim *sufis* and Hindu *sannyasis*, or holy men, shared metaphysical premises about God's oneness and reality. In the nineteenth century there emerged a sect called Brahmo Samaj, which believed in a unitary God and had Hindu and Muslim adherents. (Such beliefs still endure in East and West Bengal, providing important links between the two groups' upper classes. Also, many Muslim religious orders, such as the Surawardy, Chistai, Junayadia, Qadiria, and Naqsbandia, maintain cordial relations with like-minded Hindu, Buddhist, Christian, and even secular groups. Similarly, the Muslim Ismailias, followers of the Aga Khan, often provide a common bond among various mystical groups. While frictions do exist between Bangladesh's Muslims and Hindus, their common nationalism should not be minimized. In a crisis involving outsiders, they all are Bangladeshis first.)

Returning to the half-millennium of Muslim rule, while it was not an era of perpetual religious tolerance, neither was it noted for unrelieved persecution. After all, most Muslims were Bangla speaking and from a Hindu-Buddhist background. Indeed, folk dancing, river festivals, traditional flute music of the countryside, and many other cultural aspects were shared. More important, both cultures prospered during the early years of the Delhi Sultanate and in the later, more structured Moghul Empire. In addition, when the Sultanate declined in 1325 and when Moghul power waned in the seventeenth century and Bengal thus had a chance to be independent of

Delhi, its Hindus and Muslims cooperated to create a local Bengali government. This is critical, because under the Muslims there first emerged the idea of a greater Bengal that would include the modern states of Bihar, Orissa, and Cooch Bihar, all with large Hindu populations speaking variations of Bangla. This dream of a united eastern India still waxes and wanes but never quite dies, thanks to the unity achieved in those Muslim years.

At the outset the Muslim conquerors couldn't agree on what they thought of Bengal. Some called it a "hellish paradise," a "Paradise from which bread flows," a "Paradise of all the world." One Moghul emperor so enjoyed Gaud's comforts that he renamed it Jannatabad, "City of Paradise." Others hated the area because of the enforced idleness of the rainy season and because the rivers flooded and, over time, often changed course (an event which forced the Muslims to abandon first Gaud and then Hazrat Pandua, a nearby city). Such ambivalence was passed down the ages, as evidenced by Pakistani attitudes in this century.

Still, in this period Bengal reached its zenith as a prosperous agricultural land and world center of cotton and silk spinning. The Muslim rulers helped achieve this by uniting all of northern India into a single social system, thus stabilizing trade along the nearly two-thousand-mile route from Chittagong in the southeast to the Khyber Pass in the northwest. The Muslims also facilitated trade by building roads, such as the Grand Trunk that linked what is modern Bangladesh to Afghanistan, and by protecting shipping in the Bay of Bengal and around the Indian coast all the way to the Middle East. This made trade possible with the Arab world, Burma, Thailand, Java, China, and Japan, as well as with Africa and the faraway Mediterranean. Spices from the Moluccas and heavier cloths and manufactures from the West were traded for silks, cottons, rice, mustard seed, and jute from Bengal, tea from China, and brass, raw cotton, and indigo from western India. So great was Bengal's balance of trade with Delhi that specie never left Bengal, even after taxes were paid.

Visual testimony of this era's glory exists in the architectural remains in Bangladesh and West Bengal. For instance, Gaud, already grand under the Palas and the Senas, blossomed further under the Muslims, as attested by its remaining gates, walls, and mosques, especially the Golden Mosque. And when Gaud declined, Hazrat Pandua was built nearby on a newer, grander scale by Muslim kings. Its ruins are still considered beautiful. It too testifies to the area's past grandeur. Likewise, other mosques, for instance at Bakrganj, Dhaka, Sylhet, Dinajpur, and Jessore, remain monuments to that golden age, which has not been equaled. Also, near Dhaka are dramatic ruins of the ancient capital of Sonargaon (Golden City), once the terminus of the Grand Trunk Road. In Dhaka are found the ancient Lal Bagh Castle and numerous old forts and religious monuments. Finally, in Murshidabad, in West Bengal south of Gaud, is the last capital of Muslim Bengal.

Perhaps the greatest Muslim contribution was in music, which comple-
mented the native music and in part was influenced by it. The sitar, dotar,
harmonium, and tabla are Muslim additions to the local culture.

So wealthy was Bangladesh under the Muslims that Vasco da Gama sailed
there, rounding the Cape of Good Hope and entering the Indian Ocean in
1498. Reporting to Portugal's king, he described Bengal as a country that
could export "grain and very valuable cotton goods, a country that abounds in
silver." By 1536 the Portuguese were trading at Chittagong and living along
the Bhagirathi River in Radha above what is now Calcutta. The Dutch came in
1615, the British in 1651, and the French in 1674. Europe's merchants flocked
to Bengal for its cottons, silks, food, and manufactures. So great was Bengal's
trade that the four European countries fought for supremacy. Taking Bengal in
1757, Britain set the stage for conquering all of India. Meanwhile, thanks to
Bengal's wealth and army, the British were able to both conquer India and
send home vast riches that helped underwrite Britain's supremacy in the
eighteenth, nineteenth, and early twentieth centuries. Indeed, without Bengal
the British Empire is unlikely to have survived Napoleon.

An Army in Search of Gold

Park Street Cemetery in Calcutta is where the original British settlers of
Calcutta were buried. It is a strange place, not exactly Christian. There are
few symbols of Christianity but many Greek kiosks in semicircular marble
and large numbers of age-blackened obelisks, as if its owners belonged to
some secret Egyptian order. There's an aura of the occult, of some secret
formula for the grave that avoids the cross or the R.I.P. of a simple stone in
an English churchyard. There are some notable graves, such as that of Rose
Aylmer, who died in 1800 and of whom Walter Savage Landor wrote his
classic poem.

> Ah what avails the sceptered race,
> Ah what the form divine!
> What every virtue, every grace!
> Rose Aylmer, all were thine.
> Rose Aylmer, whom these wakeful eyes
> May weep, but never see,
> A night of memories and of sighs
> I consecrate to thee.

Indeed, her memory is the most human touch the British left in Park
Street Cemetery. For it is a place that is haunted in its way, perhaps on
purpose, perhaps to make us realize that unlike the Muslims, Buddhists, or
Hindu Aryans, the British did not come to proselytize but to make money.
They did not come to India to learn but to earn. They were merchants, not

scholars; men of craft, not of vision. They did not come to stay but to earn enough to leave. Only those like Rose, who died before she could escape, stayed on. And perhaps that is the sadness at Park Street, that here are buried the losers, those who could not take their money and run home.

In 1750 the British East India Company, which ultimately ruled British India, was not particularly successful in terms of power or wealth. With trading posts at Surat, Bombay, and Madras and a small station at Calcutta, it was a middling enterprise without either a clear view of the future or a plan for empire. It was only when a French company attempted to push the British out by allying itself with native princes that the British were forced to fight. As it turned out, after their initial panic they developed an overwhelming desire to rid India of the French, permanently. This they did in 1757.

But it was not until 1765, eight years after the Battle of Plassey that finally defeated the French and the independent king of Bengal, that Britain realized it could be an imperial power. This historic event occurred when Britain took over the *diwani*, the administrative power of the Bengal treasury. Thus there is truth to the statement that Britain garnered its empire in fits of absentmindedness. For it had its mind on gold, not empire. Only when empire promised a better return to London shareholders did it become interesting.

The foregoing is not a Marxist tirade but an introduction to Bengal's eighteenth-century conquerors. A friend, a historian in Calcutta, once described the British as an individually admirable people, good in all small things, evil in all large ones. He stressed the honesty of the police, the integrity of the courts, the decency of district collectors and magistrates, and the painstaking overall effort to understand India. He described the ability of the British to spark a new vein of literature in Bangladesh, the depth of their personal friendships, and the vigor of their railroad building, shipping, and commerce. But he added that despite their many admirable qualities and enduring legacy, they were a people who deliberately destroyed Bengal's cotton industry in order to create an Indian market for English-made cottons; established India's opium trade with China; took gold out of the country by selling the tax share of crops on the international market—even in years of famine; shipped to England about one-fifth of Bengal's liquid wealth; kept slaves on their tea plantations; treated the indigo farmers like serfs and all the natives with racist superiority, then savagely crushed their mutinies; built railways instead of much-needed irrigation systems, because England wanted to sell steel and locomotives; and forced the Indian government to buy the East India Company, even though Britain, through its viceroy, controlled the government. Thus when it was forced out of India in 1947, Britain bequeathed a great sense of legal justice and law, a love of democracy—and a de-industrialized, beggarized Bengal. The latter was partly because as late as 1943, when Bengal reeled under the massive famine, Britain exported grain to help sustain its World War II endeavors.

It had always been so, as Edmund Burke, the great Tory leader of Britain's House of Commons, attested in 1783, only a generation after the British conquest.

> The Asiatic conquerors [of Bengal] very soon abated of their ferocity because they made the conquered country their own. They rose or fell with the rise and fall of the territory they lived in. Fathers there deposited the hopes of their posterity; the children there beheld the monuments of their fathers. Here their lot was finally cast; and it was the normal wish of all that their lot should not be cast in bad land. Poverty, sterility, and desolation are not a recreating prospect to the eye of a man, and there are very few who can bear to grow old among the curses of a whole people. If their passion or avarice drove the Tartar lords to acts of rapacity or tyranny, there was time enough, even in the short life of man, to bring round the ill effects of the abuse of power upon the power itself. If hoards were made by violence and tyranny, they were still domestic hoards, and domestic profusion, or the rapine of more powerful and prodigal hand restored them to the people. With many disorders and with few political checks upon power, nature still had fair play, the sources of acquisition were not dried up, and therefore the trade, the manufactures, and the commerce of the country flourished. Even avarice and usury itself operated both for the preservation and the employment of national wealth. The husbandman and manufacturer paid heavy interest, but then they augmented the fund from which they were again to borrow. Their resources were dearly bought, but they were sure, and the general stock of the community grew by the general effect.
> But under the English Government all this order is reversed. The Tartar invasion was mischievous, but it is our government that destroys India. It was their enmity, but it is our friendship. Our conquest there after twenty years is as crude as it was the first day. The native inhabitants scarcely know what it is to see the grey head of an Englishman; young men, boys almost, govern there, without society, and without sympathy with the natives. They have no more social habits with the people than if they still resided in England; nor, indeed, any species of intercourse but that which is necessary to making a sudden fortune, with a view to remote settlement. Animated with all the avarice of the age, and all the impetuosity of youth, they roll in one after another; wave after wave, and there is no other thing before the eyes of the natives but an endless, hopeless prospect of new flights of birds of prey and passage, with appetites continually renewing for a food that is continually wasting. Every rupee of profit made by an Englishman is lost forever to India.

Nothing changed, as Romesh Dutt, a career Indian British civil servant who loved England, described in a book 118 years later.

Of all the evils Britain perpetrated in India, none was worse than its deliberate policy of destroying what was then the world's most developed and efficient cotton industry. As a British historian of the time, H. H. Wilson, wrote,

It is also a melancholy instance of the wrong done to India by the country on which she has become dependent. It was stated in evidence [in 1813] that the cotton and silk goods of India up to the period could be sold for a profit in the British market at a price from 50 to 60 percent lower than those fabricated in England. It consequently became necessary to protect the latter by duties 70 to 80 percent on their value or by positive prohibition. Had this not been the case, had not such prohibitory duties and decrees existed, the mills of Paisley and Manchester would have been stopped in their outset, and could scarcely have been set in motion, even by the power of steam. *They were created by the sacrifice of Indian [actually, Bangladeshi mills in Dhaka] manufacture.* Had India been independent, she would have retaliated, would have imposed prohibitive duties on British goods, and thus would have preserved her own productive industry from annihilation. This act of self-defence was not permitted her; she was at the mercy of the stranger. British goods were forced upon her without paying any duty, and foreign manufacturers employed the arm of political injustice to keep down and ultimately strangle a competitor with whom he could not have contended on equal terms.

Even Adam Smith in his *Wealth of Nations* had hard words for the practices of the East India Company, which he thought had a monopoly in both Bengal and England. In the one it was the largest buyer and in the other the largest seller.

As for Edmund Burke, shortly after he denounced his country's actions in India, the British government tried to restore order to Bengal and to help it recover from the outright robbery that had occurred in that first generation. Lord Cornwallis, who as a general had lost the American Revolution to George Washington at the Battle of Yorktown, was sent to India as governor-general. He reorganized the land tax system so that taxes were fixed and not subject to unexpected demands. Law and order were restored. Young candidates for the East India Company were trained in languages. And to keep them from dealing on their own, laws were passed to forbid private trading and new salary scales were introduced. Rather than antagonize the natives, Christianity was not preached. The message of Christ was not to disturb the flow of money to London. Having interfered in India's worldly wealth, the British were not about to offer the natives a better life in the next world—an afterlife most of the British probably did not believe in anyway, as the Park Street Cemetery seems to suggest.

Cornwallis's new tax structure laid the basis for recovery of the country's agriculture, and the introduction of jute, tea, and indigo gave the farmers new cash crops. However, throughout this period severe export tariffs were maintained on textiles, and East India Company officers set the price for locally made products, while negligible tariffs were put on British-made cloth that used U.S. cotton produced by slaves.

By 1810 India's normal exports had declined dramatically and opium was grown to replace the cloth that once had gone to China. (Bengalis never forgot this occurrence. In the early twentieth century, the Indian independence movement's first act was to boycott British-made textiles.) In the meantime, Britain's strangling of Dhaka's cloth trade caused the city's population in the first half of the nineteenth century to drop from 150,000 to 30,000. By midcentury much of Dhaka again was jungle.

In time, Britain did palliate its rule; and ultimately Bengal recovered from the depredations that had resulted in the deaths of one-third of all Bengalis in the first twenty years of British rule. Indeed, the Bengalis' recuperative power is evidenced by the fact that not only did they overcome the devastation Burke described, but they played a vital role in British expansion of its rule in India.

The British invasion was unlike any that had preceded it. While all other conquerors had entered the subcontinent from the west via the mountains of Afghanistan, Britain invaded in the east, a fact that surprised India's rulers. Moreover the British depended on sea power, hitherto not a major factor in subcontinental warfare. Because it established its beachhead there, Britain needed Bengal to be not only stable but also prosperous enough to finance further expeditions across India. Ultimately, though it was raped and plundered by its newest rulers during the latter half of the eighteenth century, Bengal enjoyed so spectacular a recovery that in a period of a century after its conquest of Bengal, Britain became master of all of India and Burma.

As a matter of fact, despite the ills to which it was subjected, during this period Bengal recovered its confidence, and some parts of its culture flourished. English education became important for the upper classes, and Bangla literature underwent a revival. A host of writers, educators, and religious reformers came on the scene, so that by the century's end Bengalis became prominent throughout Indian society. Before long, Bengali doctors, lawyers, poets, philosophers, and soldiers began playing important roles in the British Empire. A renaissance occurred in Bengal, helped, it is true, by the fact that funds from the expanding British-Indian Empire flowed through Calcutta. It was said then that "what happens in Bengal today will happen in the rest of India tomorrow."

By the 1890s, however, as Indian wealth continued hemorrhaging for Britain's benefit, widespread disaffection had arisen in Bengal. It is brilliantly documented in Romesh Dutt's two-volume *Economic History of India*, printed in England in 1901. The disaffection in Bengal also had been spurred by the liberal policies of William Gladstone, four times prime minister of Great Britain, who was pushing for home rule for Ireland—an eventuality that many Indians believed would apply to them by analogy.

Seeking to forestall Indian agitation for independence, the British sought to inflame Hindu-Muslim rivalries. In 1905 Lord Curzon, Indian governor general for six years, divided Bengal along communal lines, separating the

Muslim East from the Hindu West. So severe was the shock that an immediate outpouring of nationalist fervor struck Calcutta's educated classes, most
of them Hindu and many from East Bengal. The more rural Muslims of East
Bengal also were upset, but the British tried playing to their prejudices—to
no avail. The vehemence of their anger, their boycott of British cloth, and
other factors resulted five years later in a humiliating reversal of the decision
and the humbling of Curzon. Meanwhile, Bengal's victory reflected the importance it still played in British India. But later Britain took revenge by
moving its Indian capital from Calcutta to New Delhi in 1912. To build their
grand new capital, they took Bengal-based revenues, depriving Calcutta of
its role as the second city of the British Empire, after London. Thenceforth,
Calcutta began deteriorating, as did the rest of Bengal.

Even worse, the vindictiveness of the British continued, partly out of fear
that their rule in India was fast drawing to a close. To the every end, Britain
played on communal fears. Thus one secretary of state for India reminded
the viceroy in 1927 that while in public it was good to decry Hindu-Muslim
strife, in private one must remember that such divisiveness helped Britain.
Ultimately, Britain had its final shot when it succeeded in dividing Bengal in
1947 along the lines it had used in the short-lived effort of 1905.

The move of the capital to New Delhi was one of several factors that
impacted adversely on Bengal. The first was the opening of the Suez Canal
in 1870, for Bombay was much closer to it than was Calcutta. Ultimately, the
canal, coupled with an expanded rail system, sounded the death knell from a
trading perspective for Calcutta, as industrial and financial power shifted to
the west, where, thanks to the needs of World War I, India's clothing industry was reborn. In the process Bengal became a backwater of empire, so
unimportant that when famine struck in 1943, it took months before it
became a major government issue. By then it was too late. Bengal was pau-
perized.

Unlike the time when Muslim power declined and Bengal led the world
in wealth, when the British departed in 1947 all of Bengal had been reduced
to beggary and had become a byword for poverty and backwardness. As this
is being written, Calcutta is having another movie made about its poverty
and Dhaka has played host to a meeting of the Least Developed Countries. It
is difficult to imagine how it feels to fall so low.

How low Bangladesh has sunk from the days when Jean Law, one of its
first European visitors, reported that "in all of the official papers, firmans
and parwanas of the Moghul Empire, when there is a question of Bengal, it
never ends without adding these words, 'The Paradise of Nations'!"

Yet, to be fair, one must also recall the good parts of the British legacy.
Bangladesh's legal traditions remain based on laws and precedents set in
British times. Dhaka University, built at the time of the partition debate in
1912, is designed along British educational lines. The English language has

enriched the nation's heritage and given it concepts of constitutional government, science, and the arts that make its current culture vibrant. Its railroads
and ferries are built along British lines. British architecture graces its cities
and countryside: Dhaka University's Curzon Hall, the East Indian Railway
building in Chittagong, the charming, climatically adapted bungalows on the
hilltops of tea plantations, the Supreme Court building, the stately old
houses of the Civil Lines in Dhaka's Ramna area, and the beauty of the
central Maidan.

Finally, there is Calcutta, founded by the British in 1690. Contemporane-
ous with Boston, Philadelphia, Baltimore, and Charleston, it was designed to
be one of Asia's major industrial cities. Once the heart of British India, it
now is the capital of West Bengal State and remains, along with Dhaka, the
intellectual center of East India. Ironically, Calcutta may be the largest monument to British India, reflecting in its architecture, museums, monuments,
libraries, and scholarly societies all that was good and, in the chaos of its
administration, all that was bad.

Overall, though, despite its chaos and poverty, Calcutta is an intellectually and commercially vibrant entity—not the "Black Hole" of its ill repute.
This pejorative term refers not to the city's abject poverty but to a jail cell
where many Britons were said to have died. Also misused thanks to the
British is the name *Bangladesh*, which, in declining areas of London sometimes becomes a verb: *Bangladeshized*. This too is part of the British heritage.

It is an irony of history that the period from 1912, when Britain decided
to move its capital from Calcutta, to 1947, when it left India, saw both
Bengal's greatest decline and the demise of the British Empire. Indeed, that
dual decline reached its nadir in 1943, when Britain took food from starving
Bengal to support its own war effort. It was beggars stealing from beggars.
As Britain and Bengal had prospered together, so they declined together.
And in the midst of this slide, perhaps it is fitting that the British moved
their capital to Delhi, "that graveyard of empires," just twelve years before
they were run out of India. A few years after the British left Delhi, Le
Corbusier, the French architect, was to opine, as he viewed the ruins of the
Moghul, Lodi, and Afghan empires, that there was found the archaeological
heritage of New Delhi and that "the British ruins would be the greatest ruins
of all."

The Tragic Era

Although the British played on Hindu-Muslim antipathy and even exacerbated it to an extent not seen in previous centuries, they didn't invent the
problem. It had been there since Alberuni accompanied Mahmud to the
subcontinent in 1045. By 1947 neither Hindu nor Muslim in Bengal wanted
to live together. In the ferocious mood of those days, Muslim Bengal, which

had most of the people, joined its Muslim brothers eleven hundred miles away in the Indus Valley to form Pakistan, a nation physically divided by India. Meanwhile, Bengali Hindus, who felt closer to their caste-cousins in northwest India than to their racial and linguistic Muslim cousins, voted to take the western part of Bengal, essentially Radha and Maldah along the Bagraritha River, and become an Indian province. It is the two groups' striking unanimity on the separation issue that justifies Nirad Chaudhuri's description of Bengali Muslims and Hindus as separate ethnic groups: people who dress, look, and behave differently are ethnically different. Thus Ashkenazi Jews are not ethnically identical to Sephardim, and the Welsh are not the same as Scots, although both are Celts.

Reflecting from the safe vantage point of forty-six years, however, one is still puzzled about how Bangladeshis could have believed that they could belong to the same nation as a people eleven hundred miles away who, though of the same religion, did not share their language, race, cooking, music, art, or historical experience, cordial though their relations might be. As for today, while union with Hindu West Bengal probably is impossible for Bangladesh, its Hindu Bengali cousins are its most important customers and nearest neighbors.

It is difficult to gauge now just what those years as a province of Pakistan meant for Bangladesh. The history is still too close and the memories are too painful—the murders, rapes, wounds, and pillage inflicted on 350,000 Bangladeshi intellectuals, leaders, and common people, evidence of which abounds at the Bangladesh Museum, in a display even larger than that of Zainul Abedin's paintings. Moreover, during the first few years after liberation, Bangladeshis were on their knees again as the result of the war, floods, and drought. Only now do the people's liberation dreams begin to seem realistic. Now they must reflect on what those years of attachment to Pakistan contributed. One thing is certain, however: almost no one believes Bangladesh would have been better off remaining part of Pakistan.

Bangladesh is a poor country, though not as poor as in Zainul Abedin's paintings. And only the tourists of poverty come to see it in its current plight. There definitely are tourists of poverty, and Bangladesh is definitely part of their itinerary. For example, a British couple finances annual vacations in the dry season by being licensed to raise money from English donations to help Bangladesh.

But Bangladesh has not always been poor. It has had moments of greatness through a long and fruitful history. It had a trade known by the ancient Greeks and Persians, by the Japanese and Chinese, by the islands of Southeast Asia. Nearly all the words used in cotton clothing, including the word *cotton*, originated in this land. (Other such words are *shirt, pajama, taffeta, muslin, shawl, gingham*.) Its weaving methods were "borrowed" by the British to start their own cotton industry, which grew to replace the industry of what is now Bangladesh as the largest producer of cloth. Its brick-making techniques inspired British architecture. And its impact on the growth of British industry cannot be denied.

Thus, when you visit Bangladesh, by all means view the people as they are. But for your sake and theirs, remember that you are dealing with people who know what development is.

4

Aspects of the
Bangladeshi Mind

Iɴ ᴛʜᴇ ʟᴀsᴛ ǫᴜᴀʀᴛᴇʀ ᴏF ᴛʜᴇ nineteenth century, a young, exceed-ingly brilliant, and sensitive British political agent became aware that wars being fought in India's Northwest Frontier region bordering Afghanistan, some two thousand miles from the British capital in Calcutta, were being financed to a significant extent by money raised among poor Muslims in what is now Bangladesh, right under the noses of the British government, and that up to one-fourth of the volunteers fighting these wars against Brit-ish rule were from Bengal. W. W. Hunter decided to investigate this conspir-acy. More important, he made the British government pay attention to the fact that over half of Bengal's people were Muslim, a fact that, if it had been known by the original East India Company hands, had been overlooked by their successors, who had made the Hindu Bengalis their allies. Ultimately, Hunter was credited with helping found the Muslim League and with help-ing Muslim Bengalis redefine their position in the world, because as a result of his research the British reassessed their position in Bengal and generally in India.

Seeking to learn how the leaders of the "Mussalmen," as Bangladeshis prefer to be called, were able to organize the conspiracy, Hunter discovered that by 1871 the Muslims, who had ruled Bengal until the British arrived 114 years earlier and under whose stewardship the nation had prospered, had been reduced to penury by the British. The lands of upper-class Muslims had been given to Hindus who formerly had worked as bailiffs for Muslim land-lords. Their educational system, which had provided historical, scientific, legal, and artistic training, had been destroyed by the English, who had revoked their tax-exempt status. Their role in government and the courts had been turned over to Englishmen or Hindus, so that their representation in the civil service had been all but eliminated. And they were unwelcome in the military, which they had dominated. What choice had they but to rebel?

Hunter's book, *The Musalmen of India,* marks the beginning of modern Bangladesh. For the conspiracy it reveals pinpoints the moment when the Muslims forsook hope of returning to their past glory and began attempting to reassert themselves. The Muslims began looking to the future. Thanks to Hunter, the British virtually rediscovered Bengal's Muslims—especially the fact that the Muslims, not the Hindus, were by far the majority. As a result, the British colonial government began to address Islamic needs and realities. For instance, Muslim educational needs were specifically given priority: Arabic, Persian, and Urdu were introduced into school curricula, funding for poorer Muslim students was made available, and jobs and seats in educational institutions were reserved for Muslims.

The British were not motivated by altruism, however. For by this time they had become concerned that the Hindu minority they had empowered in Bengal had become too influential in a province that itself was the most powerful in all of India. Seeking to break the power of the monster it had created, the British decided to inflame Hindu-Muslim tensions. In 1905 the British viceroy, Lord Curzon, announced that Bengal Province would be divided for administrative reasons, although the implications were decidedly communal. Thus one part (now West Bengal) would be Hindu and the other (now Bangladesh) would be Muslim. So fateful was this decision that almost all the history of twentieth-century Bengal dates from this moment.

The decision to divide Bengal sparked a major change in the way Hindus and Muslims viewed each other. Hitherto, though there had been friction, dating from the time the Muslims had conquered the area, neither Hindu nor Muslim Bengalis thought of themselves as a separate nation. In the entire period of Muslim rule, from 1200 to 1757, when the British conquered the Muslim government, Muslim and Hindu had lived together in relative peace, with Muslims in political control while influential Hindus occupied high places in the government administrative system and the lower classes of both groups lived in relative harmony as tillers or landowners. Now the two sides were divided.

The Hindu leadership, which represented the zamindari (landlord and tax collector) class of East Bengal and which dominated Calcutta society in the West, railed against the decision. These leaders emphasized the unity of language, race, culture, and soil of Bengal (an approach not without appeal to some Bengali Muslims who also loved the land and language). Between 1905 and 1911 the Hindus staged a near revolution. There were terrorist episodes, huge marches, and general strikes, and they boycotted British goods. In retrospect this turbulence is widely recognized as the beginning of the free-India agitation that ultimately led first to independence from Britain and then to the emergence of Bangladesh.

Most Bengali Muslims favored the partition and relied on the British to maintain it. And although during this furor the All-India Muslim League was founded, in 1906 by Nawab Salimullah of Dhaka, this organization was unable to do much to change the balance of power, which continued to favor the Hindus. The Muslims were too poor and too far removed from power to offset the richer, better-organized Hindu movement, which fought partition.

In fact, so strong did the Hindus remain and so violent was their protest that in the royal durbar of 1911, when high British officials heard the complaints of the people and King George V was crowned Emperor of India, England reversed its decision, much to the disappointment of Muslims. To placate the Muslims, the British made two crucial decisions: they offered to (and ultimately did) build a university in Dhaka for East Bengal's Muslim majority, and they punished Calcutta's powerful minority Hindus by moving the viceroy's capital to Delhi. This move marked the beginning of the end of British rule and the decline of Bengal as a province.

Equally important, the upheavals transformed Muslim East Bengal (Bangladesh) by igniting a secular form of modern nationalism, one that was based on language, race, and culture. Although the fire burned at a low flame for many years, ultimately it flared up in Muslim Bengal in 1971 in the liberation war against Pakistan. For Bengal's Muslims are both Bengali and Muslim, and the Hindu Bengalis' fervent nationalism of 1905 was to be the impetus much later for the Bangladeshi Muslims' rise against their Pakistani oppressors.

Many Muslims imbibed the ideas of Bankim Chatterjee, a Hindu who wrote historical novels of stunning beauty that expressed Hindu love of Bengal in terms that Muslim intellectuals could identify with, even though the books were violently anti-Muslim. Had Chatterjee used the British instead of the Moghuls as the antagonists, the entire province, Hindu and Muslim, possibly would have risen against the empire. For Chatterjee's novels created a love for the language and the land of Bengal, a linguistic and cultural belief structure, that was to come to fruition in the 1960s.

There was a different legacy, too. During the argument about the division of Bengal, another strain of ideas entered the political bloodstream: the concept of secularism, not simply as an idea that rose above religious differences but as a political and social paradigm that called for a revolution that would transform all Bengal into a socialist paradise.

Still another legacy of that period was the formation of several secret societies that later supplied the cadres and ideologies for secular parties that arose as the twentieth century rolled on. Indeed, some of the secret societies that used terrorism against the British in 1905 have lineal descendants today, though, just as they did in 1905, 1917, and 1931–33 when terrorism ruled, they masquerade as literary organizations. One still endures in the shadow of the Bangladesh Parliament Building, on Manik Mia Avenue.

A final legacy of that era was the emergence of a new social hostility between Hindus and Muslims, partly fostered by the British. This politicization of religious differences had an astounding effect on the course of history. For both groups were made to forget the links of language and culture that united them, and instead began concentrating on religious differences.

From a broader view, what occurred was that the momentous events of the 1905–11 era made East Bengal's Muslims aware of their political importance and of the fact that the Hindu leadership, for all its liberalism, was an anti-Muslim force. The religious split that Alberuni had described in the thirteenth century now was being played out within the British Empire, with Britain stirring up the passions. For the Muslims, two messages emerged. The first was that Bengal would have to be partitioned along communal lines. The second was that there were ways of organizing political activities along secular lines. The first, the religious message, was destined to dominate politics until the British left and divided the subcontinent. The second, the secular message, was to linger and grow in importance politically until Bangladesh emerged in 1971 as a secular state in rebellion against "Muslim" Pakistan.

The Muslim and Secular Mind

Bangladesh is a Muslim nation, socially speaking, the third largest after Indonesia and Nigeria. Eighty-five percent of its 110 million people are considered Muslim. And the religion's underlying precept, submission to one God, is crucial to understanding its people. Were Bangladesh not Muslim, it would not exist as a separate nation but would be part of Hindu India.

Unfortunately, outsiders today often view Islam with fear, as a hotbed of militancy, reactionary policies, and terrorism—an image fortified by many events in recent years. But in truth, only a minuscule number of the world's nearly one billion Muslims are involved in these dramatic events. Most Muslims do not even live in the Middle East or North Africa; they are in Asia, somewhat isolated from the events of recent years. Bangladesh is a case in point.

Islam in Bangladesh never has been the primary political mode of thought. Nor has it been able to present itself as a complete ideological system. In the 1920s and 1930s, when limited autonomy was granted to Bengal under the British, a politician named Fazlul Huq ran secular election campaigns and won the Muslim vote only by calling for just rent laws and better working conditions. Such secular concerns have continued to form the basis of Bangladeshi politics. Only in one period, 1945 to 1953, was the country ruled by the Muslim League, a very secular, modern party compared to today's Muslim parties in Iran. That Muslim League government formed an alliance with the political left as protection against a hostile Hindu India. Since 1953, Bangladesh's political orientation has been militantly liberal and secular.

This last point is critical to an understanding of Islam's role in the mind of Bangladesh. Before India's partition in 1947, Bangladesh's politics was divided roughly between two parties. The first was the small but influential Muslim League, founded in 1906 and comprised of old families that wanted to integrate Islam into political life. For unlike most of Christianity but like Judaism, Islam sees no division between politics and religion. The second was a much larger secular movement led by Fazlul Huq, Huseyn Shaheed Suhrawardy, and Abul Hashem, who represented widely popular senti-ments. This movement was influenced by European labor and communist movements and was spread in Bangladesh by young graduates of English colleges in Calcutta and Dhaka.

Throughout the twenties and thirties, when the British granted limited provincial authority, the Muslim League never was able to muster a majority without allying itself with secular parties. When it did win in 1946 and participated in the formation of Pakistan in 1947, its leaders began ignoring the underlying Bangladeshi aspects of the problem. After all, many of the most avid Muslim Leaguers were not "sons of the soil" (Bangladeshi-born) and had linguistic and cultural roots in northern India or in the minority sects of the Shi'as, the Ismailis (followers of the Aga Khan).

In 1948 the first Pakistan president, Mohammad Ali Jinnah, who had been born in western India and knew little of Bangladesh, visited Dhaka. When he insisted that Urdu (an Indo-Aryan language related to Farsee, or Persian) be Pakistan's state language, growing disenchantment with Muslim League leadership erupted and created an opening for rekindling the old secular party networks.

By the early 1950s a secular party, the Awami League, rose phoenixlike from the ashes, due to the dynamism of two leaders, Suhrawardy and Sheik Mujibur Rahman. This party absorbed the older secular parties founded by Fazlul Huq before the formation of Pakistan. It immediately became the largest party, first in what is now Bangladesh and later in all Pakistan. Re-cruits came primarily from families that, though Muslim, had opposed the first partition of Bengal. The goal of the party was to make Suhrawardy the secular, democratically elected prime minister of Pakistan, and it succeeded. But Suhrawardy was dismissed from office, and military rule came shortly thereafter. The Awami League outlived Suhrawardy and in the 1960s be-came the leading party under the leadership of Sheikh Mujib, who was to lead the rising against the Pakistanis. A second secular movement, divided between pro-Chinese and pro-Soviet wings, was the National Awami Party, or NAP, of Maulana Bhasani, one of Bangladesh's truly indigenous leaders. After 1963 this party swerved toward nationalism and provided the radical rhetoric for that movement through two newspapers, *Dainik Sangbad,* published by Ahmedul Kabir, and *Ittefaq,* published by a major figure in the country named Manik Mia, whose son, Anwar Hossein (Manju) still runs the paper. Finally, the standard parties of the West, communist and socialist, also played important roles.

In the meantime, the Islamic parties suffered, identified as they were with the policies of the central government of Pakistan, which used appeals to religion as a means of social control. For example, in January 1964 the Pakistan government used the theft of a relic, a hair from the head of the Prophet Muhammad, that occurred in Srinagar, India, more than twelve hundred miles away, to promote a pogrom against Hindus. (This pogrom took the life in Dhaka of the author's brother, a Catholic priest and Islamic scholar.) However, such violence had less and less appeal to voters, as the secular parties emphasized social and economic needs in combination with appeals to Bengali solidarity in language and culture.

During this period, greater emphasis was placed on the language and culture of Bengal, with special emphasis on Tagore and Kazi Nazrul Islam, the humanism of M. N. Roy, and the more liberal currents that entered from the West and Eastern Europe. Tagore's songs, with their unitarian but gnostic themes, became the rage in a society that is greatly moved by music. Similarly, the music of the revolutionary poet Kazi Nazrul Islam, who combined utopian socialism and nationalism, had a profound effect on what was becoming a deep inward awakening of national Bengali sentiments—an awakening identical to that of the Hindus in the late nineteenth century when Ram Mohan Roy, Bankim Chandra Chatterjee, Swami Vivekananda, and Dwarkanath Tagore created a new sense of nationalism that fueled the 1905 revolt against partitioning Bengal. A third poet, Lalan Shah, the Baul troubadour, offered a more open and humanist outlook that differed from the severe puritanical aspects of Islam. The difference was that only in the late 1960s did the elites of Muslim East Bengal feel the pull of culture strongly enough to revolt against a foreign, non-Bengali oppressor, even though that power was Muslim.

And as in 1905, when young men took a vow of purity to serve secret societies to win Bengal's freedom, so too in the 1960s did young men, in secular imitation, join secret societies—nationalist, Marxist, Maoist, or militantly secular—and dedicate themselves to Bangladeshi independence. According to a conversation this author had with Bhagat Singh, an Indian Army general who was active in the Liberation War, these secret societies were supported by funds from India and elsewhere. Moreover, the movement, at times reinforced by professional agitators, some from India, grew stronger, with students going to the countryside and staging *jatras* (musicals) or dramatic plays to arouse the masses. During this time, Dhaka University became a political institution that unofficially trained cadres for political activities, a tradition that continues.

In the late 1960s, when calls for independence were made, the small Islamic parties remained loyal to Pakistan, while the secular ones remained true to the people's agitated demands that their language be used and their wishes be heard. When civil war came, many Islamic party leaders, including Ghulam Azam, who had earlier in his life been a student leader in the Bangla Language Movement and now was head of the important Jamaat-e-Islam, allegedly sided with the Pakistani army against the popular rising. This so discredited all Islamic parties, including the Jamaat and the Muslim League, that only now are they regaining limited credence. (Even as this book is being written, the role of Jamaat is still being debated hotly in the Bangladesh Parliament by those who favored independence. At issue has been whether Ghulam Azam is a Bangladeshi citizen and whether he should be tried for war crimes. As of early 1993, Ghulam Azam was in jail, pending a decision on his fate.)

This history helps explain why Islam has not been an explicit political force. Thus in 1991 it was no surprise that the two militantly secular parties, the Bangladesh Nationalist Party and the Awami League, won more than two-thirds of the votes in national elections, with religious parties garnering only about 5 percent.

Nevertheless, the country is indelibly, eternally Islamic, if not politically at least socially, as, for example, in the United States, where Christianity is a social but not overtly political force. The distinction between religion as a social and as a political force is major. Still, Bangladeshi minorities are treated as equals, despite minor tensions. For instance, though Hindus comprise only about 10 percent of the population, because of their merchant class makeup and role in intellectual pursuits, they are found throughout the nation, in trade, as teachers, doctors, and so on. The same goes for other, much smaller, minorities—Buddhist, tribal animist, and Christian—whose rights and, where family matters are concerned, religious laws are protected.

Generally speaking, most Bangladeshis are devout, praying Muslims who feel themselves to be part of the larger Muslim world, and they are dedicated to the laws of their religion: charity, pilgrimage to Mecca, fasting during Ramadan, a sober life, and a belief in the majestic, unitary God of Islam. That austere, straightforward way of living infuses every aspect of life.

Were it not for religion, the social fabric of Bangladesh would rend. For it is Islam that preaches the brotherhood of man, provides charity for the poor and help for the widow and abandoned woman, and has permitted many Muslims to support liberal and even socialist causes, due to its condemnation of usury and overweening government. Finally, it is Islam that provides the moral glue of society, that gives justification for a campaign of moral house-cleaning when the society loses its way.

Islam is not a church in the sense of a structured hierarchy, like that of the Methodists or Episcopalians. There is no one bishop, Archbishop of Canterbury, or Missouri Synod to make policy for all Muslims year by year, much less day by day. Religion tends to be congregational in structure, built around village or neighborhood mosques and unified by a community of feeling, a numinous air, best signified in the austere gravity of the call to prayer that begins before dawn and ends, five prayers later, shortly after sunset. The uniformity and simplicity of beliefs and public straightforward-ness gives Islam a unique ability to unify the faithful without regimentation. And in a nation of large, extended families there is surprising patience with a backslider who skips his prayers, does not keep the fast, or fails to attend mosque on Friday. There is, however, little respect for those who practice usury, do not share with the poor, or fail to care for the old and infirm or to provide for fallen women or widows. And there is anathema for those who do not care for their mothers and fathers in old age. Finally, there is a certain dislike of those for whom the pursuit of personal wealth or prideful con-sumption is a major goal or practice.

As a poor country, Bangladesh would be lost without the billion or so little charities that occur daily thanks to Islam's commands. Widows in vil-lages are kept alive by provision of jobs or community charity. No obvious organization exists, but each household seems to make sure that a widowed neighbor is cared for, even if only a cup of dry rice is sent. In some public marketplaces, merchants leave bowls of coins for beggars, each of whom will take only a single coin. This does not mean that there are no beggars on the streets of Dhaka or Chittagong. What it does mean is that they are a minority who are forced to beg in a large society that does not have welfare systems. Countless others are cared for at home in the extended family or in the village. Jobs often are rotated among unemployed landless labor to help each household, and a poor family often receives gifts of cloth or food. Similarly, the community cares for the lame, the halt, the mentally ill, and the retarded. Divorced women are looked after by their fathers or brothers as a matter of course. And unlike Hindu law, Islamic inheritance law pro-vides for some, if not equal, inheritance for women. More important, village elders inherit a tradition of common law principles to settle disputes without recourse to civil courts, a system that is a major underpinning of the social system.

It is true that Islam does not treat women as well as men. But it is well not to judge too harshly, especially when Islam in Bangladesh is compared to some neighboring religious practices. Thus Islam never demanded that a wife join her husband's funeral pyre, as did Hinduism until the early nine-teenth century. Nor did Islam ever forbid widows to remarry, as orthodox

Hinduism still does. In comparison, Islam in Bangladesh is enlightenment itself. A Muslim woman may divorce her husband and a widow may remarry. Moreover, few Bangladeshi women cover their faces and bodies with a *burqua*, the loose-fitting gown and mask; most do not even use the *chador*, or veil; and by and large they are not nearly as restrained in dress as are their sisters in the Middle East or Pakistan. (However, in periods of social tension, even many Bangladeshi women begin adopting stricter rules of dress. Examples occurred in 1982 after martial law was declared and in 1992 when the popular Muslim leader Ghulam Azam was arrested.) Moreover, in the cities, women have basically the same freedoms as do their Western counterparts, except for the right to flirt or appear promiscuous. While they are friendly and open, Bangladeshi women are quite modest compared to their Western cousins.

In a similar vein, there is a touching centrality to the role of the mother in Bangladesh that has no Western comparison, in terms of the respect and love tendered to her, especially by sons. To love someone or some cause as one loves one's mother is the highest love one can suggest to a Bangladeshi. Indeed, there seems to be an underlying Bengali folk cult, perhaps stretching back to pre-Aryan times, of the Great Mother, who is sometimes interpreted as nature or as the land of Bengal and other times, in great spiritual emotions, as a benign force that permeates Bangladeshi culture. For instance, young radicals, who take a vow of purity for patriotic reasons, vow to view all women as they do their mothers. Islam, too, creates a beautiful image of the mother, one which demonstrates that behind the screen of *purdah*, or apparent separation of the sexes, women play a far more powerful role than outward appearances indicate. Woe to the foreigner seeking to understand Bangladesh's social life who ignores what women at a social gathering have to say. For Bangladeshi women are powerful in economic life (two of the richest people in Bangladesh are women business leaders), and women have a role in all professions. Too often, Westerners misinterpret the fact that Bangladeshi women have none of the outward signs of power. Actually, they have the substance of power—power that Western women often lack.

Lastly, in terms of postliberation Bangladesh, there is no other Muslim nation that so encourages young women to go for higher education (one of the most noted Islamic historians, Sufia Ahmed, is a woman), allows wives greater access to contraceptive services, is more respectful of women working, or has more openly active women in politics. Thus two of today's three major parties—the Awami League and the Bangladesh Nationalist Party—are headed by women, one of whom, the BNP's Khaleda Zia, became prime minister in 1991. And there is no reason to doubt that the other, Sheikh Hasina, daughter of Sheikh Mujibur Rahman, the nation's "Father," has a very good chance of being Begum Zia's successor.

On the other hand, a macho male image exists and there is no doubt that male privileges are abused constantly. Mothers cater far more to their sons than to their daughters; male children are treated better and get more education, as most of those in school, especially in the villages, are boys; men are fed before women; and men have the power to divorce and the right to have up to four wives simultaneously (though even two wives is rare nowadays, especially in the cities). Still, a popular joke goes as follows: when an American gets money he buys a car; when a Hindu gets rich he buys more land; when a Muslim makes a little extra money he takes another wife.

In the broader context, Islam has been a blessing for Bangladesh, because by nature it is international and outward looking, at least vis-à-vis the other forty Islamic nations. It does not preach racism, and indeed is a truly international religion. Moreover, it has a long tradition of scholarship: theological, philosophical, political, legal, military, artistic, literary, and scientific. It also has its own educational system, which has been one of the precious ornaments of learning for centuries.

It was the Muslims, after all, who saved Plato and Aristotle for the West during the Dark Ages. The works of the Muslim scholars Averroes and Avicenna formed the basis for the rekindling of learning that became the Renaissance in Europe. Maimonides, the great Jewish scholar, and St. Thomas Aquinas, the Catholic scholar, owe their work to Averroes, because the latter preserved the works of Aristotle within his own writings. (One prominent and fertile school of political thought explicitly credits the teachings of Al-Farabi, a medieval Muslim scholar, as the major source of its own ideas. Known as the Straussian School and located primarily at the University of Chicago, this school influences a great deal of serious political thought in the United States.) Similarly, Muslim Arabs saved geometry and mathematics by teaching Europe the basis of modern Arabic counting. (Arabs, by the way, refer to their numeral system as the "Indian system," because it was learned by men who followed Alberuni to India.) And it was Muslims who introduced the compass, the rudder, and gunpowder to Europe and whose philosophy influenced Western practices of chivalry and respect for women.

As for Islam's educational influence on Bengal, before the English conquest, education in Bengal was financed by the proceeds of crops grown on tax-exempt land. This privilege underwrote a wide educational system that Bayley, an early British scholar of Islam, described as producing the best education available in India until that time. Even after the British revoked the tax-exempt privilege of Muslim schools, Bayley noted, at least 100,000 Bengali students still attended school, making the Muslim education system the largest at the time within Bengal—larger than anything the British had built. Thus it is not surprising that ever since 1875, when the British at last allowed an Islamic university to be founded in India, at Aligarh, higher education in Muslim Bengal has flourished, so that Bangladesh now has broad-based universities in Dhaka, Chittagong, Rajshahi, and Jahanginagar, as well as engineering and agricultural universities and a fairly new Islamic one.

And as for Islam's relationship to the rest of the world, it undeniably has close links to Christianity and Judaism. It too preaches that there is only one God; reveres Moses and Jesus as prophets; believes, as does Judaism, that religion is based on a set of laws; and has many dietary laws in common with Judaism. Finally, Islamic nations are far more tolerant of Christians than, say, Christian Spain was of Muslims, and are more tolerant of Jews than Jewish Israel is of Muslim Palestinians.

In short, the history of the Islamic world, the West, Christianity, and Judaism is so entwined that Bangladeshis often express amazement that many non-Muslim visitors look down on Islam as a religion and a culture, instead of understanding that Islam has a Judeo-Christian heritage. Even the Crusades and the founding of modern Israel act as shared experiences between Islam and its parent and sibling religions.

Turning to Islam itself, it is important to understand that many strains exist in Bangladesh. Most Bangladeshis, among them the majority of rural dwellers, are Sunni Muslims, whose traditions date to the Prophet Muhammad and who believe in a very old tradition of laws, the Prophet's sayings, and local adaptations. A far smaller number, mostly of the upper class, are Shi'a. Their roots go back to the death of Hasan and Husain, the Prophet's grandsons, and while they are fluent in Bangla, their first language is Farsee, as their ancestors came from Persia. A third, more liberal, group consists of the Aga Khanis, or Ismailis, who trace their origins to the Middle East. Another sect is the Ahmadis, whose roots lie in Pakistan.

Within these strains are subsects. For instance, one Sunni offshoot is the Wahabi, whose members are influenced by the militant, puritanical Saudi Arabian version of Islam. Another is a strain whose members follow a particular guru or pir, such as the currently popular Pir of Atroshi. (Some pirs come from India or Pakistan.) Then there is the Tabliq, a nonsectarian movement aimed at personal improvement within Islam. On occasion, more than a half-million Tabliqis have appeared at conferences and rallies. There also are diverse religious-based parties related to secular movements, such as a Libyan version of Islamic socialism, a mostly Shi'a group that follows the Iranian way of life, and other, socialist, sects that follow Saddam Hussein. In addition, various orders of teachers and *mullahs* (religious leaders) exist, whose members indoctrinate youth into Islam and to whom their followers remain loyal.

Lastly, as in every Islamic culture, there exists a hard-core Islamic puritanism that is as fundamentalist as any found in Saudi Arabia or Iran. This brand of Islam, which has been evident in various nineteenth-century reform movements, is a political, social, and religious mix that righteously reappears whenever the society lapses too far into offensive behavior, such as scorn of religion, licentious behavior, breakdown of family life, or failure to care for the poor. Thus Islam is not a uniform mass but a beautiful tapestry that contains myriad designs to suit every need.

At present, the best-led, biggest political party representing hard-core Islamic beliefs is the Jamaat-e-Islam, led by Ghulam Azam, whose citizenship is being debated. The party has three layers: an inner core of leaders, a level of organizers, and one of followers. It has about 250,000 members who have been vetted for loyalty and willingness to work. The party stages large, extremely well-disciplined rallies and continues to grow. More important, many university teachers report that the brightest students are turning for leadership to Ghulam Azam. His snowy-white hair, clear, warm eyes, artistic hands, and calm manner make him more of a father figure than most leaders.

Even before he was jailed, it was not easy to meet him. His house, in a clean but lower-middle-class area of Dhaka not far from Magh Bazaar, could be reached only by circuitous means. One of the nation's most intelligent leaders, Ghulam Azam is soft-spoken, conceptually logical, truthful, and disarming. While the Jamaat publicity department puts out excellent newsletters with his views, only up close is he really understood. He is a man with clear ideas of what a Muslim state should be.

As for his political party, the Jamaat draws on the works of its founder, Madudi, a man who began writing in India in the 1930s and whose followers built up the party there and in Pakistan. Descended from its Indian and Pakistani predecessors, the current Bangladeshi Jamaat also draws membership from the Tabliq, a more free-flowing movement, and from disgruntled rural people fed up with secular parties. It gains doctrinal support from the Afghan Mujahedin and from the Muslim Brotherhood in the Middle East, as well as from Cairo University, where Islamic studies have been centralized. The Jamaat also is in contact with Middle East Muslim oil people, some from the religious states, and receives input, too, from such "secular" governments as that of Qadhafi and Saddam Hussein. It is not yet the largest party, but it is poised, given the right situation, to take power. However, it has yet to win the true loyalty that is given to the nation's secular parties.

The Ancient but Living Verbal Tradition
in the Bangladeshi Mind

Islam and secularism are the dominant forces of thought in Bangladesh among the elites. However, there is a more ancient mind that everyone in Bangladesh, Muslim, Hindu, Christian, or atheist, shares. It is not a system of thought. It is barely articulated by words and books. Yet it exists in the deepest recesses of the mind, because it predates all current religions and, of course, secularism.

While Islam is by far the predominant social, economic, and political force, and though religious Muslims consider all history before the Prophet to be inconsequential, Bangladeshi culture has a multifaceted texture, thanks to its ancient animist, Buddhist, and Hindu heritage—not in a religious sense but in a deep under-level of the mind, the bottom of a split-level mind.

Even during the great medieval Muslim era, when the invading Muslims denounced the Sena Dynasty's imposition of Sanskrit and financed the translation of many writings from Persian or Sanskrit into Bangla, not only Muslim texts but also Hindu epics, such as the *Ramayana*, were included. Likewise, some scholars maintain that the early Muslim saints, who worked tirelessly to convert the Bengali masses, used philosophic concepts borrowed from local traditions. From the start of the modern revival of Bangla under the British, it was recognized that the entire Bengali culture had to be included. Thus Islam itself fostered a broader concept of Bengal. Moreover, it always had been the Muslim custom to try all civil and family cases of law according to the religion of the litigants, so that Hindus, Buddhists, and, later, Christians went to law on terms they morally accepted.

This generosity of outlook endeared the Muslim leaders, both soldiers and saints (*ghazis* and *sufis*), to the indigenous people and thereby solidified Bengali culture in the *madrassahs* (religious schools); in the laws, which showed great toleration for Hinduism; and in the general culture of music, art, poetry, and custom. Indeed, at the peak of Muslim rule in the century before the British, Muslim Bengal had mostly Hindus within its borders, as it included Orissa and Bihar, which the British, like their Muslim predecessors, maintained to form their provincial presidency of Bengal.

Rare is the Bangladeshi who does not know most of the Hindu legends and holy stories by heart, having learned them at home, at school, or from itinerant theater groups that perform *jatras* (dramas) in a tradition dating back at least two millennia. (Nowadays, jatras are staged at harvest time or during *melas*, or fairs, that travel from district to district. Also, mendicant Hindu *sadhus*, or holy men, wander from village to village, where they are greeted with respect by Muslims and Hindus alike, as are Buddhist *bonzes*, since Buddhist tales also are well known.)

The same goes for Bangladeshi music, some of which, at least in sentiment and melody, dates back to before the Buddha and maintains ancient traditions. Thus a common cultural thread unites the Muslim philosopher Kabir, the Hindu reformer Shankara, the Hindu medieval mystic Chaitanya of the devotional Bhakti movement, the eighteenth-century Bauli mendicant mystic Madan Baul, and his Bauli successor Lalan Shah. For they all composed songs in Bangla, songs whose theme was the oneness of God; and their music ultimately influenced the beloved poets Rabindranath Tagore and Kazi Nazrul Islam, the latter of whom died after Bangladesh's independence.

It is worthwhile to pause here and mention that song and poetry are very much part of village culture in Bangladesh, where television and radio have not yet destroyed the capacity of the people to enjoy group singing or to listen to traveling bards who read or sing poetic works. Bangladesh is a land that loves its poets, and this in itself is part of the numinous life of the spirit in the villages.

What is important about the music is that it represents a type of Bengali folk religion that transcends the teachings of any single sect, by blending poetry, song, and the folk beliefs of simplicity, piety toward all nature, the oneness of God, and the equality of all men into a numinous level of both *bhakti* (devotion) and *jnana* (immanent enlightenment). So powerful is this folk religion that in the nineteenth century the sensitive Bengali Raja Ram Mohan Roy founded a new cult called Brahmoism, which sought to transform this folk religion into a new humanist form of Hinduism. While many Muslims were and are attracted to the Brahmo beliefs, Roy's and his successors' basically Hindu outlook discouraged most Muslims from formally joining. However, Roy's efforts left a cultural legacy of the oneness of humanity and God that still floats numinously within the context of Bangladeshi culture.

What is important about this is that the songs and poems, the sweet, pious belief of this folk culture, endure among a people whose rural and rustic life-style cultivates it. Thus there is an indefinable yet palpable unitarian humanist quality to Bangladeshi culture that is never formalized into more than music. One hears it on ferries as minstrels ply their trade, along the waterways as weary boatmen row homeward, by the shore as women wash their laundry, and along the roads as other women pound clay to a hard finish on a new roof. This folk belief structure is neither a heresy nor at odds with Islam, Hinduism, Buddhism, or Christianity. It is a simplified version of the thoughts of hard-working people seeking to grasp the essence of life and its meaning.

Everyone has a favorite of Lalan Shah's verses to best exemplify this folk belief. Here is the author's (translated for him by Brother James).

> Where is the Lord, the empathetic one?
> Search for him with the sentient guide.
> The mind blurs the eyes,
> The mountain is often lost behind the hair,
> What fun, O my Lord, you always see,
> While sitting on the shore.
> If I am so fortunate to meet Him in the world hereafter,
> How shall I possibly recognize Him
> For yet I haven't had any sight of Him?
> You should love him intelligently.
> You may find the treasure after which you've set
> Your heart not far away.
> Lalan says search your own soul's home,
> It may not be far away.

As with Lalan Shah's poem, the aim is to lead the hearer to the presence of Him without trying to erect a doctrine or belief structure, to part the curtains but not to describe the room. It is this wider basic belief pattern that Tagore tried to systematize into a humanistic religion, as had Ram Mohan Roy. But this belief pattern eludes the grasp of all who would try to possess it. For it is this wider outlook, which embraces all the world's religions but itself is not defined, that is the core belief of Bangladesh.

Some have called this a secular or a humanist belief, and have tried to tie it to Western secularism or to the hard philosophical humanism that rejects the transcendence that religions seek to attain. In a sense, this unique Bangladeshi folk religion resembles both humanism and secularism, but it would be unwise to deny the implied supramundane power that it suggests.

Taken in its narrow sense, this monist world view can suggest a materialist philosophy. And this is surely the sense in which most of Bengal's secular political party leaders attempted to frame it. Thus when Bangladeshis fought for independence on a political platform of nationalism, socialism, secularism, and democracy, their leaders' words unquestionably had resonance among the people. But when, after independence, the nation's new leaders turned the four concepts into a godless, hard-sell jargon of left-wing rhetoric, the people deserted the Awami League in droves, just as they again rejected the party in 1991. For Bangladeshis are too close to this folk belief to accept the nonsense of jargon, of social science and ideology, even when Islam, by its support of Pakistan, was in discredit. Thus the Religion of Humanity that Tagore and Ram Mohan Roy found among the people was, as my friend the late Supreme Court Justice Syed Mohammad Hossain, a lifelong secular humanist, said as he stepped down from the bench in disgust with the military government in 1984, "a religion after all—one which the people believed in as such, not an ideology."

In this sense, the culture of Bangladesh is a timeless wonder, a tradition so old that were the Buddha to reappear he would hear echoes of all he had taught. Likewise, were Kabir, Shankara, Chaitanya, Madan Baul, Lalan Shah, Tagore, and Nazrul Islam to return, they would find the essence of all they had sung of, there to be heard and seen in the paintings of Sultan or Zainul Abedin and in the flute, the echtar, and the dotar of the country boatman.

And they would sense—in the rhythm of people's lives; in dark, sunburned, naked backs straining to plant the sheaves amid the wet paddies; in thatched village huts on Meghna char lands; among singers at a harvest wedding; in the scent of a dung-and-straw perfumed fire; in the unsteady walk of a newborn goat; in the hot bite of chili; in the roly-poly amble of water buffalo; in the sweetness of fresh rice; in the round, happy eyes of Bengali daughters—that the belief goes on, and on, and on, like the river Padma itself.

Poverty and Rusticity

In addition to the Bengali culture and Islam, there is another vital aspect of the Bangladesh mind: the constant awareness and nearness of cataclysmic plunges into poverty. No one can escape the fear of poverty or live beyond its chill grasp, even those at the highest levels. Few have sufficient wealth to ever feel secure of the vagaries of a change of fortune, the demands of corrupt government officials, or myriad other factors, such as the famines of 1943 and 1974, which threatened massive starvation.

As a result, Bangladesh's middle and upper classes are rife with vicious rumors and are staggering under the weight of fear and insecurity that paralyzes thought and creates an hysteria unknown in the West or modern Japan. This undercurrent discourages experimentation, creates skepticism about new courses of action, and plays into the culture's traditional value system, which is based on shunning those who seek wealth or disrupt societal values rooted in rule of elders, as in the villages. Even more, it kindles a corrosive suspicion of other people's motives, a suspicion that runs deep within those who lead the country.

Those who are relatively well off do not merely hate but indulge in paranoia. If someone disagrees, the tendency is to see a false motive. If someone who is disliked is successful, he is suspected of paying or taking bribes, particularly if he makes money in a new way, such as going into a new kind of business. Instead of crediting another's imagination, the tendency is to impute pecuniary corruption. Such attitudes discourage entrepreneurial activities and make success something to hide behind false humility. Thus, in the late 1980s, one of Bangladesh's economic pioneers was imprisoned for a year by the military government because he had the audacity to establish lucrative trade with Japan.

Such corrosive hate also is expressed in litigation, where landlords sue one another over petty slights or, worse, fabricate criminal charges and bribe judges or even opposing lawyers. Legal spite and corruption also are a hallmark of many lawyers and some judges, where a ferocity of attack and counterattack are the means of salving hurt egos. From a broader view, however, this characteristic is not part of the upper-class mentality so much as a statement about the drives and insecurity found when people live on the edge of poverty.

To understand this point it is worthwhile to follow a devious trail. In a fit of pique, the English historian Macaulay once wrote a devilishly cruel description of the Bengali character that still hurts deeply:

> What the horns are to the buffalo, what the sting is to the bee, what beauty according to the Greek song is to woman, deceit is to the Bengalee. Large promises, smooth excuses, elaborate tissues of circumstantial falsehood, chicanery, perjury, forgery are the weapons, offensive and defensive, of the people

of the Lower Ganges. All these millions do not furnish one sepoy to the armies
of the [East India] Company. But as usurers, as money-changers, as sharp legal
practitioners, no class of human beings can bear comparison.

Another commentator called Bengal a "low lying country of low lying people." Such sentiments are correct if applied to the rich and clever merchants
of Calcutta and Dhaka, where, from the earliest days of British rule, there
gathered the shrewdest businessmen Bengal and India could muster. Indeed,
today such descriptions fit Calcutta's great wholesale market around Old
Clive Street, now Netaji Subhas Chandra Bose Street, where Banian merchants, Hindu and Muslim, whose ancestors cheated the British as often as
possible, ply their devious ways with Japanese and German trade. That is
the world that Macaulay saw. The same world exists today in Motijheel or
Karwan Bazaar in Dhaka or in the business district of any town in Bangladesh.

However, while corruption, chicanery, perjury, and smooth promises today more than ever shape the Bangladeshi upper-class character, such traits
are not the essence of its rancid aspect. Fear is—the almost olfactorily palpable fear: of poverty, of enforced self-denial, of hunger. This fear does not
make the Bangladeshi more greedy or dishonest. What it does do is create
jealousy, cynicism about human character, and slanderous, loose talk about
others' corruption.

It is this fear of failure and poverty that drives mothers to bribe teachers
to give their children good marks or tempts them to encourage their
university-aged offspring to buy illegal copies of upcoming tests or to take
crib sheets to SAT exams. Huge fees are paid to professors to "tutor" children
who will then get higher marks than those who cannot afford "tutoring."
Understandably, such corruption filters down to village schools. And all this
is done because education is viewed only as a means of overcoming poverty.
So perverse has the system become that in 1987 Dhaka University students
staged a huge rally demanding the right to cheat. And what learning does
occur is based on rote, in a system characterized by an enormous shortage of
library books and laboratory equipment and an air of overweening corruption and fear.

Coming of age in such an atmosphere, the nation's future leaders, educators, politicians, lawyers, businessmen, and others imbibe a sense of envy,
distrust, and suspicion that constantly fuels both the left-wing movements,
based as they are on envy of wealth and desire for confiscation, and the calls
for fundamental moral reform of a religious nature. Even worse, the fears
generate isolation and despair among the country's hard-working masses.
This is especially so since there exists a mafia that works with politicians,
labor unions, political parties, and, yes, even with religious parties, to undermine the courts, universities, and election machinery, a mafia that is tied into
both government and foreign intelligence agencies. So obvious are these

characters, with their white unbuttoned shirts, Western pants, sunglasses, and teams of Suzuki-riding election riggers, that they have become part of the scene, found in the best houses and clubs and hovering around the money lenders in the bazaars. They personify the element of fear that is part of the existential angst of the middle classes of Dhaka, Chittagong, and a few other major cities.

The other side of this fear is the increasing emergence of hard-eyed men and women—in the government, civil service, military, and all political parties except the Jamaat—who callously rake off a percentage from every transaction. Also, military officers' wives ostentatiously shop in the best stores, followed by their servants and government drivers; "businessmen" shamelessly say that they must add 25 percent to all government contracts to pay off ministers as well as the president, his wife, or his mistress, it seems no matter who is in office; and sometimes one must bribe the tax collector to receive a tax form in order to prevent being jailed for failing to pay. One American organization even had to bribe the telephone company to get a receipt for a payment.

There is an old saying that evil people succeed because they stick together, while honest people often are isolated, afraid to protest. As recently as 1990 the reigning prime minister said that all political parties, except the Jamaat, were taking bribes from the government. Remarkably, no party protested. No one in the government bothered to deny it, and the press demurred. Given the press barons' political proclivities, no one was surprised.

The foregoing has no relevance to Bangladesh's desperately poor—up to fifty percent of the people—who have simple needs and desires, who are willing to work under any circumstances for any wage, and who calculate for only one day at a time. For them, the race is run every day for food, minimal clothing, and shelter. Poverty is a hot spike in their minds, the pain of which they live with twenty-four hours a day, sixty minutes an hour, sixty complete seconds every minute. With poverty as a way of life, they have not the leisure for theories or envy. Their sleep is not disturbed by the quiet terrors of those who have some wealth. Theirs is the sleep of exhaustion; the terror they face awake.

More than half of Bangladeshis are desperately poor and landless. With a marginal rural or urban existence, few own land or a hut they can count on having on the morrow. Most never have a chance to go to school, to receive health care, to have their teeth treated by a dentist, to relax in a tea shop, to go to bed on a full stomach. Their women are old and sagging of breast before age thirty; they eat *pan* (a narcotic leaf) to ease their hunger pains and have children who die of frightful diseases. The men often expire at their labors before full maturity. Widows, orphans, cripples, and men prematurely old and alone are common, as are abandoned women who have become prostitutes to survive. (Bangladesh has thousands of poor prostitutes; Narayanganj, a Dhaka suburb, had over five thousand in 1985, according to a study.)

And none are so poor as those who live in the slums of Dhaka, along the railroad tracks at Moahkali, in the slums on the road to Narayanganj, or in the garbage heaps on the road to Comilla. There, in filth and with space so small they barely can sit down, the poor, the widowed, the ill live in a situation that would make the poorest in Dickens's London weep.

And among these poor one finds the haunting presence of perhaps 5–10 percent of all Bangladeshis, especially around the cities, who are living on the brink of starvation. So many skeletal frames, so many sunken eyes, so many emaciated laborers, so many sallow, feverish mothers, so many swollen-bellied children. This presence is everywhere in cities and small towns, although it is not as noticeable in the villages, where family support systems and village social life offset the worst problems, except in years of scarcity.

As for the middle and upper classes, they are never far enough from this specter of abject poverty, from the haunting memories of hunger or the shame of being weak and dependent on aid, to avoid the tensions, social backbiting, envy, and paranoia that have become as engraved in the Bangladeshi mind as has Islam or the ancient cultures.

And related to the nation's poverty is the fact that Bangladesh is rustic, both in physical conditions and attitudes. Physically speaking, it is both predominantly rural (more than 80 percent of the people live in 65,000 villages) and, as my friend Dr. Richard Baxter Eaton once said, it fits the English philosopher Thomas Hobbes's description of a "state of nature" where people's lives are "nasty, brutish, and short." For more than 80 percent of the people live in houses made of mud walls or bamboo lattice with thatch roofs, sleep on mats, burn dung and straw or rice husks for cooking, live among cows and domestic fowl, drink and bathe themselves and their animals in the same water sources they use as latrines, and are exposed to the elements in the rainy, hot, and cool seasons in ways that people in modern countries cannot imagine—or, as Aleksandr Solzhenitsyn said of life in the Gulag, a man who lives in warmth can never understand a man who is cold, so that those of us raised in the modern world have trouble understanding those who live in what can only be called premodern villages, and those of us who are accustomed to wearing shoes can never understand those who wear rubber flip-flops or the millions who have never known what it is to wear something on their feet.

Moreover, poverty in the Bangladesh countryside is relative. Only the very rich, especially the tea planters, still live baronial lives. Most large landholders own fewer than fifteen acres, compared, say, to the average two-hundred-acre farm in Pennsylvania or Ohio. Most people own under five acres, and more than 40 percent hold less than two acres, which is equivalent to being landless, since it is not enough to be self-sufficient. Vast numbers of people have no land but huddle in tiny hutments at the mercy of big landholders. And Muslim inheritance laws, which eschew primogeniture and split property among sons and daughters, even married ones, generation after generation, exacerbate this situation, as the land is ever subdivided.

Although such conditions represent poverty by anyone's standards, given the climate, life in the countryside often isn't quite as bad as it first may appear to be. Also, an important distinction must be made between "poor" and "primitive." Take the Bangladeshi villages. All are poor and primitive to one degree or another. However, some are far less poor but no less primitive. Moreover, all are environmental wonders. Their trees shade and cool them. Usually they are well watered by streams, rivers, and ponds, as well as by *dighis*, or tanks. Their building materials suffice as protection against the elements. The presence of animals energizes life. And using dung and straw for fuel is not only economical but energy-efficient. The crucial missing things that would add much to the quality of life are electricity, mainly for lighting, natural gas for cooking, and refrigeration centers for farm produce. All these would make the villages less poor and primitive without disturbing the environmental balance.

In fact, that is what is happening in many villages. Modern seeds, fertilizers, and sprays have been introduced, as have tubewells, which draw on plentiful ground water, and rice-husking machines, which relieve women of the mind-numbing task of using a *dheki*, a mortar and pestle. Some villages have been electrified, bringing not only lighting but also many appliances, purchased with money sent by relatives who work in Middle Eastern Muslim nations. Such money is one of Bangladesh's chief sources of income.

However, despite such touches of modernization, which are raising living standards in many villages, a primitive, some would call it parochial, mindset remains. For instance, villagers believe that other villages smell different, are not as friendly, or have people who are less honest. More important, intervillage feuds passed down for generations are commonplace, so much so that nationwide elections are contested along narrow village or clan lines and regional hatreds, as between Noakalians and Sylhetis or Tipperans and Bograns, run deep.

In short, parochialism is the salt of rustic life. Thus every *gram*, or hamlet, tells its legends with slightly different emphasis, based on its own history. Each has its own *gram devata*, or local god, and seasons its food, builds its huts, manages its fields in ways different from its neighbor. And riverside villages are unlike those slightly inland, while the latter are different from villages still farther from the water.

This parochialism is passed down the generations by elders' word of mouth. The same goes for traditions. Women learn to paint their hut floors with rice-based white dyes, with brick dust, or with dust from coal or charcoal. They learn to paint powerful images of peacocks, the sun, the moon, or flowers, as well as perfect circles drawn freehand. Among the elders are those who know every strip of village land and how it has changed hands or been divided over four or five generations.

The elders, mostly men, are an institution unto themselves. It is they who resolve disputes and whose decisions are law on most matters. As a non-Bangladeshi friend once said, the only qualification for being an elder seems to be that the man be over sixty, an age that Bangladeshis and most Asians consider to be venerable, as until recently very few achieved it. My friend is half right. Age is a factor. A young man with a good idea and sound reasons will not be able to innovate without the elders' approval.

As to the elders, they are not necessarily the richest men. They achieve their position after a lifetime of proving that they have learned and can apply precedents and of demonstrating intelligence, restraint, and wisdom. While an old fool is considered just that, elders are an elite whose job is to produce solidarity among the decent villagers, to oppose the mafia gangs that prey on the village, to represent village interests to government, to defend villagers from corrupt officials, and, most important, to transmit from generation to generation accumulated wisdom—about crops, irrigation, time to plough, how to anticipate floods, and the myriad decisions that keep village republics functioning. The elders are not elected. They have no legal power. Yet their word is more the law than that of any mullah or government official. The reason is that the village unit predates both Islam and modern government and doubtlessly will outlast at least the latter.

This does not mean that the mullah is powerless. He exerts enormous influence on all aspects of village life, from the establishment of the *maktab*, or mosque school (the most important village school, as even the British were forced to recognize), to matters of health and family, support for the poor, and many secular issues. Like the small town parson in the United States, the mullah often is the best educated villager.

Another important aspect of village life revolves around "clannishness," a word that in the West has lost its depth of meaning, its resonance. Here in the villages, clannishness is as essential to life and dignity as rice and *dhal* (a lentil), as water and air. Nearly all villagers can identify up to seven or eight generations of their forebears, as well as cousins three, four, and five times removed. Consanguinity is part of the life-support system, for it provides role models, patrons, friends, and, often, love—for "cousin-love" is one of the most sensuous aspects of Bangladesh life, often resulting in marriage, among all classes. One reason is that by marrying a cousin one maintains the "good" family line and avoids marriage with hereditary enemies, those considered not good enough, or those who consider themselves better.

Another advantage of keeping things within the family, albeit an extended clan, is that once one moves into the larger society, relatives are always available to smooth the way: to provide introductions for jobs, to help arrange school entry, to stop or divert some official action, to provide a "home" when one is in need. On a larger scale, a huge patronage web exists that affects all clan members. Thus one may be expected to return a favor done one's grandfather. Such family networking, in villages and cities alike, is one of the strongest bonds, as well as causes for divisiveness, in Bangladeshi society. Woe to him who speaks and does not know to whom he is speaking. For it may well be that the person so spoken to is a relative of your worst enemy.

This concept of clannishness affects Bangladesh in numerous ways. A woman is not known by her name but, for instance, as "Samsuddin's Ma," the mother of her eldest son. Friends or acquaintances, even foreign ones, are called "cousin," "brother," or "uncle," depending on relative age. Shajehan Kabir's *bhai* (brother, but actually friend), A. M. A. Muhith, who is older than I am, is my uncle, or *cha-cha*. On meeting someone for the first time it helps to ask elders what they should be called. Thus does the tradition of the clan affect social intercourse.

As to tradition, it remains powerful in the villages because their security margin is narrow. Since a flood or drought can destroy the way of life, there is a hunger for knowledge of the tried and true, as well as tales of why it is true. For example, in the nineteenth century, bright young engineers from England's steel industry tried to introduce a steel-bladed plough to replace the wooden schooner that had been used from time immemorial. When force was threatened, the villagers relented. However, the steel plough sank deep and the oxen had difficulty pulling. Worse, it raised the more acidic, deeper laterite clay that made the soil less rich in delta loam. The experiment failed, and many farmers lost their crops. The ancient wooden schooner still is used effectively on small plots. Similarly, horror stories of marriages to other clans are the spice used to instill prejudice in children. Often the stories have a ring of truth, as some families have a history of drinking too much, being less literate, or farming less well. While such tales can be malicious, tradition remains important. Tradition settles land disputes, inheritance rights of wives, daughters, and sons, and other crucial day-to-day matters. It provides law and standards of behavior that villagers respect. And while tradition occasionally has bent as customs changed—in the early nineteenth century, for instance, grooms paid a bride price to their in-laws, but after the spread of male education in costly British schools a dowry was demanded of the bride's family—nevertheless, village traditions are like common law, adding new cases and precedents.

Another vital aspect of rural life is widespread illiteracy. Village literacy is aural and artistic, not lineal and written. An elder who hears and understands the principles of village life is as literate as his well-educated son, even if he is illiterate in the modern sense. (Much of the Jewish Bible was not written down until near the time of Christ, but was handed down by men who faithfully memorized every line.) However, in a modern world with changing technologies, literacy is becoming ever more dependent on lineal and written records. Unfortunately, in most villages, education is a double-edged sword: it is viewed with suspicion and fear as well as with awe. For it is well understood that official posts go to those educated in secular schools, whereas a madrassah education is respected for itself.

One aspect of the rustic life's dependence on aural traditions is love of poetry. People in Bangladesh take their poetry seriously and listen with an intense interest to bards recite it. Indeed, poetry is one of the most effective modes of political rhetoric. This will be touched on in later chapters where politics is discussed and the war of the poets is a theme in the liberation movement of Bangladesh.

Still another crucial part of the rustic Bangladesh village mind is its belief in, its certainty about, its respect for austerity—in style, belief, virtue, practice, and language, in art, agriculture, and business, in life: economic, social, and political. To this day, the most rustic village will respect the naked Hindu sadhu, the traveling Muslim preacher, or the sufi seeking enlightenment through poverty and escape from the material world. In the villages live rich farmers with only the plainest of furniture and housing, clean, simple, and practical, like the Shaker style in the United States. Dress is simple: white pyjama and kurta, plain saree, conservative-colored lungi. Ostentation, decorative dress, and fancy shoes are signs of the unenlightened, the cruel, the heartless. This austerity arises not from Islam, Hinduism, or Buddhism but from the very austerity of life in the village, where these religions learned it, where the margins are small, where death always hovers, where the elements are both blessed and severe, where a person's true value is measured over a lifetime, and where wisdom, not knowledge, is respected. Bangladesh is a nation that admired the Buddha, the Vedic Aryan Brahmin scholar, the sadhu, the sufi, the simple Muslim preacher who lived a virtuous life. It is a nation that was moved by Gandhi and that admires *pirs* (holy men) who so live. It is nation that respects the Muslim *ghazi* (warrior), a man of great patience and austerity, at ease in the saddle or on the battlefield; it is a nation where saving, investing, and doing business with honor, giving value for the price is valued. This austerity is part of the Bangladeshi mindset. And it is no insult to this aspect of the Bangladeshi mind that one of the country's vices is the opposite of austerity: disgusting ostentation. For often a nation's greatest virtue is offset by the opposite vice. The truly rich and the truly wise in Bangladesh, and the two are seldom identical, are people of the most severe simplicity and subtlety of life. In this, they bring to the fore the most rustic virtue: austerity.

But such a virtue can stand in the way of progress in the modern sense, progress that depends on consumption and consumer demand. Thus this writer once heard Kabir Chowdhury, a Dhaka University literature professor, poet, and world-class intellectual, castigate women who wear fancy sarees. "We should have only one color saree for everyone and white kurta and pyjama for men," he maintained. Another professor condemned the multiplicity of automobile models or annual changes in fashion. While neither man is a Luddite, both are unaware that such concepts, if followed, would reduce Bangladesh to a more primitive society than it is. Widening of markets opens employment choices that command the use of a nation's diverse talents.

This same drive for austerity has created in economic speech a number of near Luddite ideas that affect the country. There is constant talk, even by economists who know better, of the need for autarchy in food, in clothing, and so on, or for eschewing modern for more labor-intensive machinery. Such ideas are a throwback to ancient Elizabethan mercantilism that envisions the nation as a subsistence farm. Such talk, and it is endless in Dhaka, ignores the fact that Japan, Germany, and Switzerland, the world's richest countries, are not self-sufficient in food or anything else but compete, adapt, and depend on the world market, whose existence underwrites their wealth, as they learned after attempting to establish autarchic empires in World War II. Yet this autarchic drive in Bangladesh, despite its prevalence among nationalist, socialist, and hence xenophobic elements, arises less out of fascist ideology than out of the drive for austerity that still informs the Bangladesh mind.

This is unfortunate, as compromises are possible and even desirable. For instance, a Bangladeshi friend's name is synonymous with wealth and power. Privately he is austere: his car is undistinguished and without air conditioning, his large house is simply furnished, and he dresses and eats with great simplicity. Yet he does not suggest that others do likewise.

The final important aspect of the rustic Bangladeshi mind concerns the spiritual outlook, which differs from that of educated Muslims, Westerners, or modern East Asians. Many villagers follow animist beliefs and customs. Spirits may inhabit trees, ghosts may roam, fairies may beckon young men, the evil eye may fall on a child. Such spirits often must be propitiated, as when young brides cut their hair if they have trouble conceiving or a widow makes a wish while bathing in a sacred river during the full moon. What's important is not whether the spirits exist but that the villagers' mental life is extremely imaginative and able to operate in a world of greater sensitivity to nature, to the animal world, to land, stream, and terrain, than that of most city folks. (Although some of the more mystical devotees of the environmental or New Age movements in the West have minds filled with similar images, they lack the experience of the rustic life.)

Perhaps of greater interest is the fact that such animist beliefs and the trappings of rusticity are present, too, in the most sophisticated circles in Dhaka, whose members have Harvard or Oxford degrees. For by and large, Bangladeshis are not products of Western education but truly are a rustic people living at or near the state of nature. They are superstitious, seek the advice of astrologers, and respect the prophecies of pirs. Two examples come to mind. First, it is said that during the Pakistan era, a Bangladeshi-born governor appointed by the Pakistan government believed the governor's mansion to be haunted and lived a miserable life there as a result. Second, before murdering Bangladesh's first president, Sheikh Mujibur Rahman, in 1975, the would-be assassins consulted a pir to establish the best date.

Finally, so ingrained is such thinking in the minds of the upper classes that a grand lady of Bangladesh, English educated, once expressed outrage at the thought of her country's being industrialized. "Such a policy," she declared, "would destroy my dear Bangladeshis." She viewed them as premodern rustic villagers and did not want to see them turned into modern people.

Thus, as we have seen, the rustic life, its parochial, traditional, clannish, and austere style, still haunts the Bangladeshi mind and affects all aspects of life, even in the largest cities, even among the best-educated minds.

Land and Language

Land and language are integral to the mind of any culture, not least that of England, where every part of the nation evokes unique images and where the language, spoken and written, always is enunciated in a near reverential way. Russia has the *rodino*, the peculiar mix of land, language, and culture that is crucial to the Russian mind. In both Japan and Israel, race, language, religion, and belief in the "holy land" are combined in a powerful cultural brew. Bangladesh has a similar mix, one that is as beautiful as that of any nation.

As to the land, there is sufficient evidence in poetry and legend to state that the soil, the climate, the terrain, the water, the plough, the boat, the yeoman farmer, and the *sareng*, or pilot of a vessel, are the subjects of very deep love. Likewise, the singer on a ferry boat, the Baul minstrel in a town square with his patchwork dress and winning ways, the film sequences on television depict enduring love of the countryside. On all such subjects Bangladeshis can be maudlin. They can bore a stranger to tears with the love of leisure, of the flute, of lying under a blue sky with a straw between one's teeth, of the rainy season, and of that strange darkness that descends at almost the same time every day, when a pure black all but obscures the orange flame of the lantern on a fishing boat's bow on the Meghna. Even Bangladeshis born and bred in London for two or three generations still come "home," don saree or lungi, bathe in the river in the morning mist, brush their teeth at the dighi, and stretch out in a kutcha hut as if they had never lived any other way.

For Bangladesh has a benign countenance; it is truly the paradise of nations. That Bangladeshis love it with total absorption is one of the facts of history, from the time when the Gangaridae defeated Alexander, to 1757 when the nation lost to the British, to the 1830s when the first rebellion began, to 1857 when the great but unsuccessful uprising against British rule, the Mutiny, occurred, to 1875 when W. W. Hunter noted Muslim support of the Afghan rebellions, to 1905 when resistance mounted against partition and a true modern secular nationalism first emerged, to 1917 through 1945 when the nation increasingly resisted the British, to 1947 when the nation voted for Pakistan, through 1971 when the Pakistanis were overthrown. No one reading history will ever doubt Bangladeshi resolve to continue fighting for this mystical land, whatever the outcome. Certainly after more than two thousand years the love of the land, in song and painting, in poem and gardens, must be recognized as a valid claim. To paraphrase Warren Hastings, Bangladeshis love their land and have suffered much for it.

Likewise the language. Bangla (or Bengali, as it is sometimes called) is a member of the Indo-European language family with a long history of use. Obviously, ancient Bangla is very different from the modern variety. Yet there is evidence of continuity, both of the true spoken vernacular, the *chalti bhasa,* and of the written language, which is attested to by a stone fragment from Akbar's time, three hundred years before Christ; by the Pali script of the Pala Dynasty, of which banana-leaf manuscripts still exist; by more standardized scripts from the early Muslim period when modern Bangla began to be formed; and by the late-nineteenth-century great learning revival that was precipitated by the Western invasion.

Throughout this nation's history, there have been attempts to replace the language. The Sena Dynasty tried hard from the eleventh through the early thirteenth centuries to force Sanskrit on the people, just as the Moghuls later tried with Farsee, the language of modern Iran, or Urdu, now the official tongue of Pakistan. Through it all, the people resisted, savoring their distinctive vocabulary, script, and enunciation, even as their language adopted words from Marathi, Hindustani, Persian, Arabic, Portuguese, Orissan, and finally British and American English. Unlike Gaelic, Celtic, Welsh, and Hebrew, which once were eclipsed but in this century were revived, the Bangla language has had a continuing evolution without ever having declined. Bangla is a mother tongue, a being, a spirit on its own. It never fails to give pleasure with its many words which, with minor modification, deepen and expand shades of meaning. In terms of the number of speakers—110 million Bangladeshis, 65 million West Bengalis, and 87 million Biharis, not to mention 32 million Orissans and 23 million Assamese who use a related tongue—Bangla is one of the world's top ten languages. Moreover, it long has been a language of commerce, literary expression, government, law, science, and history. Bangla is the raw material of all that Bangladeshis are and want to be. And it is one of the most powerful nonreligious objects of this country's affections.

The combination of land and language first emerged as a potent political and ideological force in 1905 when the British attempted to divide Bengal. There appear to have been two reasons for the British action. The first and most obvious was to spark Hindu-Muslim rivalry, thereby preserving British rule. The second was that newer parts of Britain's Indian Empire resented the nineteenth-century Bengal revival, wherein Bengal, the oldest part, was providing the largest number of civil servants, legal experts, engineers, and intellectual leaders. For the Empire's capital was in Bengal Province, in Calcutta, which had most of the good schools and a group of people eager to take advantage of this. Furthermore, as Calcutta was the major port city with first access to government contracts, it was truly the "second city of the empire," after London. Thus, in the 1890s, Gokhale, an early leader of Indian thought who came from western India, aptly said, "What Bengal thinks today, India will think tomorrow."

It was against this background that Britain announced the partition of Bengal, a move that would split up this powerful, dangerous, unwanted partner in empire. For by the turn of the century, Bengal had become nearly equal to its master, furnishing a large part of the Empire's monetary return, many skilled personnel in government and trade, and a high percentage of intellectuals. If Bengal's Muslims and Hindus ever united and rebelled, the reasoning went, Britain might lose India. So the British decided, under an apparently sincere guise of administrative reform, to divide Bengal into Muslim and Hindu halves, placing a lieutenant-governor in charge of each. As Sir Herbert Risely wrote in a government paper, "One of our main objects is to split up and thereby weaken a solid body of opponents to our rule. . . . Bengal divided will pull different ways. . . . Bengal united is a power." Thus just when the Bengal elite felt strong enough to challenge British rule, the British struck first.

They did not expect what followed. For in the next year, 1906, the Japanese defeated the Russians in a war, the first defeat of a European by a non-European power in over a century. The effect on Asian confidence was devastating for the Europeans, especially in Bengal, where Lord Curzon, the governor, wrote that "the reverberations of that victory have gone like a thunder clap through the whispering galleries of the East." Ultimately, the events of that fateful year forever diminished British prestige in India and made Britain totally distrust the Bengali *babu*, or gentleman; the word became a term of disdain.

There flared up a campaign of raw modern nationalism, compounded of race, language, and land, a campaign whose fires still smoulder. Bengali leaders used the writings of the great Hindu poet and novelist Bankim Chatterjee as a voice of their movement, and his song "Bande Mataram" emerged as one of the most powerful, evocative hymns of Bengali nationalism. Mahatma Gandhi used it during the independence movement, as did Bengali nationalists in 1971 when Bangladesh revolted against Pakistan.

Mother, I bow to thee!
Rich with thy hurrying streams,
Bright with thy orchard gleams,
Cool with thy winds of delight,
Dark fields waving, Mother of night,
Mother free.
Glory of moonlight dreams,
Over thy branches and lordly streams,
Clad in blossoming tree,
Mother, giver of ease,
Laughing low and sweet!
Mother, I kiss thy feet,
Speaker sweet and low!
Mother, to thee I bow.
Who hath said thou art weak in thy lands,
When the swords flash out in twice seventy million hands,
Seventy million voices roar
Thy dreadful name from shore to shore?
With many strengths who are mighty and stored,
To thee I call, Mother and Lord!
Thou who savest, arise and save!
To her I cry who ever her foeman drave,
Back from plain and sea,
And shook her free.
Thou art wisdom, thou art law,
Thou our heart, and soul, and breath,
Thou, the love divine, the awe,
In our hearts that conquers death.
Thine the strength that nerves the arm,
Thine the beauty, thine the charm.
In our temples is but thine.
Thou art Durga, Lady and Queen,
With her hands that strike and swords of sheen,
Thou art Lakshmi lotus throned,
And the Muse a hundred-toned.
Pure and Perfect without peer,
Mother, lend thine ear.
Rich with hurrying streams,
Bright with orchard gleams,
Dark of hue, O candid fair,
In thy soul, with jeweled hair
And thy glorious smile divine,
Loveliest of all earthly lands,
Showering wealth from well-stored hands!
Mother, Mother mine!

Mother sweet, I bow to thee
Mother Great and Free!

This song evokes the basic emotive complex of love of the land, the soul, and the spirit of the motherland, sometimes identified with the wise love of the Hindu goddess Durga, and sometimes fiercely with another aspect of Durga, Kali, the dreadful name heard from shore to shore. Chatterjee's books called for the formation of secret societies of men and women who would take vows of poverty and would sacrifice themselves in acts of terrorism. Such groups were in fact founded to oppose the division of Bengal. And boycotts of British goods, theater, and public events followed in a frightening, spiraling cycle of revolt that at first was purely Bengali in thrust but later was generalized into India-wide agitation. Organizations were formed throughout Bengal, groups whose lineal descendants live on today. As for "Bande Mataram," the British outlawed it, so inflammatory was it. Its popularity is one of the most dramatic examples of song and poetry uniting to form the basis of a political movement—an example that was also to affect the liberation movement of 1971.

In 1905 the uprising was confined mostly to the Hindus, who, occupying most of the best positions under the British, had the most to lose. Muslims would have gained a semiautonomous province where Hindus would have been prominent only as merchants and zamindars. Still, looking back, it would be wrong to view the Bengali Muslims of the time as mere agents of the British, as many Calcutta Hindus do. For the Muslims, too, loved the land, the language, and the melody of "Bande Mataram," even though they had little use for Durga and Lakshmi and couldn't swear allegiance to the anarchists' oaths, since they were Hindu oaths to the goddess Kali. Nevertheless, the memory, the excitement, and the patriotism aroused by those times was strong enough to create an enduring nationalism in what is now Bangladesh, a sense of nationalism that still runs deep in the Bangladeshi mind.

Sixty-six years later, when modern Bangladesh was formed in a liberation war against Pakistan, Bangladeshi Muslims played on all the strings of nationalism—race, love of land, and cultural superiority—and used parties and organizations that traced their antecedents to 1905. In that struggle, language was the mainspring of agitation and was such a powerful issue that many Indians feared that all of Bengal, Hindu and Muslim, would unite.

But nationalism can heal and bind, or it can become a force for xenophobia and inward-looking self-pity, a trait that Nirad Chaudhuri calls the natural attitude of the people of the subcontinent. And so the Bangla language movement today is being put to xenophobic uses. It is aimed at cutting Bangladesh off from the world by appealing to hate, an often self-pitying hate that animates many members of the upper class. The modern language movement has none of the generosity exhibited by the British-educated nineteenth-century intellectuals who reinvigorated Bangla by translating works from other languages, helped by the great German scholar Max Müller and by French scholars at Pondicherry and Chandernagor, as well as by Belgian priests at Saint Xavier's in Calcutta.

That tradition basically has died out, so that, for the most part, all but the tiniest segment of Bangladeshis today lack access to the vast storehouses of knowledge accumulated in other languages. This writer has surveyed the libraries of Bangladesh and is aware of the poverty of important knowledge to be found there. Still worse, a conscious decision has been made to discourage such access, a decision which is destructive, self-absorptive, and due to nationalism's xenophobic side. As a result, a sort of "language fascism" has emerged, a phenomenon that is the greatest danger to the nation today, as it is aimed at turning Bangladesh into a hermit nation. The implications are enormous. For instance, many outsiders have noticed this side of the Bangladeshi character, and thus have been discouraged from investing or expanding trade. This surly, twisted-lip, self-pity side does Bangladesh a great injustice.

Interestingly, Bangladeshi self-pity seems to be a hallmark of a certain segment of the upper class. The more educated the people are, the more this self-pity becomes apparent. A hierarchy of fears and resentments seem to be the underlying factor: fear and resentment of Western racism, real and imagined; fear of poverty, instilled by British depredations; fear of famines, dating to memories of the Liberation War; hatred of the aid-givers. So deep are these feelings, so assiduously comforting is the resulting hate, that some Bangladeshis have lost all ability to reason.

Foreigners who, in empathy, try to justify this self-pity neither gain friends nor serve the truth. For it has long been realized by Bankim Chatterjee, Rabindranath Tagore, Kazi Nazrul Islam, and countless other leaders of modern Bangladesh that self-pity, isolation, hatred, ingratitude, cultural superiority, and chauvinism are an aberration the nation can ill afford. And self-pity, as a well known mullah says, "makes a people stupid." Thus Bangladesh, a nation that has been part of the English-speaking world since 1757, is on the verge—at least in some powerful circles—of reverting back to a language enclosure, before the work of translation is complete.

The Brahmo Mind

Parallel to the nationalist movement there is a cosmopolitan, urbane outlook, which is common to all aristocracies but has no peer elsewhere. This outlook is not communal, and therefore it embraces all of Bengal, seeing itself as above the fray. It is an educated outlook, combining all that is best in Bengali, Hindu, Islam, Persian, and modern world culture, including strong links to Japan, China, France, and Britain. Even more, it is a cultivated out-look, not an atavistic one.

Those who follow its precepts intermarry and tend to be Anglophiles, having attended the same schools in India (Saint Paul's, Mussoorie, Dera Dun, and Saint Xavier's), in Bangladesh (Notre Dame and Holy Cross), and then in Britain (Oxford, Cambridge, the University of London). Many of the older generation (over fifty) maintain close friendships in Calcutta, while the younger set, separated by the Pakistan-India rivalry, have formed their rela-tionships at British schools, where the culture of South Asia today is being forged.

Nevertheless, though all that is good in England has helped to form them and their outlook, it is not quite accurate to call this set Anglophile. For their true tradition is older and native to Bengal. Lacking a better word, let us call them *Brahmo*. This term will need some qualification, but it is central to all that is best in Bangladesh, a best that is in danger of being lost.

Let us return now to a theme discussed earlier, to the intellectual, spiri-tual life lived by the Brahman scholar, a life of learning, of rearing a family, of retirement to contemplation, then of spiritual preparation for death. Let us recall Megasthenes, who came among men at the peak of their intelligent lives, meeting in a grove and discussing the meaning of life and death. Let us hark back to the scholarly cross-cultural work of Alberuni, who came to understand the Hindus and gained their confidence. Let us recall the transla-tions into Bangla of both Hindu and Muslim works by the first Muslim conquerors, and the Muslim love of study and the great tradition of scholar-ship begun by Alberuni.

Such examples express a gentlemanly, courageous ideal, based on old-fashioned concepts of self-discipline, integrity, philosophical balance, and wisdom—wisdom that transcends a particular tradition, without compro-mising the principles that illumine that tradition and make its preservation vital. This behavioral ideal runs like a golden thread through Indian and Bangladeshi history, personified by men and women, scholars, judges, law-yers, civil servants, diplomats, and businessmen, who meet these high criteria. Few are self-consciously part of an elite; most are simple yet sophis-ticated. They can be found in some of the best homes in Dhaka, Chittagong, and other cities, homes where culture, not money, talks.

The term *Brahmo* has been chosen to describe this group because it refers back to the religious movement called Brahmo Samaj, based on Hinduism and founded in Calcutta in the 1830s by Ram Mohan Roy. Brahmo is an extremely sensitive, humane version of Hinduism. Though fostered within Brahmo Samaj, Brahmo somehow outgrew the religion's unitarian beliefs and created a modern, open, and secular sensibility within the Bangladesh matrix. Ultimately, Brahmo's puritan manners, integrity of truth and mean-ing, and careful language created a civilized life-style that today informs

Bangladesh society at its best, the way Quakerism lends style to Philadelphia, Puritanism influences Boston, and Pelagian humor affects High Church nobles in London. What is important is not the religion—for the religion of Brahmo Samaj has been almost forgotten—but the sensibility that it represents.

During the latter part of the nineteenth century, the Brahmo style affected most members of Bengal's upper class, especially in Calcutta. Its modernizing outlook made it the ideal behavioral vehicle for that age. It also offered a way for the educated elites both to find common cause with a purified version of the local culture and to mix easily with the English. And it permitted Muslim and Hindu to meet on equal footing on neutral territory, thanks to its vague unitarian theology. In many respects, Brahmo's style and belief structure is similar to Unitarianism in the United States, to Reform Judaism in Germany, or to the principles that guide the Ethical Culture Society in New York.

Brahmo is characterized by infinite concern for the ideas, beliefs, sensitivities, and needs of others, as well as by patience, self-control, self-deprecation, ironic humor, and, above all, a sense of personal responsibility and integrity. Its style is most beautifully expressed in the classic works of Rabindranath Tagore, Ram Mohan Roy, and Sir Romesh C. Dutt and in the contemporary writings of Nirad Chaudhuri. It also is expressed in some current Dhaka wallahs, including Kamaluddin Hossain, former chief justice of Bangladesh's Supreme Court; the economist Rehman Sobhan; the author Hamida Hossain; and a host of scholars, poets, writers, and artists, some of whom still keep their links with old friends in Calcutta.

While such Brahmos are first and foremost patriotic Bangladeshis, they represent an element of their society that views their nation as part of a wider international community: South Asia (India, Sri Lanka, Burma, and Pakistan); Asia as a whole; the Islamic world and its one billion people; the Third World of developing nations; Britain's former Asian colonies in the Commonwealth (of which Bangladesh is the oldest); and Europe, especially England, where so many were educated, so many have family, and from whence so much of their culture derives, dating to the era of Ram Mohan Roy and the days when European scholars came to appreciate the subcontinent's past and provided the basis for the modern view of India and Bangladesh. Such a sensibility is preserved in the Asiatic Society, in both its Dhaka and its Calcutta branches.

What is fascinating and important about the people who have this sensibility is that for the most part they are ever open to new ideas; they form opinions tempered by experience and reflection, maintain truths not swayed by the exigencies of the moment, and can both defend their views or revise them to fit new information. Moreover, with intellectual capacity and learning rivaling the best anywhere, they represent the best of Bangladeshi thought.

Their weaknesses also are both legion and detrimental to the land they love. For the Brahmos do not represent the people. They are, often as not, unwilling to dirty their hands in politics by seeking to ameliorate many of the evils perpetrated by successive leaders; and they are ill-informed about and thus incapable of gaining civilian control over the military, which has dominated Pakistani and Bangladeshi politics since independence. They also are essentially ignorant of Asia as a whole, especially of Japan, Korea, Indonesia, and Southeast Asia. And crucially, as we shall see, owing to a dangerous mix of left-leaning party politics and their hands-off political approach, they have failed on both sides of the Bengal border: in Bangladesh they have often failed to help spur a forward leap; in West Bengal, due to their flirtation with Marxism, they have contributed to a decline.

In Bangladesh, given their predilections, they have been unable to establish their intellectual superiority by offering a vision for the future, to use study and reflection as tools to guide the nation, to offer new projects, to recognize new needs, to use new revenues for social purposes, to create a nongovernment brain trust or think tank. Bangladeshi Brahmos have no magazine, no television talk show, no organization to express their ideals. Worse, they often are overshadowed by development intellectuals from foreign aid agencies who, because they control the money, can silence the locals.

To understand the Brahmos' strengths and weaknesses one must contemplate the influence on them of Tagore, a man who, through his songs, poems, essays, novels, plays, sentiments, unitarian religion, and pious outlook, exerts the pivotal influence in all of Bengal: on Brahmos, Muslims, Hindus, Buddhists, and Christians.

Tagore was born in 1861 into one of Bengal's richest Hindu-turned-Brahmo families, whose British ties dated to the original invasion in 1757. His father, a disciple of Brahmo Samaj founder Ram Mohan Roy, helped turn the movement into both a religious and a social force by welcoming members of other faiths.

Because Tagore was viewed as a genius with diverse talents, from a young age he exercised enormous influence in Calcutta and beyond among leaders of the final renaissance that occurred in British Bengal late in the nineteenth century. Moreover, his tendency to mystical religion rivaled that of the sufis, of the various mystery brotherhoods of the Muslim orders, and of the Bhakti movement led by Chaitanya and Kabir, and his sound common sense and directness matched him with the best of the pragmatic thinkers of India's elites.

Interested in politics only insofar as it concerned the deeper life of India, he espoused mildly communistic ideas, though not necessarily Marxist ones, wanting the nationalist movement to consider social reforms before political freedom, actively opposing the Bengal partition, and endorsing the peaceful aspects of the countermovement to keep Bengal in one piece.

Tagore's diverse writings, permeated by a sense of the universe's beauty, love of children, and simplicity and by a consciousness of God's presence, helped the West understand the Bengali people. Tagore was best known for his mystical poem the "Gitanjali," a partial translation of which had been published in the West when, in 1913, he won the Nobel prize in literature. With the prize money he founded his own alternate educational institution, Santiniketan (about ninety miles from Calcutta in West Bengal), where he tried to introduce concepts of humanism, holism, and love of workmanship associated with the socialist guild movement in England and where, ahead of the times, he tried to encourage a more natural, less industrial society. His school attracted the beautiful people: poetically attuned young men and women with pure ideals of selflessness. Among them he fostered a certain romantic escape from the world of everyday power, money, and success. About the time of World War I, his ideas greatly influenced the young of Bengal who, two decades later, helped lead the independence movement.

At first his influence was far greater among West Bengali Hindus, who still retain Tagore's ambiguous legacy of mild communism—a legacy that has had a lasting impact on the Brahmos as well. Over time, however, his influence among the Muslim masses grew stronger, so much so that a Tagore cult emerged in East Bengal during the Pakistan era when the Bangla language came under siege. The Pakistanis fanned the flame when they banned Tagore's songs and poems from radio and television. In this setting, Tagore became an icon of Bangladesh expression, a symbol of sorts of the greatness of Bengal culture compared to that of West Pakistan. His influence is another example of the role of poetry in Bangladeshi politics.

And herein lies the crux of the ambiguity of his legacy. For despite his enormous, enduring influence—evident every time the national anthem of India or Bangladesh is played, every time his songs are sung, every time his poetry is recited—he did not see himself as an icon. It says something about the Bengali mind that Tagore has been elevated almost to sainthood. Had he lived in England and written in the English tradition he would have been remembered merely as a great bard.

The difference can be attributed in part to Tagore's sense of the mystical based on experiences of his youth, according to his best English translator, Brother James, a Holy Cross religious who spent most of his life in Bangladesh and was one of the first to render Tagore's complete "Gitanjali" into English. Another reason is Tagore's romanticism, which melds readily with the rustic tendencies, traditions, and numinous mysticism that permeates the music, poetry, and sentimentality of a still pristinely parochial country that enjoys the sound of its own language. This romanticism dates to when, as a young man, he helped manage his father's estates in East Bengal, near Kush-tia (where, he believed, the most pure Bangla was spoken and from whence the great Baul bard Lalan Shah also hailed).

In the heat of the independence movement such associations came to express the people's yearnings, so much so that when victory came, the ruler of an independent Bangladesh, Sheikh Mujibur Rahman, quoted Tagore twice, to the effect that hopefully Bengalis now would hold their heads high in Golden Bengal. Bangladesh's independence was due more to Tagore than to any other native force. Indeed, as Calcutta poet Ira De says, "Today, Tagore is probably more of a force in Muslim Bangladesh than in Hindu West Bengal, where he spent most of his life, because only in Bangladesh is there an emotional drive to preserve the language, and Tagore exemplifies the pure language. In West Bengal we are losing the love of the language that we had many years ago."

The trouble is that the Tagore tradition went to Bangladesh after leaving a sad legacy in West Bengal, a legacy that can be blamed as much on West Bengali Brahmos as on the great bard. For Calcutta and West Bengal long have been a major seat of a romantic, democratic sort of communism that, while not anti-industrialist, has contributed to Calcutta's being one of India's least-developed cities and to West Bengal's being one of the poorest prov-inces. Under the communists (all of them middle-class, educated, and sensi-tive) who took power in the late 1970s, West Bengal began a descent into East Bloc drabness—so that despite Calcutta's natural beauty, it has not modernized as have Delhi, Bombay, Bangalore, and Madras, and it is not as modern as Dhaka. When one recalls that until the 1930s it was the "Second City of Empire," it is hard to believe that today it is not, in the opinion of many foreign observers, even the first city of the Bangla-speaking world. And while rural West Bengal has improved after years of neglect under India's Congress Party, the state has become a byword for backwardness in the past fifteen years while Dhaka has zoomed forward. Television programs are now produced in Dhaka and watched in Calcutta.

Calcutta is a city where the telephones barely work; where the univer-sity, once the greatest in India, no longer is in the top five; where mass transit consists of a mile-long subway in a huge city choked by auto fumes; where cooking, more often than not, is done with coal, even in the best homes and despite the presence of offshore natural gas; and where electric power is more unreliable than in Vietnam during the war.

Tagore is not to blame for this and would have protested the decline. But his escapist passivity infected the "intellerati," particularly the Brahmos, so that they came to accept the most terrible backwardness. In fairness, how-ever, Bengali life in Calcutta among the Brahmos is gentle, intelligent, and sensitive, providing an example of one of the most civil middle- and upper-middle-class elites to be found anywhere. This civility is due to Tagore's influence.

In contrast, in Dhaka, where Tagore's ideas helped liberate the country and where his romanticism is saved for sentimental times and his common sense prevails, communism never took root, owing to the rural, rustic way of life. Today, as Bangladesh strives to modernize and industrialize, telephones work, rural areas are booming, the electric grid system is being expanded, and new industries are being formed. While Tagore has receded in importance in Calcutta and West Bengal, his image replaced by communistic heroes, in Bangladesh he is revered as the country surges forth in a capitalist direction.

As for the upper-class Brahmos, they continue sitting on the sidelines, haunted by, vaguely yearning for, and dreaming of the socialism, romanticism, and austere life Tagore visualized in his more poetic moments. As a group they thus far have been intellectually incapable of separating themselves from Tagore's mystical, poetic, romantic, and sentimental legacy and of confronting the economic and political realities of the world. To overcome this, the Brahmos need to stop posing as intellerati and to find a new impetus for action. In the meantime, however, the general decency of their outlook, the quiet manner of their expostulation, the deeper and more reflective aspects of their ideas, deserve to be emulated. Civilizations begin with manners; all else follows.

Before leaving the strain of thought in the Bengal mind known as Brahmo, it is worthwhile to pause and recall that thirty-five thousand Hindu and Muslim intellectuals were massacred by the Pakistan Army in 1971, many of them from the arts and the universities, intellectuals who, if anything, were close to the Brahmo sensibility here discussed. Their tragic absence is a wound to Bangladesh that has not yet healed, however much their passing has been forgotten, or so it seems.

The Military Mind

Throughout the Pakistan era and well into the Bangladesh one, the military has run circles around the nation's so-called intellectual politicians. The intellectual leaders of the major political parties have ignored the need both to formulate major foreign policy and defense directions and to comprehend the nature of power. Instead, they have squabbled about who will lead and how to attain a socialist democracy and represent their constituents' internal concerns. In contrast, the military's disciplined thinking, governing experience (within its own ranks), sense of its opponents' weaknesses, understanding of the needs of its civil service partners, and decisive planning have made it the nation's most effective political force—one that has ruled for most of the two decades of independence.

The politicians have yet to recognize the nature of the threat. For so enthralled have they been by their narrow world view that they have never comprehended that their first job is to come to power by demonstrating that they are in a position to lead. To achieve this, they need to reverse themselves: to quit disdaining the military and come to understand it—by joining it, even briefly, at some point in their career, as future politicians do in most modern nations, East or West, and by studying its history and ethos (a carefully honed political program based on two-way loyalty between officers and men); and, crucially, they need to show that they comprehend the exigencies of governing, as well as defense and foreign policy. All this must occur if Bangladesh's civilian politicians are ever to command the respect of the military that would make the latter comply with civilian rule.

One reason the military has prevailed is that in contrast to its civilian challengers, it seems to truly understand the implications of how Bangladesh long has been governed, that both under the Muslims and the British, Bangladesh was ruled by two lines: civil and military. The reason in the former case was that the Muslim religion always has distinguished between holy warriors (ghazis and sufis) and preachers (mullahs). Under the Muslims, power was divided along the executive (civil) and military lines. Thus, the local prince or *nizam* controlled the *nizamat*, the administrative structure of the military, the courts, and the secret police; the *diwan*, the top civil service and financial official, controlled the *diwani*, the administrative structure responsible for the civil service, taxation, et cetera. The diwani was tied to bankers who financed the government. The British also established two lines of power: "civil" lines, located around the Ramna section of Dhaka, and "military" lines, in an area called Kurmitolah. What appeared to be civil rule was carefully backed by the military, and the two lines were linked by British political intelligence agencies and the police, who watched the subject peoples constantly, as so clearly outlined in the popular Paul Scott novels, *The Raj Quartet*, and portrayed in the BBC's "Jewel in the Crown" series. It is this latter system that characterizes military government in Bangladesh; it governed the nation for twelve of its first twenty years and was nearly perfected under the most recent military ruler.

Having established the importance of the Bangladesh military, it behooves us to understand something about its leaders. Perhaps their most distinguishing characteristic is that they are almost a caste: different in looks, education, manner, and viewpoint. Although Bangladesh's last two military leaders, General Zia Rahman (1975–81) and General Hossain Muhammad Ershad (1982–91) were both sons of the soil, true Bengalis, they also represented a less definable category: a senior officers corps, the *ashraf*, descended from the Turkic and Afghan immigrants who first brought Islam to Bangladesh. As Bangladeshi as five hundred years of residence and intermarriage can make them, these officers nevertheless follow a different value system whose underpinning is a ruthless sense of power. (Those who believe that government is as much about governing people as representing them maintain that such a value system is essential.)

While in manner some of them have an aura of Sandhurst and Colonel Blimp, most reflect an older tradition of canniness and calculation, a tradition that stretches back to the great military leaders of Bengal: Mahmud of Ghazni; Muhammad Ghori; Qutubuddin Aibek; Bakhtiyar Khilji; Fakhyuddin, Sultan Sekunder, who founded a fort at Takdala near Dhaka; Sheikh Islam Khan, who made Dhaka the capital of Bengal; Ibraham Khan; Samsuddin Ahmed; Gayasuddin Khan; Kasim Khan; Alivardi Khan, the last great independent king of Bengal; and Shaista Khan, who established Bengal as independent in the Moghul era. These were rulers trained in the art of war and governance, justice and administration, and they commanded obedience by their knowledge and courage—trained in the generous thought of the virtuous state, as taught by the Muslim political philosopher Al-Farabi. Many in today's officers corps come from military families that have served their country from the days of the face-off with Alexander to the independence war against Pakistan. To a large extent this group has intermarried for countless generations.

Bangladesh's military officer corps lives apart, in garrisons and cantonments, where they are shielded from everyday concerns. Behind their guarded walls the cantonments are quiet oases of neat houses, barracks, mess halls, officers' messes with gymnasiums, low-priced stores, hospitals, libraries, schools, and well-maintained vehicles and greenery. Everything is provided in return for the complete loyalty of the troops (*jawans*), officers, and noncommissioned officers (*harildars*). Similar to many Western military bases, the cantonments contain training institutions where all personnel, regardless of rank, receive instruction, day in and day out, sometimes for decades. All soldiers are trained, cross-trained, upgraded, and sent through a hierarchy of schools, some abroad, so that more than in almost any other profession, a soldier is both student and teacher and an officer is an intellectual. In peacetime an army trains for all eventualities. That is its nature, its promise. As that training progresses, it includes intelligence, strategy, and national priorities and strategies, diplomatic, military, and economic (as represented by the military-run Bangladesh Institute of Strategic Studies, which has no civilian counterpart). Thus Bangladesh's military receives a veritable extended university degree whose only civilian counterpart exists in the civil service and judiciary.

Moreover, there are the equivalents of West Point and Sandhurst: armed forces schools and academies for preinduction training at the high school and college levels, where military virtues and culture are inculcated and the winnowing process begins. There are even special schools where young officer aspirants or inductees can cram for the difficult entry-level examinations.

Not a few Bangladeshi men who attended these schools but did not choose to join the military remain proud of their school and examination results. More telling is a fact everyone knows: broadly speaking, the military-run schools are not as corrupt as the civil ones.

In this way the military officers mold new caste members (even those who come from "outside") into clones of themselves, via a difficult, painful, seemingly endless series of tests and objective measures, physical and mental. The result is men who know how to command, because they have been taught how to think. And because the tests of leadership are objective, there is respect for those who have excelled. Thus does the military caste exist and perpetuate itself.

Many who now command were trained in the Pakistan Army as noncommissioned or commissioned officers. Only a few fought in the Liberation War, mostly because the Pakistanis transferred them all and jailed many. Consequently, with certain notable exceptions, especially General Zia Rahman and those who joined his rebellion in Chittagong in 1971, the Freedom Fighters who fought the Pakistanis were recruited from among the general populace and were trained by the Indian Army under General Baghat Singh, who years later died fighting for Sikh independence in India.

Indeed, in the first eight years of independence, until General Zia was assassinated in 1981, there was open warfare between Pakistani-trained soldiers and Freedom Fighters. This period also saw the formation of radical cells within the army and of a powerful group of irregular army troops, called Mujib Bahini, which fought the army; the well-planned murder of Bangladesh's first leader, Sheikh Mujibur Rahman, by Pakistani-trained soldiers; a military mutiny under the leadership of one Colonel Taher and a countercoup by the pro–Awami League General Khalid Musharaf; the emergence of General Zia; a five-year campaign to destroy radicals in the military and restore the chain of command, a campaign in which hundreds of officers and men and, ultimately, General Zia died; and the murder of General Manzur, the last of the major Freedom Fighters. This culminated in a 1982 coup by General Ershad, who had helped President Zia establish a new chain of command.

What is crucial about this tale of bloodletting is that the military caste that achieved final victory made decisions and fought decisively—as opposed to the attempts of President Mujib's civilian advisers to deal with problems by using theory and rhetoric. The military faced internally all the fissures that were present in the body politic, and had to act.

Again, this tale of bloodshed is crucial only because, after years of conflict, the military was the first national institution to establish unity, by resolving once and for all what the country's goals should be. For the military infighting mirrored the ideological contradictions that existed among the civilians, conflicts that the still-warring civilian establishment has yet to confront. Ultimately, the military came out in favor of a Western, market-oriented, social welfare government rather than the East-oriented, socialist government that had been favored by the best and brightest of the civilian leadership. In fact, in 1974, the civilians had passed a constitutional amendment that resulted in the formation of a one-party state, called *Baksal*. This event vested President Mujib with vast powers. The dreadful mistake was that having learned nothing from history, the civilian politicians had not thought it necessary to secure agreement from the military and civil service. As a result, a fissure appeared in the national unity that had seemed so certain at independence. The quake came on August 15, 1975, when President Mujib and his entire family, except for a daughter in London, were massacred by the military, which took control for most of the next fifteen years. Though in 1991 the civilians again came to power, they remained divided because they could not solve by reason what the military had solved by force. They still do not comprehend that, right or wrong, the military formulated and committed itself to a vision for the nation as a whole, a vision the civilian politicians cannot agree on.

It is perhaps no surprise, then, that many Bangladeshis, including civil servants, labor leaders, social leaders, and rural dwellers, admire the military's courage and welcome its rule. A similar phenomenon exists in Pakistan. This fact leads many outsiders to believe that something about Muslim states makes them prefer military rule. There may be something to this, not in the sense that Muslims are antidemocratic but that perhaps there exists an atavistic predilection for rule by the cantonment, for firm, commanding rule by the nizamat.

If there is such a predilection, one must wonder whether there really can be a civilian democratic government without a cadre of military-trained civilians capable of commanding the respect of the armed forces and the civil service. Can barristers and political intellectuals be expected to lead a government without some appreciation of the military and without a sense of command, well-defined objectives and policies, and a vision for leadership? A related question is whether a credible, effective civilian leadership can emerge as long as the ashraf intellectuals maintain their traditional sense of superiority vis-à-vis the army—an attitude that heightens tensions and makes compromise impossible. In truth, ashraf intellectuals will not even admit that the army has a place in the political picture, and they refuse to develop policies whereby civilian leaders, the military, and the civil service could cooperate. Having discussed these concepts in depth with nearly every civilian Bangladeshi leader since 1971, this author has no doubt that only a handful really understand the hard political fact that in a nation-state the military represents the one truly national institution, the ultimate sanction behind civilian rule. That is true even when the civilians regain control, as they did in 1991. The issue, given the predilections of the populace, the civilians' antimilitary stance, and the Bangladeshi intellectuals' traditional political inclinations, is how long a civilian government can endure. The outcome depends on what the civilians do in power. For as long as the military remains an organized force, it will continue dominating the civilians, unless the latter make a determined effort to provide the firm leadership that makes military rule unnecessary.

There is only one way for civilian power ever to return permanently, and that is the hard way: with leaders who are able to control both government lines, the civil and military, the nizamat and the diwani.

The New Class

Since independence, a new, modern entrepreneurial elite slowly has been emerging, much to the disbelief of many foreign "experts" and the disdain and disgust of the traditional ashraf class (comprised of old families in jute, tea, and the import trade), the Brahmo class, the civil service, the judiciary, the law, and the military. This new class, some members still chewing betel nut and clad in lungi and kurta, others in slacks and button-down shirts, has been upsetting traditional class relationships and revolutionizing Bangladesh in many other ways, thanks to its flashiness, its electronic gadgetry, and its propensity for things Western, especially capitalist enterprises. In fact, this new elite is establishing a Hollywood culture in the midst of the Oxbridge world of the Brahmos, as we shall see.

From the perspective of this new class, 1972 was a critical year, the year that made its existence possible. It brought independence, which is a prerequisite for development, and it rid the country of the dominant old merchant class, consisting mainly of Pakistani Muslim Biharis and Hindus left over from British days. While the ashraf intellectuals debated policy at seminars, helped found government agencies with such alphabet-soup names as BART, BIDS, BISS, and BARC, and attended political rallies to be harangued by politicians, and while the army fought its bloody internecine war, these new, mostly young businessmen went to work. Though they took various paths, they had one important thing in common: they chose businesses that were nontraditional in Bangladesh, the ones which the British patronizingly call "cottage industries" but which the Japanese and Americans call the backbone of commerce and industry: small, family-owned enterprises.

The members of this new elite specialized in computers before they became household items, set up construction companies or brick works, built small garment factories or pharmaceutical plants in out-of-the-way places, sold pan and betel nut (both of which have narcotic effects), made ceramic toilets and sinks, produced printed textiles, opened architectural or civil engineering firms, and manufactured plastics, electric clocks, and electrical components for the power grid.

Some became smugglers, reviving old trade links with Burma, India, and Nepal. Others opened movie theaters or licensed the right to make heavy-duty truck and auto batteries. Some rebuilt old auto and truck engine parts. Others bought machine tools and made nails, nuts, bolts, gears, O-rings, and E-rings. Still others established welding shops, trucking companies, and bus lines. Many went into wholesale and retail trade in markets that began booming everywhere.

This new class worked in the shadow of Bangladesh business, which was dominated by a Chamber of Commerce that represented traditional indentors and importers, espoused a socialist ideology, and supported mammoth government projects, such as those of the Bangladesh Engineering Corporation, the Iron and Steel Corporation, the Jute Board, and the Bangladesh Trading Corporation, all designed to funnel imports through a specialized single agency. The Chamber of Commerce in many ways had absorbed all the intellectual fads of the 1960s without ever learning the history of what makes business work. As a result, the new class ran rings around the so-called "best men."

While the nation's intellectuals wasted billions of takas (the local currency) on these failed projects, the little men persevered quietly, almost anonymously. Many, working in undershirt and lungi in filthy sweatshops worthy of the name, expanded slowly into other lines, such as molded privies, chinaware, irrigation pumps, shoes, or wrought-iron objects. Meanwhile, though the Chamber of Commerce huffed and puffed and ignored the little guy, slowly, almost imperceptibly, the number of little guys proliferated, and some even became big guys. Then, suddenly it seemed, in the 1990s wherever one went in the world one could find many, many things made in Bangladesh.

In short, a mini-industrial revolution is under way in this land, with operators who can distribute goods nationwide, get goods from anywhere, and make almost anything. As one man in Old Dhaka promised not long ago, "If we can't get it, we'll make it; if we can't make it, we'll steal it, somewhere in the world; if we can't steal it, then what you want hasn't been invented; and if you want us to invent it, we'll do that, too." Such determination and confidence are signs of the new class.

This new elite, as a whole, is as unprincipled as any group that has arisen in Bangladesh. Unlike the Brahmos and Brahmo-influenced ashraf, this new *banian* class is interested only in money and too readily uses its management skills for nefarious purposes, such as to rig an election or to bribe government officials for contracts that once automatically went to the ashraf elite. Indeed, the rise of the new class has made corruption a very competitive business, with bigger bribes being paid more often by young men too impatient to wait for legal change in tiresome regulations left by British, Pakistani, or Bangladeshi regimes. It is important to understand that this phenomenon does not represent a decay in the morals of Bangladeshi businessmen or government officials. The "your turn to curtsy, my turn to bow" minuet between government and contractors is as old as government itself. After all, what is government for if not to divide the taxpayers' or, in Bangladesh's case, the aid-givers' money?

Rather, what has decayed is something that had been the *sine qua non* of Bangladesh's small talk and harangues for decades: Politics—politics first, politics now, politics forever—has lost its relevance. The entire premise of twentieth-century Bangladeshi thought, as taught in schools and universities and editorialized and harped on by newspapers, has been the centrality of government and politics as the solution to humanity's problems. This belief in the importance of the state has been the central doctrine of intellectuals, economists, sociologists, even literature departments, which have romanticized the idea. Thus higher education has had one major purpose: indoctrination of students, who are recruited by the political parties and turned into activist political fodder. Proletarianizing of students has been a way of life since the beginning of the language movement in 1952. Students became the soldiers of politics, professors became the indoctrinators, and universities became political institutions hiding behind academic freedoms. Obviously, not all students, professors, or even universities fell into this trap. The worst offenses occurred at Dhaka University, which once had a sterling reputation but, by the middle sixties, had become a crucible of political agitation, demonstrations, and political outbursts. Student activists from one party fought those from others, occasionally killing someone; nonactivists were harassed; students went on strike or protest marches and left campus to agitate among workers, farmers, and others. So politicized did the campuses become that many Bangladeshis still equate the university with politics or brag that students are the vanguard of change in the country.

In truth, the students, manipulated by the politicians, have played a major role in all political movements since independence, including the ouster of the Ershad government in 1991. But at what price? Instead of learning the liberal arts, the essence of education, they are distracted. Instead of having the leisure to study, to read, to reflect, they are co-opted by politics before they can understand what they are fighting for or against. In such an atmosphere, classes are devalued, learning is arrested, and students never know a quiet afternoon of tennis, music, plays, or social activities. Instead they become cynical, politically crafty, and alienated, by age twenty. They do not read the ancient classics of Islamic philosophy, the poetry of Rumi, or the ancient law texts of pre-Muslim India. They do not have time for Hobbes, Locke, Bentham, Mill, or Burke. They are not taught the discipline of calculus or chemistry. They are recruited to nearly full-time agitation, almost when they arrive on campus.

While many grow beyond this, some do not. And it is those who remain corrupted, who grow up to be cynical, empty, and heartless, who form the basis of the new Hollywood class. They outgrow the ideals of politics before they graduate, carrying away only cynicism. They see politics not as a system or a set of rules but as a brutal game. They lose faith in politics and in the system. Soon they see that politics is a matter of power and money, something to be manipulated for profit. And as they outgrow politics they come to see law not as something to be obeyed if the fabric of society is to be maintained, but as being out of date or a scam. For many of the laws were written right after independence and were aimed at killing individual initiative, at a time when there was hope that socialism could be achieved. Today, though meaningless, these laws remain on the books, passports to graft and corruption.

The new entrepreneurs see that the laws were written by the old bureaucracy to funnel graft into certain hands. Today the grafters exist at many levels of the bureaucratic system, and bribes have gotten ever larger as each civil servant through the hierarchy takes his or her share. In fact, so ingrained has bribery become that even the police threaten to serve false charges on citizens who have money and might find it easier to pay off than to go to court. Thus politics and the laws that result from it have lost their meaning, and an attitude of political libertarianism has arisen that translates into an individualist ethic saying "take as much as you can get." And that's what the young are learning today. Instead of being taught ethics, character building, and normative, honest ways to behave, much of Bangladeshi youth is learning by example—from their leaders.

A case in point is a bit of gossip that made the rounds in 1989 and, true or false, was widely believed. It seems that President Ershad was lounging at the pool (whose surrounding wall has a plaque saying it was a gift from the Japanese people) at the exclusive Kurmitolah Golf Course in Dhaka (which Ershad allegedly used as a playpen for his doxies when not golfing). His current girlfriend, the wife of a cabinet secretary, was beside him. Up rushed Ershad's wife who clawed at and mangled her rival. Trying to separate the women, Ershad fell, hit his head, and knocked himself out. While Ershad was hospitalized in Dhaka, his girlfriend was rushed to Bangkok for facial surgery. It wasn't the infidelity that so outraged Ershad's wife, the story went; she was furious because the girlfriend had received a lucrative business contract. What makes the story both important and believable is that it is so typical of Dhaka's tawdry Hollywood morality and *Dallas*-like greed. In such a world, politics becomes a soap opera whose chief end is the pursuit of wealth. In Bangladesh the seeds of this soap opera were sown nearly two decades ago, before the country even had a chance to catch its collective breath after the ferocious civil war. Indeed, since the fall of the Ershad government, new scandals concerning aircraft and the current foreign minister or the opposition leader's new lakeside house keep surfacing. Hollywood tawdriness is now part of the culture, institutionalized in fact.

The corruption began in 1972, right after independence, at Dhaka's Intercontinental, the country's only world-class hotel at the time. The action occurred in the hotel's ground-floor Saqi Bar, where rich and spoiled young bucks came to ogle the "feringhi" (foreign) women at the pool. A common sight there was Sheikh Mujib's son, the splendid Kamal, and his friends, including a man whose nickname was Manju. They could be seen lining up empty beer cans, which cost six dollars each when full and usually were flown in from Bangkok, chilled of course, high in the sky by an RAF advisory team. Alongside, Kamal's cousin lit cigars with hundred-taka bills, worth about fifteen dollars each. (At that time, the old Pakistani currency was used with the word *taka* imprinted by a red stamp.)

Meanwhile, upstairs in Room 1100 were dealers in government favors who smuggled tens of tons of Red Cross material donations across the border to Calcutta, where they could be found in the marketplace with their Red Cross labels intact. During the day, Room 1100 was used for "business" deals; at night it hosted an orgy of sorts, where men who during the day bemoaned the rape of Bangladeshi women by Pakistanis themselves ruined the virtue of other Bangladeshi women.

The depoliticization of Bangladesh's youth began, then, in the early days, with the new class, all in their twenties and basically uneducated, as they had spent their college years in leftist political discussions and in undisciplined dormitory life, in a totally politicized university, where the purpose of education had been prostituted to make young and tender children into alienated haters of the world, before they had written their first poems, before they knew of love, honor, and integrity. In the name of patriotism, all during the 1960s they had been used by grown politicians to do the dirty work, to man the demonstrations, to go to the countryside, to fight other student groups with weapons supplied by Bhagat Singh, the Indian general. (Ironically, Bhagat Singh was to die in the Golden Temple in Armritsar in 1983 helping Bhinderwale, a young Sikh extremist, a member of the new class that arose in India.)

What happened was that their young minds grew cynical. For they saw that only power and money counted, since they came of age just before and during the corruption of the immediate postindependence period (corruption so widespread that it led to the assassination, in 1975, of President Mujib by soldiers scandalized that "politics" only meant getting rich). Based on their learned cynicism, these pampered young students came to hate the laughable ideals taught in the name of socialism. They gave up on politics and began preying on the state.

This depoliticization carried over to the 1971–89 period, when diverse political parties—the Awami League, the JSD, the BNP, the Jatiya—continued whipping up student passions, encouraging them to demonstrate, fight, or terrorize in exchange for money, weapons, girls, or the spoils of crime.

Thus, as they attended Dhaka University, which due to the upheavals was closed over half each year during most of this period, successive classes of students received guns. The biggest supplier was the Awami League, to be followed by the splendid Kamal, then by the BNP, and finally by the Ershad government, which operated via an infamous "student" leader named Litu. In fact, by the late 1980s, so bad had the problem become that anyone with money sent their children overseas for higher education. For instance, in 1990, Molotov cocktails were thrown on Dhaka University's campus and a student was killed in a gun battle while this author crouched under a desk in a library research room.

Thus, the cause of the lack of morals, depoliticization, and cynicism in Bangladesh today is this new class, epitomized by the erstwhile Ershad Cabinet, where the morals of a fictional "Dallas" became those of the real Dhaka. In 1991 this situation precipitated a further crisis at Dhaka University, sparked by more killings and long shutdowns. And, as of this writing, the crisis continues. It did not end with the demise of the Ershad era, because Ershad did not start it. And it will continue until the political party that did start it is shamed into ending it.

In fairness, this section cannot end without touching on one who tried to fight the corruption as best he could. He was a young army colonel named Taher. In 1975, after President Mujib's murder, he led a mutiny of soldiers in which they confiscated vast amounts of material goods that symbolized the corruption around them—televisions, air conditioners, fancy furniture, et cetera—that belonged to the corrupt elites. Piling them up, the mutineers set them afire, in what was to be the last howl of hate against the new class, at least so far. Unfortunately, Colonel Taher was fighting a future that no one could restrain. He was executed by firing squad by President Mujib's successor, General Zia. Despite Taher's efforts, the corruption continued.

Realistically speaking, it was just as well. For Colonel Taher was a throwback to the austere Bangladeshi rustic farmer; and, in favor of the new class created by "progress," the politics of the last twenty years had destroyed, perhaps forever, the values that earlier class had represented in its state of grace. Moreover, Taher was the last gasp of romantic Tagorism, someone who realized that the harsh materialism of the Saqi bar and Room 1100 had become the only ideal cherished by students who knew no better, because they had no culture. They had never read Tagore in a reflective way, they had never heard of Alberuni, Kabir, Kazi Nazrul, or even of Homer or Mill. Like Tagore, Taher had wanted youth to have a complete education, one in harmony with nature and with their own time. He realized that the new class had been deprived of basic values, had not been trained in character, and only had been trained to hate. In his howl of burning the signs of corruption, Taher missed a chance to destroy the university itself, as Tagore had done symbolically by founding his own school when he saw the univer-

sity in Calcutta being politicized. It would not be overstating the case to say
that Taher was the last Tagorian. For after Taher raged at what modernity
had become under the half-educated new class, Tagore literally became an
icon, no longer associated with reality.

The Anglophile Mind

It is hard to recall today that for 190 years Bengal and Bangladesh were
as much a part of the English-speaking world as were London, New York,
Ottawa, and Canberra. Over nearly two centuries, English law, English science and education, English art and architecture were as much a part of
Dhaka as of Manchester. One can still glimpse the remnants of this heritage
in Dhaka, that mixture of Greek, Roman, and Gothic architecture that the
British used to grace their own cities. For instance, one can visit the beautiful
maidan, or park, in its center, the lovely homes in Ramna where the "civil
lines" were found, the classic Anglican Church in Old Dhaka, or the grand
Supreme Court Building. One can also attend a session of Court where the
judges wear wigs, view army uniforms and customs and note their British
origin; examine the university structure, which has colleges along English
lines; or listen to the accents of the ashraf class. Though it often seems to
have been overpowered by the new Bangladesh, the British inheritance still
permeates the society in deep and lasting ways.

It has been nearly half a century since Great Britain left India. Much has
changed. It might be said that American, Soviet, and East Asian influences
have displaced those of Britain, quantitatively and qualitatively. Certainly
the British legacy has been vastly submerged in cities that have grown far
larger than they were in British times. Calcutta has grown from three to
twelve million people, Dhaka to four million from less than a half-million at
the end of World War II. Yet Dhaka and Calcutta are British cities that owe
their distinctive characters to the Empire. Even today, by burrowing deeply
enough, one will find the British legacy at these cities' cores, be it in sports,
law, parliamentary practice, military customs, civil service conceits, or culture. For much of modern Bengali culture, Hindu and Muslim, derives from
movements begun in British times and strongly influenced by British
thought. Without the British legacy the ideas that have held the nation together could not have been developed. It was the hope of national independence, political freedom, and state planning that made the transition from
colonial status to modern development possible. Without the British legacy
there would have been no modern Bangladesh. The nation's deepest core
symbolically has more to do with the advice of the British and the Commonwealth High Commissions than with that of any other foreign government.
This is due not to conspiracy but to the inherent logic of thought as it
evolved over 190 years of British rule.

Though Britain had trading stations and small colonies at Surrat, Bombay, and Madras, it did not gain real power in India until after the Seven Years' War, which began in 1754, a war against the French fought in the West Indies, North America, and India that left Britain, under Clive, as undisputed military leader among the foreigners in India. Although France held Chandernagor and Pondicherry, Holland controlled Chinsura in Bengal, and Portugal had Goa, Britain controlled the sea and had the most powerful army. When Clive defeated the French, the British were poised for further conquest. The first major battle occurred when the Nawab of Bengal, against the advice of his bankers, the Jagat Seths, decided to fight the British by conquering Calcutta and imprisoning certain British leaders, who ultimately died in captivity in a prison cell known to history as the infamous "Black Hole." In 1757 Clive attacked and defeated the nawab at the historic battle of Plassey, fought upstream along the Bagaritha, then the major branch of the Ganges.

The Plassey battlefield, in West Bengal just across the Bangladesh border, is not often visited nowadays. Marking the spot is a line of trees along a hard road at whose end is a commemorative obelisk. To one side is a more modern monument to the Muslim gunners who fought the British. Beyond the battlefield, which is surrounded by rice fields, is the river. In the distance a majestic banyan tree still stands, a relic of a copse of trees in which the British huddled. Nearby, adjacent to the flood-control dike which the Nawab of Bengal used as his defense line, a Hindu farmer kneads the soil of his irrigated paddy with his feet, walking like an Italian squashing grapes at harvest. The wind is still, the sun bears down. Something about the land suggests a mute awareness that when Clive won at Plassey, he conquered Bengal, the richest province in Moghul India.

The defeat of the nawab, the last of the Moghul rulers, led to the Anglification of Bengal, to the planting of Western civilization among a people of the Orient. These people were to live longer under Western rule than those anywhere else in Asia, except in some of the old Portuguese colonies such as Goa, Macao, and Bantam. Bengal, the first real province conquered and ruled by the British in India, was one of the richest places on earth. The British victory led to a period of some twenty years of pure plunder on the part of the conquerors, Clive and the East Indian Company, culminating in a complete disruption of trade that forced the British government, at Burke's insistence, to impose a more imperially responsible government, first under Lord Hastings and then under General Cornwallis.

The rule of Hastings and Cornwallis could not make up for the plunder (for instance, Clive had taken more than a hundred shiploads of gold and silver from Murshidabad after the conquest, and his employees had used their power to extort millions of rupees from the people), for the famine (one-third of the populace died in 1770–71), for destruction of the cotton-weaving industry by British government policy (so as to transfer cotton processing to England), or for the fact that vast sums of wealth were transferred to the motherland. However, the British did launch a more liberal and respectful form of government that was to win the respect, if not the love, of the Bengalis.

Hastings, for instance, frowned on racial prejudice. He not only showed respect to Bengalis but set an example that many would follow afterward. He fostered the study of native languages at the College of Fort William in Calcutta, where young East India Company employees learned Sanskrit, Persian, and Hindustani as well as Bangla. He founded the Asiatic Society in order to systematically study the people among whom he lived. And he favored keeping intact as many of the courts, laws, and customs of the country as possible. Although he was to suffer all kinds of calumny, including impeachment, when he retired, he survived the wrath of his enemies and today is respected above all others in the long line of British governors and viceroys, by both Englishmen and Bengalis.

Hastings brought to the Bengal government a new sense of solidity and vision, a vision that Clive (who in a fit of depression after leaving power slit his throat with a knife after excusing himself from a hand of bridge with friends) did not have. Hastings raised the art of government to include a real concern for Bengalis. He restored both order and a sense of the future, so that when Cornwallis arrived the time had come to institute a meaningful, just taxation system. Cornwallis began reorganizing the system by fixing a single tax on land, one that remained unchanged for more than a century. Indeed, thanks to this tax, to the restoration of law and order, and to fair and liberal politics pursued by its British rulers, Bengal in the nineteenth century enjoyed sustained agricultural prosperity, punctuated only by natural disasters and famines, and was the British Empire's main revenue source, just as it had been one of the principal pillars of the Moghul Empire. Only in the last five decades of British rule did the province become poor relative to the rest of India and the world.

As to Bengal's educational and cultural advancements, Calcutta University was founded in 1857. India's first university, it came into existence long after many lower components (colleges) of the British University system had been established, beginning with Presidency College in 1830. The creation of Calcutta University sparked the first renaissance in Bengali thinking since the British conquered the Moghuls. The introduction of European Enlightenment ideas of secularism, science, economic theory, and law quickly attracted the imagination of the Bengali mind and precipitated the rise of intellectual fervor. Ultimately this fervor led to the creation of more colleges, to the spread of Western learning, and, more important, to a new flowering of Bengali prose and poetry. Among these new names were Madsuddan Dutt in poetry and de Rozio in prose.

The Bengal Enlightenment occurred in Calcutta, a city founded and designed by the British that was the most modern in India until 1912, when Britain moved its capital to Delhi. In the nineteenth century, Calcutta was the most beautiful city on the plains of India, one of palaces and gardens, where the decisions of the largest empire ever governed by a Western nation were made. In this atmosphere of learning, scholarship, and art, the Bengali intellectual flourished. At first the intellectual stage was dominated by Hindus, as they were the major beneficiaries of British rule. But over time, especially in the late nineteenth and early twentieth centuries, Muslims entered the stream of debate and culture. By 1900 more Bengalis had modern educational degrees than did people from anywhere else in India, and most civil service ranks open to Indians were filled by Bangla-speaking people who served throughout the country, much to the irritation of other groups and regions. Bengalis also dominated the professions of law and medicine. When a Muslim university opened in 1875, it was modeled on Cambridge, just as Calcutta University had been modeled on the University of London.

This educational blossoming was supplemented by British scholarship around the Asiatic Society, the National Museum, and the National Library. These institutions literally recreated the history of India by organizing it and applying modern historical methods. One result was new discoveries and perspectives on the history and culture of Bengal and, indeed, of all of India. At the same time this new learning opened vast vistas of national pride for all Indians and formed the basis for what later would be an independence movement. Importantly, however, while it focused on India, this learning was filled with British concepts about government, religion, and philosophy that influenced all Indians, at least indirectly.

Nearly all the learning of the Bengali Enlightenment thus emerged from British sources, which underpinned the fabric of the new university in Dhaka, built in 1925, and of other universities, which came later in Rajshahi, Sylhet, and Chittagong. Today the Bangladeshi mind remains deeply influenced by British thinking. But the British educational influence also has been fostered in other ways. Thousands of Bangladeshis have been educated in or have visited Britain. Many have moved there and maintain close links between the two countries. One can hardly visit London today without meeting Bangladeshis everywhere, in the universities, restaurants, banks, and stores and at the golf links. Such continual contact, reinforced by Britain's very efficient cultural institutions in Dhaka and Calcutta, to this day maintains these ties.

Moreover, thanks to Britain, Bangladeshis are barristers not lawyers, physicians and surgeons not doctors, readers not assistant professors. So deep is the inheritance that English language usages and customs have been translated into Bangla, judges wear wigs, generals wish to be field marshals, and civil service titles match. In short, Bangladesh has inherited from its erstwhile colonial master the civil lines and the military lines, complete with their links to the intelligence service and the police.

At its best this inheritance is in line with the pre-British Moghul system. At its worst the system has been made more efficient and therefore more tempting to a local "viceroy" to take power. In a very real sense, this is a part of the British legacy that goes deep into the nation's psyche.

All of Bengal, ruled from Calcutta under the British, represented Britain's power base in India. The security of the capital in Calcutta demanded that the base province be the most policed part of the country. Such precautions became more important in the latter half of the nineteenth and early twentieth centuries when Bengal's rich landowners, including most of those in modern Bangladesh, became restive and sought a greater voice in governance, which Lord Curzon refused to consider. As we have seen, what he did instead was to attempt to divide Bengal. This devastating fiasco sparked random acts of terrorism and assassination of officials, led by a revolutionary movement that operated underground in secret societies and kept British authorities in a perpetual state of alert for more than half a century. It was this history that made Bengal different and cemented the relationship between the military and civil authorities, along with the police and intelligence services.

Still another aspect of British rule has been superimposed on this Muslim nation. From an international perspective, Bangladesh looks west toward Mecca and London and, more recently, toward the United States. Those who can afford it travel westward. Every Muslim male is obliged to make *hajj* in Saudi Arabia at least once in his lifetime, if he can afford it. His religion came from the west, via the Muslim armies. Later his cultural links spread westward to Delhi, which was the Moghul and Sultanate capital; then to modern Pakistan, which became Muslim before Bangladesh did; and then to Iran, the Gulf states, and the entire Muslim world, or *Uma*. Bangladeshi Muslims pray to the west, toward the sunset. It is there that they find their God.

To this influence have been added London and the English-speaking world. Most educated Bangladeshis have relatives who live in London or who once did. The BBC, via short-wave radio, is a must among the upper classes, because it represents an old institution, a familiar voice speaking of a place that has evocative resonances, of sports Bangladeshis play, of people who are their own.

The unfortunate aspect of this is that despite their proximity there is less feeling and information about their brethren in West Bengal. Bangladeshis also know little about Burma, their southeastern neighbor, and less still about Thailand, East Asia, or even Malaysia and Indonesia, which also are predominantly Muslim. The United States is the exception, as many students now go to school there.

Bangladesh, therefore, often appears not to be in Asia, much less on the Indian subcontinent. There is something *sui generis* about its mindset. It seems to have no integral link to other factors, yet it does. It is interesting that the Bangladesh National Museum has little in it of the British era. The reason is that the era is not yet over.

In summary, the Bangladeshi mind, in its Islamic, secular military, land and language, rustic, new class, and Anglophilic manifestations, represents a pattern much like the seasons. Each of the moods becomes apparent over the course of the year; each is part of a mindset that reinforces all the others. Speak with an educated Bangladeshi long enough and all these aspects will show themselves.

5

I Am the Cyclone;
I Am Destruction

Near the paintings of Zainul Abedin in the Bangladesh Museum is another exhibit that in terms of space and visual impact is nearly as powerful as Abedin's vision of the 1943 famine. This exhibit, a photographic one, highlights the other important era in Bangladesh's modern history: the Liberation War of 1971. The exhibit depicts some of the murders perpetrated by the Pakistan Army: a ricksha driver on the floor of his vehicle; Bangladeshi leaders massacred en masse at Dhaka's Rayer Bazaar shortly before the war's end, especially a Hindu doctor shot in his dhoti; a pile of skulls belonging to intellectuals who were murdered at the war's outset at Savar, about twenty miles from Dhaka, where there now stands the stately Shahid Minar, or Martyrs' Monument. The pictures are stark, mounted on white boards, with black explanatory text. The exhibit's atmosphere is that of a midcentury newsmagazine's prosaic journalism. It evokes the apprehension of viewing the journalistic endeavors of any war: horror at the stark barbarity.

Yet this exhibit lacks the majesty and imaginative power of Zainul Abedin's paintings. It seems to emphasize the aphorism that history is a mass of facts, while a work of art states the truth with simple elegance. Indeed, nearly all Liberation War art seems devoid of the poetic thoughtfulness, the blend of color, scene, symbol, and artistic composition, that characterizes Abedin's work. It is not that the latter is any less stark or horror-filled. It is more so. The difference is that Abedin captures the power of the human spirit in the face of the horror. Somehow the power of what occurred during the Liberation War never has been captured by art. For down deep there remains a smoldering uncertainty about those days that still makes them difficult to deal with.

The reason is not any secret history but three problems that art has not been able to digest. The first is that political stories by nature always portray mankind's least noble aspect: the give-and-take of politics and the squalid search for power. The second is that there is a limit to what man the artist can do in the face of such human cruelty. There is little really good art about any of the political atrocities of this century, from Auschwitz to the Gulag, though Aleksandr Solzhenitsyn certainly has tried to bring art to the latter. At least in this century there seems to be a need for stark black-and-white photos and stark print to express political murder, not only in Bangladesh but also in Europe. The third problem is that nearly all political movements based on mass uprisings, where expectations are at a zenith, result in disappointment. Witness the Terror of the French Revolution, the Gulag of Soviet communism, and the failures of a host of Third World movements, which have left legacies of squalid dictatorships and economic decay. In such an atmosphere it is hard to focus on the innocents who suffer from the aftermath of high expectations. In the ennui of the after-moment, there is not enough energy left even to focus hate. Bangladesh, too, has had its moments of such ennui in the aftermath.

Such is the legacy of a war of savage cruelty that was followed by a nearly gnostic evocation of Golden Bengal, then by the coming of Baksal (the second revolution which, like the Terror in France and the Bolshevik Revolution in Russia, followed the first revolution), then by the restoration in August 1975, when Sheikh Mujibur Rahman was murdered. The liberation struggle encompasses all that happened from the beginning of the language movement in 1966 to the death of the Sheikh.

There are really two stories here: that of Bangladesh and that of a generation of political and intellectual leaders who saw their beliefs evolve from a movement of reform within Pakistan to one of liberation and who saw their beliefs in a multiparty state evolve into the totalitarian beliefs of Baksal. The two stories, of Bangladesh and of that now-disappearing generation, are not identical, though they are intertwined. Of the two, the story of Bangladesh is a glorious one. The story of a generation, however, is less clear-cut. Let us begin with Bangladesh.

The Emergence of Bangladesh

True to a tradition that stretches back to before the Buddha, there have been those in Bangladesh who have resisted the presence of the caste-conscious Aryans, the Hindus. At first as outcastes, as dasas and namasudras, the Bangladeshis tended to retreat into the watery swamps of the river deltas, out of reach of the more civilized landlubbers to the west. There they held out as long as possible. At the time of the Buddha they rose up and left Hinduism in large numbers for the certainties of the Buddha's casteless society. For twelve hundred years they were attracted to the Buddha's path and resisted any attempt to force them back into the caste system. When, in the tenth to twelfth centuries, the Sena Dynasty tried to force them into the caste system and to Sanskritize their language, they resisted in the face of great cruelties. They endured this struggle until the emergence of a new casteless society in the form of Islam, under which, for the next half-millennium (1200 to 1757), they lived without fear of Hindu caste rules.

When the British wrested control from the Muslims, they initially catered to Bengal's Hindu minority, playing off that minority against the formerly powerful Muslim majority. During the first 120 years, the British destroyed the bases of Muslim society: the madrassahs, the courts based on Persian and Muslim law, the army, and the government system. The Muslims were driven from politics and deprived of social influence. Only in the 1890s, when the favored Hindus began challenging British rule, did Britain make the Muslims their new favorites. Finally, as we have seen, in 1905 Britain divided Bengal, creating a Muslim majority state in the province's eastern part. When the Hindus protested because they thus lost their power in the east, the Muslims remained silent, not necessarily helping the British but grateful to their new leaders, Bamfylde Fuller and Lancelot Hare, the British lieutenant-governors of East Bengal who fought for a Muslim Bengal. This is not to imply that Bengali Muslims were pro-British. Like the Hindus, they wanted independence. But when it came they wanted to be certain that they would be able either to offset the Hindu majority in all of India or to have a separate Muslim nation, protected from the Hindu caste system. In fact, the Muslims suspected, accurately so, that when the British left India they would turn the government over to the Hindus.

Nevertheless, when Bengal was divided in 1905, the Muslims at first heeded their Hindu neighbors' appeal to remain loyal to a unified Bengal and almost joined the anti-British rebellion. But as soon as Hindu forces outside Bengal turned the protest into an All-India and Hindu movement, the Muslims backed out. For they saw that Hindus meant to maintain their superiority not only in Bengal but also in a united, Hindu-dominated India. Yet in that first moment of agitation, when the protest seemed to be about Bengali nationalism and not about Indian or Hindu nationalism, modern Bangladesh was born, at least in spirit. For Muslim Bangladeshis love the land, language, and soil of Bengal as deeply as they love their religion. Nevertheless, given the circumstances, the Muslims were forced to bury their aspirations for their native province, an aching desire that, as we shall see, never died, but was revived intermittently, before arising with a passion in the 1960s. Thus from 1905 to 1947, when Britain was forced out of India,

Muslim Bengal downplayed Bengali nationalism in favor of a longer-range hope of some constitutional arrangement that would protect them from Hindu caste rule.

This cannot be overemphasized. All Bangladeshis have a split-level mind. On one level they are Hindu, Muslim, Buddhist, or Christian; but on a deeper, less rational, repressed level they are Bangladeshi—in a sense that harks back to the pre-Aryan period, before Hindu, Muslim, or Buddhist thought frames existed. At this second level, their historic memory is a barely articulate tribal throwback to traditional nationalist loyalties of language and soil, as well as to the natural religion of the rivers, the moon, the sun, and the village gram devatas. Every nation has such deep wellsprings. But in Bangladesh the well has been called up in this century as never before. It still has not been given full expression.

After the 1905–12 period, the Bangladeshi Muslim underwent a rarely remarked upon conversion. Thanks to the teaching of some, like Nawab Abdul Latif, a Muslim reformer and teacher, but more to the emotionalism of the Bengal unification movement, coupled with Tagore's uncanny gift of evoking the land and the language, the Bengali Muslim made peace with his Bangladeshi heritage. He did not like the "Bande Mataram" because it made reference to Hindu goddesses; but he did like its sound and evocation of Bengal. He could not consent to Hindu raj, but he wanted a Bengali nation where Muslims would have a just place in a casteless society. And because some Bangladeshi Muslim families joined their Hindu brothers' efforts to achieve such a Bengali reality, beyond Islam and Hinduism, in the Brahmo style of life, there was planted a seed of nationalism and secularism, one that ultimately would meld with democracy and socialism to form the four pillars of Bangladesh. For secularism would offer a way for Muslims and Hindus to cooperate without reference to religion, thus freeing Bengali nationalism to flower. This numinous evocation, sustained with poetry and song, appealing like Lalan Shah to the unseen and unrevealed, formed the true foundation of Bangladesh. Even Bangladesh's national anthem is based on a Tagore poem, *Golden Bengal*, set to the music of Lalan Shah. It was written for the 1905 movement to keep Bengal united. Thus, the legacy of 1905 is embedded in the Bangladesh psyche and is restated every time the national anthem is played. However, this new sense of Bengali nationalism took years to gestate before it became, among the Muslims of Bengal, a real basis for a political movement.

This aching desire for Bengali nationalism was revived in the World War I years, when the Jaguntar, Anushilan, anarchist, and communist secret movements took root in Bengal. These were largely Bengali Hindu movements. They were violent, as opposed to the peaceful methods of Mahatma Gandhi in the Indian Congress Party independence movement. This violence, which always had a Bengali component, separated Bengal from the rest of the Indian liberation movement. The desire for Bengali nationalism arose again in the 1920s when C. R. Das, a Hindu Bengali who was an elected secular leader and author of the Bengal Pact, which eliminated religious competition from politics, and Subhas Chandra Bose, also a Hindu but unlike Das a national socialist militant radical who broke with Gandhi over the use of violence, appealed to Bengali nationalism. Das and Bose worked out a modus vivendi for Hindu-Muslim cooperation within a united Bengal, a feat unmatched elsewhere in British India. They were able to pull into the Bengal Pact Fazlul Huq and H. S. Suhrawardy, who were to become the foremost Muslim politicians in Pakistan in the 1940s and 1950s. The nationalism reappeared during World War II, when Bose joined the Japanese against the British. And it resurfaced in 1945 when Suhrawardy and Sarat Bose, Subhas's brother, tried feebly to unite Bengal rather than allow Gandhi and Nehru to divide it. Finally, Bengali nationalism reemerged in 1971 during the Liberation War, when Sheikh Mujib alluded both to Bengali unity and, at the urging of Maulana Bhasani, a rural radical Bangladeshi leader of the 1950s and 1960s who was associated with the Soviet and Chinese Communist parties, to *Purbodesh*, unity of all of east India, including Bihar, Orissa, and Assam. Thus at a very imaginative and evocative level, Bengali unity has had a long life. Culturally, but not politically, it exists today.

At the level of the real world, however, Bengali Muslims' foremost desire was to end Hindu rule. It was partly a religious issue, but a more fundamental reason was that under the British most landowners and moneylenders, or *mahajans*, were Hindus who kept their peasant tenants in a state of serfdom unmatched by any civilized society in this century. The zamindars and mahajans rack-rented and usurized the peasantry, so that at least 80 percent of Muslim Bengalis were little more than slaves to interest payments, paying illegal taxes and exorbitant rates of interest, and were beaten by an army of mafialike *gomastas* and *lathials* who worked for the ruling class. Subjected to such treatment by upper-caste Hindus, the Muslims succumbed to severe, debilitating racial inferiority.

Consequently, from 1905 to 1947, from the viewpoint of Bengali Muslims, all talk of being *bhais*, or brothers, was overwhelmed by a devastating socioeconomic and caste battle—one recognized but ignored by the British rulers. Still, the Muslims did not call for revolution, but worked within the Bengal Pact for moderate, gradual reform. Nevertheless, the class makeup of the confrontation gave it Hindu-versus-Muslim overtones.

The struggle for Muslim identity within Bengal, however, had to go through a number of battles on different fronts. The head start the Hindus achieved in higher education, coupled with the British-run civil service and economic system, had placed the Muslims at a disadvantage. These obstacles had to be overcome.

Britain, for example, staffed the schools with Hindu teachers who helped produce textbooks filled with allusions to the Hindu religion. A major outcome of this was that while most Muslims spoke Bangla, they wrote mainly in "Mussalmani Bangla," a language filled with Urdu, Arabic, and Persian words; and they produced what is called the *Puthi* literature of the nineteenth and early twentieth centuries. At the same time, the schools taught in a purified literary Bangla, developed under the British by upper-class Hindus. Thus a language barrier came into existence. In fact, the first Bengali Muslim book in literary Bangla, a song book, appeared only in 1910. And not until the 1920s were large numbers of Muslims educated in this language, because they believed that written and literary Bangla was a "Hindu" language. It took several more years before the books were stripped of their Hindu biases.

Though it is anathema to say so in today's Bangladesh, the truth is that the high literary tradition of Bangla was carefully developed in the late nineteenth century mostly by Hindus, who used Bangla to help impart to their province the sense of identity of a modern nation-state in the European style. As for Bengal's Muslims, during this period of Hindu revival they were in the throes of a deep reexamination of their Muslim roots and were writing in Puthi. Not until the first decade of the twentieth century did the Muslims begin turning to Bangla literary style and tradition, and not until the 1960s did they vociferously endorse a wholehearted Bengali ideology. Thus one result of the united Bengal movement of 1905–12 was that Bengali Muslims began the process that would lead to the language movement and the ultimate acceptance by educated Bangladeshis of the high literary tradition of Bangla developed by Hindus in the nineteenth century. Not until this transition occurred did Bangla become the language behind Bangladeshi nationalism and the great modern language it is today. Yet this effort to move from Mussalmani Bangla to the literary Bangla movement proved to be long and difficult. It was not a matter of concern to many Muslims until well into the 1950s.

Still another example of Hindu dominance concerned the spread of modern secularism, which gave the Hindus a decided advantage in political discourse. For their version of secularism, while professing tolerance, implied a Hindu majority in a so-called secular state. While Islam can be tolerant and its record is better than that of many religions, nevertheless it had to examine the meaning of secularism at a time when Hindus had mastered it as a political tool. However, as the writings of many Bengali Muslims demonstrated in the 1920s, mastery of this concept made possible the Bengal Pact, which confined politics to bread-and-butter rather than religious issues. Still, the introduction of secularism had a most profound effect that remains unresolved.

In the face of secularism, religion lost all relevance to politics. In place of religion came the idea of love of land, language, and culture in the modern nationalist sense, or love of the international humanist or working-class movements. Neither of these movements has an inherent moral system. Indeed, in this century the opposite has been the norm. Both imply a certain gnostic evocation, an enthusiasm for a more perfect future through destruction of current political structures. Both are political and have no philosophic or moral universe in the sense of individual or social behavior. Nationalism appeals to the chauvinistic aspects of racial, ethnic, and linguistic pride; socialist internationalism is based on envy of richer classes and richer nations.

However, in a quite unintended way, the secularists of the leftist parties and the humanists opened up a pit of nationalism among the newly educated people. By denying the religious basis of society and seeking to substitute socialism or some other brand of idealism for religion, the leftists opened the door to the cellar of the tribal mind, to the base feeling of race, nation, blood, and soil, the sons-of-the-soil ideology of nationalism in its most primitive form. By preaching not secularism but irreligion, the leftists, liberals, and socialists left the Bengalis with a dislike of the moral precepts that underlie all religions. Moreover, by tearing away the cloak of religion, the so-called secularists opened the field to ideologists of left and right who, without moral restraint, created an amoral nationalism that the people were ultimately to reject. In the meantime, however, this amoral nationalism was celebrated in all its nihilistic meaning, as we see in the poetry of Kazi Nazrul Islam. A more concrete example is the fact that in the name of Bengali nationalism, one of the most important Bengali nationalists of this century, Subhas Chandra Bose, cooperated with the Communists under Stalin, the Nazis under Hitler, and the Japanese against Britain, and participated in the mindless terrorism of the Bengal independence movement of the 1920s and 1930s.

Such an opening into xenophobia need not have occurred. True secularism is not antireligious or antinomian but is tolerant of all moral beliefs and, indeed, seeks to promote moral systems, the traditional religions being the most effective systems and worthy of toleration and respect. The secularism of Socrates is an example of this: Socrates refused to deny the power of the people's gods, even as he drank the hemlock. Unfortunately, such a tolerant secularism did not exist. It thus left the door open for assertion of modern radical belief.

The Political Tradition

The emergence of a true Bangladeshi political tradition can be traced to 1921, when elections were held in Bengal for the Calcutta Corporation Council, the only elective body in which locals could participate under British rule. Three important Muslim figures emerged: Fazlul Huq, who was to become the foremost Muslim politician until the end of World War II; H. S. Suhrawardy, who came to prominence in the 1930s and by the 1950s was the preeminent politician of Pakistan; and Abul Hashem, a socialist who worked among the peasants and trade unionists and provided a grass-roots base for the parties that subsequently were created.

Fazlul Huq entered politics in the 1920s, when C. R. Das, a leading Hindu and a profoundly tolerant man, arranged the Bengal Pact between Muslims and Hindus (an excellent example of a tolerant secularism that sought not to deprecate religious belief, but to foster cooperation based on mutual respect) and promised Muslims full representation on the Calcutta Council. There, Huq met Suhrawardy. The latter, who represented a working man's constituency in Calcutta and was a native of what is now West Bengal, ultimately was the leading spokesman of Muslim Bengal until Pakistan was formed. In 1937, when Britain expanded representative government, Huq was elected to and then became prominent in the new provincial assembly.

It is important to recall that the Bengal Pact enabled Hindu and Muslim activists to work together against the British, if only for a limited time. This occurred as more and more Muslims began entering the universities in Calcutta and Dhaka in the 1920s and 1930s, thus creating, for the first time, a unified Bengali intelligentsia cooperating against common foes. Young men such as Fazlul Qader Chowdhury and Sheikh Mujibur Rahman mingled in an anti-British matrix with Hindu radicals. One of their adventures was to tear down the monument to the Black Hole of Calcutta, a monument built by the British as a symbol of Bengali cruelty that was based on a fantasized number of deaths. Likewise, Muslim and Hindu students and intellectuals followed the charismatic Bengali leader Subhas Chandra Bose, who formed military-type organizations and encouraged revolutionary underground groups, some swearing mystic oaths of celibacy and self-sacrifice, others swearing tantric oaths to the Hindu goddess of destruction, Kali. Even Muslims who did not so swear admired the fire and idealism of their more fanatic compatriots who were committed to Bengali freedom. It was during this period that the Chittagong armory was attacked by such terrorists and young women shot British district officers or murdered policemen. Sharing tensions and triumphs, some of these Hindu and Muslim students became communists, some Gandhi followers, some socialists. But most important, during this period there almost arose, as in 1905, a common destiny for all Bengalis, Hindu, Muslim, Buddhist, Christian, and tribal.

This last point is crucial. For especially in the 1930s, because Bengal always had a sense of its own destiny, a more nearly formed nationalism than existed in any other Indian province except Maharastha, Hindu and Muslim Bengalis protested together against the British and against the Indian freedom movement led by Gandhi and Nehru. This intra-Indian battle always was played down. Thus while the fight against the British held the headlines, the parallel battle against the Indian Congress Party carried a subheadline. In retrospect it deserves more importance than it receives in the histories.

Essentially the battle broke into the open between Gandhi, a devout Hindu, and Bose, a secular Hindu, after the latter became president of the Congress Party. Charismatic and impetuous, Bose quickly disturbed the party's Olympian calm by inserting into the independence movement a purely Bengali point of view, as opposed to the West Indian, Anglicized view of the main leaders. A passionate advocate of revolution, Bose had no patience for peaceful means or for the Congress Party's Fabian slowness to attack. Desiring outright warfare, he began training youths in martial militias and appealed to students to take radical action. Before long the undercurrent of disagreement between Bose and Gandhi became too apparent to paper over. Gandhi called for Bose to step down as party leader. In 1937 an angry Bose too easily gave in, without playing all his cards. The result was the emergence of a real Bengal nationalism movement led by the Hindu Bose. Despite Bose's religion, his oratory and outlook attracted some Muslim Bengalis, because he appealed to Bengal nationalism, a concept that, without reference to communal background, was beginning to have widespread resonance. Years later many people pointed to a relationship between Bose and Sheikh Mujibur Rahman, at least in terms of nationalism and race consciousness. And even more saw in the Sheikh's Baksal movement a national socialist pattern evident in Bose's thinking, although Mujib played up to the Muslim majority while remaining a hero to Bangladeshi Hindus who feared the Pakistanis.

A great deal is known about Bose: his meteoric rise; his dismissal as president of the Congress; his flight from Calcutta in 1940 to the USSR and thence to Stalin's then-ally, Nazi Germany; his daring submarine voyage to Japan; and his ultimate formation of the Indian National Army, which fought side by side with the Japanese in the captured Province of India-Burma (Burma had been part of India since the mid–nineteenth century and was ruled from Delhi). But little is known about that critical era in terms of the real feeling of its youth, although Nirad Chaudhuri has described the amazing amount of pro-Japanese and pro-German feelings that existed in Calcutta and elsewhere in India during the war. Thus it is still unclear whether Bose was a fascist or a communist. His escape to the USSR with communist help suggests the latter, and had he survived the war, he might have emerged as a Bengali Ho Chi Minh. Some believe he was a fascist because he lived in Japan and Germany. (What confuses everything is that Bose escaped when the Communist Soviets were allied with the Nazi Germans during the Stalin-Hitler Pact. Interestingly, in 1990, the Indian Parliament began to investigate him by requesting that the USSR, Germany, and Japan open their archives.) What is clear is that while the mystery man left behind no fascist party, the Left used him as a hero when after the war the Indian National Army founded by Bose to help the Japanese was put on trial by the British. Whatever the truth, Bose is important to Bangladesh history because he created a model of national and socialist agitation whose form was to reemerge some thirty years later. Indeed, in Calcutta, but not in Dhaka, Bose still is revered, in street names and in a warlike statue with sword in hand that faces Delhi. Whatever he was, there is no doubt that Subhas Chandra Bose was a man of Bengali nationalism, a symbol of future strife.

As the Bose controversy swirled over Bengal in the late 1930s, Fazlul Huq created a peasants' and workers' party that agitated for reform of the zamindari relationships with the province's Muslim majority. While he was communal in the sense that his constituency consisted of Muslims who would not have trusted a Hindu, Huq did not inflame religious passions but promised reform through law. He appealed to sociopolitical issues that affected all peasants and was an able campaigner and organizer who formed Hindu friendships that ultimately paid off politically. A disciple of Das and Bose (they both were ardent nationalists and secularists who, unlike many secularists of today, were able to respect the religious beliefs of their Muslim brethren), Huq mastered politics on an all-Bengal basis. In 1936, at a time when the ultimate division of the province into Indian West Bengal and Pakistani East Bengal had not been mooted, Huq, Hashem, and, to a lesser degree, Suhrawardy formed a peasants' and workers' alliance, the Krishak-Sramik movement. Calling for radical reform in Bengal, it swept the province, giving the Muslims a majority. Bengal thus became the only province in British India to have an elected majority Muslim government.

At this juncture radical All-India Hindu nationalists—not Bengali ones—rebelled. For though Hindus were part of the coalition regime and the Muslim party was a leftist one that was demanding reform of the zamindari-peasant and owner-labor relationships, Hindu nationalists were frightened by a Muslim-led Bengal, one that also was attacking the monopoly of civil service and teaching jobs held by Hindus and calling for laws to control moneylenders, who also were Hindu. To counter the Muslims' sudden ascension to power, the Hindus called for a return to the basest sort of communal politics. To create Hindu solidarity and to antagonize Muslims, they launched a vast anti-cow-killing campaign, which ultimately led to Bengal's partition and to the communal hatred that erupted in massive riots just before the Pakistan era.

There was no one of substance left to impose calm. The reasonable Das had died, and Bose, though still idolized, had been discredited owing to his fight with Gandhi and his forced resignation from the Congress Party. The truth was that the Bengal Pact of Hindu-Muslim cooperation had ended. Much-increased communal tension filled the void. Though Gandhi and

Nehru had opposed extreme Hindu nationalism in Bengal, neither now cared enough to try to stop the growing communal rift. What they did not foresee was that their failure to act was to be one of the pivotal factors that ultimately made Bengal's partition inevitable.

The reason was that there then existed an All-India Muslim League, which, like the Congress Party, called for both an end to British rule and for an independent, Muslim Pakistan. Comprised predominantly of non-Bengali Muslim leaders from western India, this party never had made deep inroads in Bengal because of the role of Das's Bengal pact. However, it did have leaders in Bengal who were people of substance, but who lacked a mass base. As long as Bengali Hindus and Muslims got along, the All-India Muslim League could not garner mass support. But once the cow-killing campaign began and Muslim-Hindu tensions flared, the picture changed.

From the Muslim perspective, the most important consequence was that in 1937, at the prodding of the All-India Muslim League, led by Mohammad Ali Jinnah in western India and by Hassan Ispahani and Mohammad Ali of Bogra in East Bengal, Huq, Hashem, and Suhrawardy founded the Independent Muslim Party, a wing of the All-India Muslim League. This new Bengali party combined the mildly radical Praja party, which had a mass base, with the upper-class ashraf, which had no mass base but could contribute its wealth and ties to the All-India Muslim League. Thus Huq's secular party approach had to be modified because, faced with Hindu hostility, Huq and his followers had to join an outright communal movement. A major result of this new Muslim party was that nearly all hope of a united Bengal was abandoned. And while there were subsequent attempts to renew the Bengal Pact, they were feeble and doomed.

It is important to understand that the Independent Muslim Party was a mildly radical, secular-based one, with socioeconomic goals, founded on a peasant-worker alliance. For the most part it followed the precepts of the Praja movement that, created by Huq and Hashem not long before, had catapulted the Muslims to power in Bengal. Essentially, then, these three leaders' turn to Muslim communalism in the supercharged atmosphere of the late 1930s did not represent a change in goals so much as a change in tactics. The vast majority of landlords and moneylenders, who were the "enemy," were Hindu, and communal passions only added to the overall direction of the effort.

The All-India Muslim League leaders, especially in East Bengal, did not appreciate the fact that Suhrawardy, Huq, and Hashem were not communalists at heart. As we have seen, all three understood the secular outlook and had links to Calcutta Hindus in the Congress Party and to members of more radical parties. In contrast, the upper classes of the All-India Muslim League, as opposed to the Bengali Independent Muslim League, mostly were descendants of Moghul, Afghan, or Persian settlers in Bengal. Their mental outlook was not attuned to the feelings of the people, as, unlike the three native Bengali political leaders, most of them were not professional politicians. Nor were they "sons of the soil" or true Bengalis. Moreover, their education made them part of the Brahmo world. Though Muslim, they had liberal ideas, drank liquor, and socialized with the upper crust of Calcutta society. More important, most of the leading All-India Muslim Leaguers were educated in England or in the Anglophilic, Muslim Alighar University, which self-consciously modeled itself on Cambridge University, rather than in Dhaka or Calcutta. This, more than any other single factor, separated them from the Bengali masses.

It is important to pause here to note that this interplay and interface of the upper-class ashraf of the All-India Muslim League and the mass-based secular politics of the Praja movement later would play a vital role in Pakistan's demise and Bangladesh's emergence. In other words, the interplay of the 1940s would become an interface in the 1950s.

As to the new communal path of the Independent Muslim League, while it had large numbers of followers, most were loyal within the context of the socioeconomic rationales as presented by Huq and his compatriots. Uniting this unlikely coalition was the implacable conflict forced on them, as they saw it, by radical Hindu forces. By 1939 the Muslim League, with its Bengali allies, had become implacably anti-Hindu. And in 1940, at the Muslim League All-India conference in Lahore, it was Huq who called for the Pakistan Resolution, which suggested that two Muslim states be created out of British India and that they be united only in spirit, because both were opposed to Hindu majority rule and to a return of caste. (Ultimately, for reasons that many find unclear, in 1947 this idea resulted instead in the creation of a single Muslim state, with west and east wings a thousand miles apart. Untenable as such a state inherently had to be, it was years before its underlying conflicts erupted into an independence movement. Before that could happen, the mass movement had again to rediscover its roots, which first had been rediscovered in 1905, as a Bengal or Bengali nationalist movement.)

Returning to 1940, we must keep in mind that while the government of the then-united Bengal was in the hands of Huq's Muslim party, it faced an actively hostile Hindu minority in West Bengal. As for the common people, the Muslim majority and the Hindu minority, their main battle was for survival, as they continued to be preyed upon by the zamindars and mahajans. But more and more Muslims, sensitized to the Hindu backlash as a result of riots in Calcutta and elsewhere, were anxious for the British to leave. These Muslims—by no means the majority—were being educated in schools where the texts were no longer Hindu tracts, and they were learning English. For the first time under British rule, large numbers of Muslims were being brought into the mainstream of political life.

However, in 1943, Bengal was stricken by the famine that Zainul Abedin's paintings portray so starkly, so splendidly. Initially, Huq, Suhrawardy, and the British government reacted slowly, failing to grasp the vast extent of the hunger. When they did act, their attempts were stupendously inadequate. Recall the times. British India was engaged in a war to the death with Japan in Asia. The Japanese occupied Burma, just across the border from East Bengal, where vast numbers of British troops were poised for battle. Scarce food was being exported to help the British war effort. Suddenly famine struck. What little food existed in the countryside was unable to reach the cities. Thousands of Bengali boats had been confiscated and destroyed to prevent seizure in the event of a seemingly probable invasion. For the Bengalis, the war itself became a blur. Only sheer survival mattered. Three to five million people died. *Three to five million!*

In the midst of this catastrophe, one Muslim family, the Ispahanis, whose members had been active in the All-Indian Muslim League, lost enormous credibility for supposed "mishandling" of food supplies. They were not the only ones thus accused, as some Hindu zamindars also were blamed. Suhrawardy, who as Bengal's food minister was deeply involved in the food maldistribution scandal, strongly defended the very powerful Ispahanis, whose pro-Pakistani interests he represented. (Many years later, misunderstandings arising from the famine would lead to a split between the Ispahanis and Suhrawardy.) The famine hurt Suhrawardy's reputation, as he too was accused of profiteering, although it is unlikely that either he or the Ispahanis were as guilty as gossip indicated. Ultimately this conflict played a role in the breakup of the Independent Muslim League into its constituent parts after the formation of Pakistan.

The famine also did enormous political damage to the province. Not only did it divide Hindu from Muslim, but it also precipitated a breach of faith between the starving "sons of the soil" Bengalis and the All-India Muslim League merchant classes, whose ancestral roots were planted elsewhere and whose material wealth insulated them from the tragedy that swirled around them. The famine's main effect was its brutal destruction of both life and inhibitions. A poor nation reduced to its basic needs has little to lose when it decides its future course.

When the war ended, new elections were held in India under British auspices. Once again the Muslim parties, led by Huq and Suhrawardy, won a majority in a still-united Bengal. The Hindu minority objected anew. Finally, after severe riots in Calcutta and in Noakali in East Bengal, the Bengal legislature voted on whether to remain united within India or to allow the province to be partitioned. Naturally the Muslim majority preferred the status quo. But to a man the Hindus voted for partition—for the very thing their fathers had protested against so violently in 1905. Now the decision, an irrevocable one, had been made: Bengal would be divided along religious lines. One major result was that the mantle of Bengali nationalism was to fall on the Muslims instead of on the Hindus, as it had in 1905. For the vast majority of Bengalis were Muslim and henceforth would be in Muslim Bengal, part of the new nation of Pakistan.

As for Suhrawardy and Huq, they argued for an independent, united Bengal. Suhrawardy tried to work with Sarat Bose, Subhas's brother, and with other Hindus to secure a united Bengal within some framework. Moreover, sickened by the violence, he cooperated with Gandhi to calm the situation while attempting to fashion a compromise. But the Hindu Congress Party in Bengal felt more loyalty to Delhi than to the rest of Bengal, and all hope of a united Bengal was lost. Ultimately Huq and Hashem chose to live in the newly created East Pakistan. Suhrawardy—whose home was in West Bengal, the part that remained in India—stayed on there, working with Gandhi to soothe communal relations and to search for some way to put India together again. During this period he absorbed the doctrines of the Congress party. Only after Gandhi's murder in 1948 did he return to East Pakistan, in hope of helping create a secular, nationalist, socialist, and democratic state.

The Pakistan Era, 1947–71

While it is obvious why Britain divided Bengal, it is not clear why East Bengal agreed to become part of a single state instead of pushing for the two states that had been called for by the original Pakistan Resolution. No doubt part of the reason reflected religious enthusiasm. For the first time in 190 years, by becoming a single state, India's Muslims again would rule the Indus and Lower Ganges and Brahmaputra valleys—which had been the two richest parts of India in both Moghul and British times. Another reason was the shared fear of India. East Bengal's Muslims had good reason to worry. For the British never had trained the Bengalis to be soldiers, but toward the end of their rule had recruited whole regiments of Muslims from northwest India, now West Pakistan. Ironically, given what was to happen twenty-four years later, the East Bengalis reasoned that they needed their western brethren to help defend them. Finally, in the aftermath of the freedom struggle and the British departure, amid devastating rioting throughout India—rioting that did much more damage in West than in East Bengal—there was a great desire for a breather, for a chance to reorient. In the confusion of those last months of British rule, Huq's call for two Muslim states was ignored, overlooked, or forgotten. Besides, Bengal still had not recovered from the famine. And most important, a divided Bengal would have left the eastern part that went to Pakistan as an agricultural province and the western part that went to India as an industrial one, an outcome that would have done great damage to both. Unfortunately, the respite did not long endure.

Nor could it. Though Muslim, in some senses western Punjabis are more different from Muslim Bengalis than the latter are from Hindu Bengalis. For West Pakistan is part of the land area of the Middle East, partly desert, and definitely a land of dryness and austere habits. In Bangladesh, Islam is nurtured in a tropical rain forest, a tropical gothic land. People are warmer blooded, friendlier, perhaps more village simple and trusting than are the more sophisticated westerners. And while in the West martial virtues are admired and cultivated, in the East people are not martial and, if cultivated, they are Brahmo in style, Bloomsbury not Sandhurst.

The first major blunder in relations between the two wings occurred when Mohammed Ali Jinnah, Pakistan's first governor-general, went to Dhaka to announce that Urdu, a Moghul Empire language, part Hindi, part Persian, really an army language, would be Pakistan's official tongue. Jinnah thought this to be fair, since no Pakistani province spoke Urdu (the local languages were Punjabi, Sindhi, Baluch, and Pushto), and since turn-of-the-century Bengal had had a popular movement that sought to have Urdu taught in the schools, while that era's Muslims had thought literary Bangla to be a "Hindu" language. Jinnah failed to understand several crucial things. First, East Bengal was not populated by ashraf people who spoke Urdu, Persian, or English or who had been educated abroad at Aligarh in Central India, among the upper crust of Calcutta, or in London. Second, in the intervening years, most educated East Bengalis had learned modern Bangla and had become heirs to the Hindu literary, British secular, and socialist movements that had begun in the nineteenth century. By 1948 East Bengalis schooled in the 1930s and 1940s felt closest to Tagore and Chatterjee, to the secular politics of de Rozio, Bose, and M. N. Roy, or even to the British-influenced intellectual life of Calcutta, though that life might have been filtered through Dhaka University. Furthermore, many East Bengal intellectuals, Hindu and Muslim, had been educated at Calcutta University or Dhaka University, not at Aligarh, so that they had a different cultural perspective. They had absorbed the nationalism of the Bangla language and literary movement without the Hinduism, though they had been influenced by great draughts of Tagorean, Brahmo, and British liberal humanism. Third, after the first flush of independence, East Bengalis had reverted politically to bread-and-butter issues, to wit, overcoming the Hindu landlords and moneylenders, most of whom had fled to Calcutta or were preparing to go. The East Bengalis wanted land reform, better credit, better wages, more education, urbanization, and health reform. In short, they yearned for modernity. And they desperately wanted to overcome the degrading poverty of the 1943 famine.

Like Jinnah, the ruling hands of the Muslim League—Fazlul Qader Chowdhury of Chittagong, Nawab Ali of Bogra, Khanja Nazimuddin of Dhaka, Hassan Ispahani, and the upper ashraf—simply did not grasp that

Bengal's Independent Muslim League represented not the ashraf but workers and peasants, people of the political left, though not in a Marxist sense. Indeed, of all the Muslim Leaguers, only Chowdhury deliberately worked his constituency and has left a legacy that endures. The other Muslim Leaguers never really had a stake in the society.

The majority of Huq's followers wanted change and an answer to their grievances. Jinnah understood none of this. So when he announced that Urdu would be Pakistan's official language, he unwittingly set off forces that would end, twenty-four years later, in an independent Bangladesh. For the language issue, with its atavistic appeal to Bengali tribalism, to the deepest wellsprings of Bengali emotion, unleashed an incredible desire for social change, especially among the newly educated strata, a desire that ultimately boded ill for the ashraf and for the remaining Hindu landlords. In short, the lavalike force that Bose had unleashed against the British now came to the fore in Pakistan.

In 1950 a law was passed that provided for expropriation of zamindari estates and an end to their rule. Though the law promised compensation and did not go into effect until 1956, its passage led to communal tensions and sometimes to jacqueries that forced Hindu landlords from the land, so that in 1952 and 1953 many Hindus fled East Bengal. (The remains of the zamindaris, often abandoned, still exist, now held by the Bangladesh government as alien property.) While this law and the Hindu exodus did take pressure off the Pakistani government for awhile, it ignited another problem. For the agitation made both the West Pakistanis and the Bengali ashraf wary of Bengali nationalism, as it often was expressed in radical and/or Marxist language.

To counter the threat of rising Bengali nationalism, the West Pakistanis and their ashraf allies began using a Muslim minority, much as the British had used Bengali Hindus against Muslims. Called Biharis, this group, which was to suffer severely in the future, had left caste-conscious India for East Pakistan because the latter promised to be a homeland for all Muslims. Up to half a million Biharis, most of them educated, middle-class, and speaking Urdu, Hindi, or some related language, had emigrated. Not Bangla-speaking sons of the soil but possessing skills and needing work, they became, like the Cossacks of Russia during the tsars' time, a sort of "state people," as Hannah Arendt uses the term: they were loyal to the Pakistan government, nonradical, and supportive of the status quo. From the government's viewpoint, the Biharis were an asset, for they related better to the ashraf and the West Pakistanis than did the Bengali masses. As might be expected, their status and allegiance to the Pakistanis, especially during the Liberation War, hardly endeared them to East Bengal's majority. When Bangladesh became free, the Biharis were to suffer greatly. (Even today, large numbers of Biharis live in squalid refugee camps in both Bangladesh and Pakistan, unwanted by the former, unwelcome in the latter. Their plight is a disgrace to the honor of both nations, but particularly to Bangladesh for blaming all Biharis for crimes committed by a few.) Finally, Pakistan as a single state could not long endure because it never really was democratic: its system was unresponsive to local interests, local needs.

Thus all these factors—a tremendous desire for social change, a hunger for national identity, and resentment against the Pakistani Government and the Biharis—rumbled beneath the surface of East Pakistan. Meanwhile, the central government, more than a thousand miles away, across India, failed to sense the depth of the unrest. The outcome was inevitable. A new political movement had to emerge.

Not surprisingly, the impetus for this new movement came from Suhrawardy and Huq, who formed a political party, the Awami Muslim League. They soon dropped the word *Muslim*, as there was a large, restless Hindu minority, representing more than 20 percent of the populace, that might support a secular party whose platform called for social change, socialism, and democracy. As it turned out, Suhrawardy had learned a great deal during his post-1947 sojourn in India with Gandhi. For the new Awami League, patterned after Nehru's Congress Party, was able to unite Muslim and Hindu, peasant and worker (including Marxist minions who had come to India in the 1920s and had spread throughout the subcontinent), and even some of the wealthy old landlord families that once had supported secular politics in the Congress Party and had sided with Hindus during the 1905–12 era. Moreover, Suhrawardy was able to count on scores of Calcutta-educated lawyers and professors who sympathized with Western liberalism in the social-democratic, English Labor Party mold and had migrated to Dhaka. Finally, he was able to appeal to the Brahmo mind, whose outlook, fueled by the poems of Tagore and Kazi Nazrul Islam, so colored upper-class Dhaka and Calcutta thinking. In 1955 this coalition-turned-party became the majority party in East Pakistan and thereby was able to have Suhrawardy made prime minister of Pakistan, as East Pakistan held most of the seats in Parliament.

Suhrawardy's tenure lasted only a few months, not long enough for him to make major changes. A restive Pakistani military, preparing for a coup, forced him to stand down, replacing him with another Bengali, Mohammad Ali of Bogra, an ashraf Muslim Leaguer with little popular support even in the East. In 1958 the Pakistani military, under Ayub Khan, finally took power. Soon Suhrawardy was jailed and political activities in East Pakistan were curtailed. The ouster and imprisonment of Suhrawardy, who had been chosen in a free election as head of the parliamentary majority party, caused a major breakdown of faith in the system. It was a watershed never to be overcome, a harbinger of the mutual dislike and fear that henceforth was to characterize relations between Pakistan's two parts. Suhrawardy's party, the secular, nationalist, socialist, and democratic Awami League, the successor to the Krishak-Sramik movement of the 1930s, would remain the only party of note in East Pakistan. Indeed, by the early 1960s a Catholic priest wrote to his brother in the United States that he believed that East Pakistan would become independent by 1970.

The deaths of Suhrawardy and Huq in the early 1960s brought an end to a generation that had steered the country out of British colonialism into union with Pakistan. Moreover, until his dying day Suhrawardy had fought to keep Pakistan from disintegrating. Such efforts ended with his passing. A new generation of leaders had been emerging—educated in Calcutta and Dhaka, radical-to-socialist in politics, and militantly, rather than passively, secular. These leaders began seeking to identify with the Soviet Union or China at best, or at least with the more militant socialism of the British Commonwealth. Given such predilections, they were to forge deep links to India, especially to the secular, socialist India of Nehru.

The Anti-Pakistan Rebellion

The generation that had grown up during the uprising against the British had deep links all over Bengal, both Hindu and Muslim. These were the people who had been nourished by Bose, fed by the idealism of Roy and the Anushilan and Jaguntar secret societies, and influenced by the terrorism of the 1930s and by the Quit India and pro-Japanese feelings of the war years. Most of all, they were the ones who would fasten on the language issue as a means of distinguishing between East and West Pakistan, an issue that appealed to Hindu and Muslim alike, an issue that would create—and still creates—a xenophobic view of the world. For no language movement is, can be, or ever has been international in outlook. The two simply cannot coexist.

Out of this generation were to arise two major leaders: Sheikh Mujibur Rahman and Maulana Bhasani. Unquestionably, Mujib was the greater politician and organizer, but Bhasani gave the movement a visceral, radical nationalism without which it might have perished. For Bhasani, with his simple, almost Gandhian ways, was the movement's ground-level operator, someone capable of energizing the diverse elements of the Awami League. Moreover, Bhasani, whose National Awami Party contained pro-Soviet and pro-Chinese wings, never forgot that he represented Bengal and Purbodesh rather than any foreign power. He also helped found *Ittefaq* and *Dainik Sangbad*, leading newspapers that remain important; and through his Gandhi-like travels, he was able to reach the masses. That there was about him a hint of the virtuous huckster, combined with a Gandhian humility, does not detract from the crucial role he played in the independence movement. One observer, a British diplomat, describes Bhasani as the only real political leader Bangladesh ever developed.

From the passing of Suhrawardy until his own death, however, the man
of the era of the rising against Pakistan undoubtedly was Sheikh Mujib, the
heir to Huq, Suhrawardy, and Hashem. From Huq, Mujib took not only the
party organization and contacts but also remembrance that the 1940 Pakistan Resolution had called for two Muslim states. From Suhrawardy he inherited a sense of secular and socialist politics. To these he added a strong
sense of grievance against the Pakistanis that gave an almost Marxist tinge to
his nationalism. And from his own past he took a record of anti-British
activity, including imprisonment, and a host of links with friends in Calcutta. Emotionally—and unconsciously, for he was not a rigorous intellectual—Mujib sometimes seemed to be a Bengali rather than a Bangladeshi
nationalist, as the latter ultimately came to mean Muslim Bengal alone.
Moreover, he represented a nationalist, socialist, and secularist tradition that
traced back to Bose. He disliked Bengal's Muslim League ashraf and only
admitted into his confidence those ashraf who were Brahmo in outlook and
who had the upper-class pretensions of the Calcutta cognoscenti: in short,
the Anglicized intellectuals who surrounded him.

Nevertheless, from the outset, wittingly or unwittingly, Mujib served
East Pakistan's independence cause. Not an intellectual, he never believed in
a united Pakistan as did Suhrawardy, though at first he sounded as though
he favored a united Bengal. Whatever his beliefs, it was his personality that
made him the pivotal figure of his era. He represented an elemental force, a
comet in politics. Never was he considered to be particularly intelligent or a
statesman. On the contrary, he represented all forms of mercurial and emotional politics that bordered on, but for years never crossed into, the realm of
demagogy. He was a man of the spoken, not the written, word, of remembered faces and names, of slogans and well-phrased complaints designed to
play to East Bengal's merchant middle class and moneylenders, many of
them Hindu. Basically he was an intuitive force, one whose personality and
action inspired the pit of the Bangladesh mind. His desire for independence
radiated as much from the people as it did from his own intellectual outlook.
He proved to be a vessel through which the people's desires were to flow.

Mujib also understood the underside of politics and did not distinguish
between good and evil; what worked was all that mattered. Thus he is
remembered for using East Bengal's near-criminal underground to coerce
and blackmail. It seemed that all the *gomastahs*, or illegal enforcers, who had
lost jobs when the zamindari estates were broken up, made themselves
available to the Awami League, which was in opposition to the government.
The Sheikh and his compatriots used the gomastahs well—to enforce general strikes, to intimidate enemies, to silence critics. By thus infusing the
independence movement with a sense of power and ruthlessness, Mujib
introduced into politics a new class, one of tawdry and doubtful social value,
one that still remains active in the economy and in the darker side of the

political spectrum. At the same time, in defense of the Sheikh is the fact that this use of mafia power arose not from any duplicitous Machiavellian side to his character but from his simple and single-minded devotion to his cause. He never dreamed that one day this force would threaten to undo what he hoped to create.

Gaining control of the Awami League only after Suhrawardy's death, Mujib from the start added a new dimension to the party. It was a strident nationalism grounded in Bengali culture, a movement not unlike the Hindu-led Bengali revival of 1905, which had been based on submersion of Hindu-Muslim rivalry and harked back to the culture's pre-Aryan roots that scholars were then researching. By so doing, Mujib played up both the differences between Bengalis and West Pakistanis and the similarities between Muslim and Hindu Bengalis. Emphasizing secular rather than communal themes, he sang the praises of Bengal, as did the *Bande Mataram*, except that for references to Hindu goddesses he substituted Tagorean visions of Golden Bengal or Nazrulian visions of a better Bengal—visions that were inherent in the evocation of language, land, and blood. Long before the Liberation War, Mujib assumed for East Bengal the mantle of poor victims of Pakistani aggression, thereby giving Bengalis the moral exultation of being blameless.

A remarkable aspect of all this is that even before Mujib emerged as leader, the language debate was over, for Pakistan had accepted Bangla as an official language of the country. Recognizing this, Mujib inflamed another grievance: the perceived discrepancy in wealth between Pakistan's two wings, an issue akin to the one that had incited Huq's followers to pursue the politics of envy that had culminated in nationalization of the Hindu zamindaris.

Mujib also played up the superiority of Bengali culture compared to that of the military and martial Pakistani Punjabis. Thus, as we shall see, he counterposed Hindu and Muslim Bengali poetry to that of Mohammad Iqbal, the great poet of Pakistan who had been the inspiration for an independent Muslim state, while relying on the verses of son-of-the-soil Kazi Nazrul Islam. Mujib understood the aural and artistic quality of the rustic Bengali mind and the role of poetry in explicating moral positions. As Socrates long ago recognized, poets are really rhetoricians, politicians who appeal to emotive as well as reasoned positions.

On the one hand, then, Mujib emphasized the works of the unitarian, Brahmo Tagore, whose religion of humanity he compared to Iqbal's Muslim humanism. Tagore, of course, was (and remains) the only Bengali poet equal to Iqbal. But more to the point, Tagore was a Bengali native son and much beloved. Ultimately, so effective was Mujib's poet-tactic that the Pakistan government tried to ban as subversive the singing of Tagore's songs and the reading of his works, just as the British, in 1905–12, had banned the *Bande Mataram*. Of course, that is what had been intended. On the other hand,

Mujib and the Awami League wielded another literary sword in the campaign to inflame Bengali nationalism, anti-Pakistani grievances, and blood unity, and to enervate student activists: the poems, stirring marching songs, and personality of Kazi Nazrul, a secular and nationalist former British Army sergeant. So successful was this attempt that by the eve of the revolt Nazrul had become the poetic voice of the Awami League's rank-and-file.

It is enlightening to examine this battle of the poets, all of whom were British influenced but still could appeal to the very core of their people's feelings. For in a rustic society that is aural and artistic, poets and poetry can be a major means of political agitation. The reasons are that poems appeal to people who know how to listen, while the drama and acting out of long poems around a village cookfire, or *mela*, has an effect akin to that of radio and television in another world. We must remember that during the freedom struggle of India, Pakistan, and Bangladesh most people had no access to news as we know it. Instead, the traveling bard, reciting and acting out his own or others' verse or some combination thereof, often exercised over the minds and hearts of his village patrons a powerful force for change. Crucially, and of course in a different way, poetry also greatly influenced the more educated classes. Therefore, let us examine "the war of the poets."

One hesitates to stress this battle for fear of further politicizing some field of literature. It is worth taking the risk, however, since there runs through the history of Pakistan, West Bengal, Hindu-dominated Bengal, and Bangladesh the influence of three poets who gave a voice, vision, and sense of direction to vast numbers of people. Having previously discussed Tagore, it behooves us to examine Mohammad Iqbal and Kazi Nazrul Islam.

Iqbal created the word *Pakistan*, which meant "land of the pure," an acronym of the names of the provinces of Punjab, Baluchistan, and Sind, which are located in the Indus River valley area. A friend of Jinnah, Pakistan's founder, Iqbal was the first intellectual to call for a separate state, for partition of India. Were he just an intellectual, he would be only of passing interest. But he was a Cambridge-educated poet of unsurpassed brilliance whose works, unlike those of Tagore and Nazrul, can be enjoyed as much in translation as in Farsee or Urdu, the languages in which he wrote. Iqbal's poems are convincing and humanistic, embracing all of India, the homeland of Muslim and Hindu. Aware of the inspirational power of Islam (as opposed to that of secularism), Iqbal charted an intelligent world view, created at the highest levels of understanding and sensibility, a "Brahmo sensitivity." Representing the best of the subcontinent's intellectual outlook, he was a worthy opponent for Tagore, one who, taken in his state of grace, had much in common with his Hindu brother poet. It is one of the tragedies of history that Iqbal died in the late 1930s, thus robbing the world of the one

Muslim intellectual who might have reached across the communal divide to Gandhi, Nehru, and Tagore to heal the breach.

Iqbal was important because his poems had the unusual ability of speaking for the Pakistani government, for East Bengal's ashraf, and for the Bihari "state people." Reading him in Farsee or Urdu, these groups revered him. His poems appealed to all these people—rich and poor, urban and rural—who thought in terms of dignity and wisdom. Recitations of his works normally were part of all their cultural activities in the 1950s and 1960s, and during the partition movement his verse was very influential. In East Bengal, though his works had been translated and were taught in the schools, they never had resonance, because the patois of poetry there had developed differently, influenced as it was by the more romantic, gentle verses of Tagore and Lalan Shah.

Still, Iqbal and Tagore, the leading poets of Pakistan and India, of Muslims and Hindus, had much to say to and learn from one another had a situation arisen, as it had with Alberuni and his Hindu scholar friends so many centuries earlier. Yet their outlooks differed. For Iqbal had benefited from academic training at home and in England, while Tagore rarely had attended school but was at once genius, autodidact, and dilettante. Iqbal, a student of M'Taggert and the best English minds at Cambridge and, later, German minds at Heidelberg, brought to his work not only solid scholarship but also the manner of the High Table. Moreover, whereas Tagore's poetry appealed to the progressive Brahmo sensitivity of East Bengal, Iqbal enjoyed a more traditional appeal, having rejected both radical socialism and Western materialism. Finally, while Tagore took after Shelley in many ways, Iqbal resembled Dante.

Nevertheless, the two might well have changed the course of history, because hundreds of thousands, if not millions, of people knew their poetry by heart. According to an old British hand, in the 1930s it was impossible to travel from village to village in Bengal without hearing a Tagore song or rhyme. Similarly, as late as the early 1970s, this writer, visiting a Punjabi village near Lahore, heard the Dantesque *Javed Namah* of Iqbal read out to rapt villagers. It speaks well of the poets and their auditors that the cultural makeup of these countries is still aural rather than linear and written, and that poets have such deep influence because their listeners have such sensitive powers of imagination.

As for Nazrul, he was much younger than the other two, having been born in 1899, compared to Tagore's 1861 and Iqbal's 1877. Nazrul died only in 1976, and it can be said that he represents Bangladesh even more than did Tagore, in that the latter's influence seemed to be greatest among Bangladeshis who grew to maturity before partition, as was the case with Mujib and Suhrawardy, while Nazrul became influential after partition, when the anti-Pakistan movement was emerging. He ranks, therefore, as the National

Poet of Bangladesh among the youthful leaders of the freedom struggle. As much as any work of art, his poem calling upon students to rebel led to the politicization of the universities that has had such a detrimental effect on Bangladeshi education. In many ways, though he would have been mortified to admit it had he known of it, his poetry appealed to the youth of Bangladesh's politically disturbed universities and thereby, by their antinomianism, to the tawdry Hollywood values of the post-liberation new class.

Let us now turn to the political realities that influenced the paths of the three great poets. First Tagore. Having grown to maturity before the initial battle over Bengal partition, he soared to his most creative heights in that era and elevated the campaign from a crass political action to a major intellectual event. His ability to do so sustained the movement even after he broke with its terrorist aspects and helped convince the more reasonable representatives of British rule that Bengal should not be divided. Like many of his time, he sought to establish the dignity and capability of his people vis-à-vis Britain and the West, and to create an India that would avoid the West's modernization-related mistakes, as he understood them. As it turned out, while his most intense appeal was first to Bengali Hindus and second to Bengali Muslims, because he saw himself representing all Bengalis, Tagore found himself speaking for all of India. For, analogously, Bengali aspirations were seen to reflect those of the entire subcontinent. Tagore's influence, even among the British, though to a far lesser degree of course, arose from the fact that he strove to rise above the politics of the moment and to avoid indulging in communal battles. Thus he deplored the politicization of education and differed with Nazrul over criticism of Western education. He never wrote a seriously communal piece but sought to hark back to the pre-Aryan, pre-Muslim Brahmo and Bengali mind. Consequently, he is neither a Hindu nor a Muslim poet, though he is a Brahmo one in the religious sense as well as in terms of sensibility.

Turning to Iqbal, like Tagore, he sought to express the dignity of all Indian people as well as their ability to govern themselves; but he also was concerned with the welfare of his Muslim brethren. In an India not riven by British-agitated communal divisions, Iqbal might not have come to be viewed as a "Muslim" poet, for he set out to write great poetry, not to engage in communal politics. His direction changed when he realized that owing to the languages he used—Farsee and Urdu, which were not spoken throughout India—he had a relatively small audience, mainly in West Pakistan. To reach out, he turned to essay writing and politics. Ultimately he found himself drawn increasingly into and identified with the Pakistan nationalist struggle.

As for Nazrul, he both represented a much younger generation and held different world views from those of his fellow poets. Like Tagore he was an autodidact, but unlike him he was not a dilettante, although he was profligate in practical affairs and philosophically undisciplined. For Nazrul devoted his life to poetry. He did not have grander aims, such as trying to found a university or to reshape society, except through his poetry and songs. Yet he was a radical, but one who expressed his views only in an outpouring of verse and song that far surpassed in volume that of Tagore or Iqbal.

Born at the turn of the century, Nazrul enlisted as a soldier in the Forty-Ninth Bengal Regiment and served during World War I in Karachi. He learned Urdu, Persian, and English and wrote well in all three. He was thrust into prominence with the publication of one poem, which, coming as it did in the midst of Gandhi's first noncooperation campaign, appealed to the mood of the time, one destined to reappear during the movements against Britain and then Pakistan. Appearing at a time when the anarchist doctrines of the Calcutta intellectual Roy had currency, the poem, *Rebel*, is a howl of outrage that expresses the frustration felt in Calcutta in the 1920s against British rule. Powerful because it reflects Nazrul's experiences as a poor boy who subsequently traveled throughout Bengal and saw its people's sufferings, it shows the near nihilistic sense of rebellion of which Nazrul was capable. A friend of the Marxist leader Muzzafar Ahmad, Nazrul was sympathetic to Marxist goals, but was a believing Muslim. *Rebel* was an instant success. Reprinted immediately in larger press runs, it became the mood piece among university students who, forty years later, in 1960, were to lead the Bangladesh independence movement. For Nazrul's poem broke the chains of liberalism and opened up a near nihilistic vision of libertarian violence.

> Proclaim Hero, Proclaim
> Towering high is my head. . . .
> I am invincible, insolent and cruel for ever.
> I am the dancing demon on the day of doom,
> I am the cyclone; I am destruction.
> I am the terrible terror, the curse of the earth.
> I am to be stopped by none.
> I tear all things to tatters.
> I am indiscipline, I am chaos.
> I trample down all fetters, all rules and regulations.
> I acknowledge no law whatsoever. . . .
> I am the Rebel, the rebellious son of the Lord of the universe. . . .
> I am the Hero in revolt forever!
> I have risen beyond the universe, alone,
> With my head ever held high! . . .

(Trans. Mizanur Rahman, 1966)

Also important was Nazrul's *On the Song of Students*. Put to music as a march, it was sung by Dhaka students from the 1920s on. It begins:

> We are the strength, we are the force
> The Band of Students that We Are! . . .
> Under the pitch dark night, we stir out
> Barefooted across the road
> With obstacles strewn. The soil stiff
> We render red with our crimson blood
> Caused by our going strong and fast.
> It's our blood that soaks, from age to age
> The soil of this our earth.
> The Band of Students that We Are! . . .

(Trans. Mizanur Rahman, 1966)

These works, imbued with revolutionary fervor, have a bloodthirsty aspect that can be viewed as immature or simply as reflective of the times. But while these were Nazrul's bloodiest verses, others reflect his love of the countryside, his sense of economic injustice by moneylenders and zamindars, and his desire for a Muslim society. Over the twenty or so years that he was productive, Nazrul wrote thousands of poems and more than three thousand songs, many of them recorded by His Master's Voice record company. Many of his poems speak of love, while many lament tragedy. Crucially, though his outlook was Muslim, he was not a communal poet in the sense of hating Hindus. His wife and many of his friends were Hindu, and he always depicted Islam in the most humanistic, tolerant terms. In fact, Tagore dedicated a play to him, though the two fell out over Nazrul's approach to violence and his criticism of education.

His own life was a challenge. Having failed to finish school before joining the army, he found it hard to support himself. While he did work as an editor for newspapers and for his own publications, he quickly spent what little he earned. His poem *On Poverty* is a moving ode to the difficulties of being penniless, for unlike Tagore he inherited nothing. For several years, while recording his songs in Calcutta, he had money, but he spent it improvidently. His beloved son, Bulbul, died of smallpox and his devoted wife became paralyzed at about the time money began running out. In 1943 he entered a torpor, a catatonic state, in which he remained until his death in 1976.

What is important about Nazrul is his genius, his common touch, and his vigorous style. Even in translation there is about his verse a strength of expression that reaches across language barriers, a strength that even translations of Tagore cannot match. But Nazrul lacked Iqbal's constancy of philosophic approach and Tagore's majesty of universal outlook. Yet his poetry endures. For he created it in a way that reached the maximum number of people, so that by the mid-1960s Nazrul's popularity equaled that of Tagore among Bengali youth. It was his songs that they sang, his marches that they marched to, his verse and song in the *jatras* that they staged. It was Nazrul's verse that the traveling minstrels and bards read. His appeal reached across educational boundaries, for he expressed what was in the people's hearts. That is why his works were so important to the politics of Sheikh Mujib. The revolt against Pakistan had to do with culture: the immediate culture of Bangladesh and the distant culture of the Pakistanis. What Nazrul brought to the fray was a Bangladeshi language and a true son-of-the-soil and Muslim voice to counteract the fact that, after all, Tagore was dead and, besides, he had been a man of Calcutta, West Bengal, and India. Nazrul spoke only for Bangladesh. Ultimately Nazrul's role was to destroy Iqbal's legacy in Bengal by counterposing a Bangladeshi voice that drowned him out. Remarkably, Nazrul himself was a native of and lived in Hindu-dominated West Bengal and Calcutta, while Tagore spent more time in what is now Bangladesh. And ironically, owing to the illness that destroyed nearly half his life, Nazrul never knew Pakistan or the Bangladesh liberation movement. He never knew he would be named the National Poet of Bangladesh.

It is important to understand that Nazrul neither stooped to petty politics nor played to the chauvinistic gallery. Those are not the poet's roles, as Iqbal and Tagore understood. Rather, the poet's genius is to give voice to the people's values, to appeal to their higher instincts, not as they are but as they strive to be. When a poet thus succeeds, he elevates the discussion and makes his hearers wiser and more hopeful and generous. He also makes them brave and imparts a sense of mission. Tagore did this for one generation, and Sheikh Mujib quoted him often. However, for the Sheikh's followers, the poet laureate was Nazrul.

Having examined the poets' role from their own standpoint, one must note that politicians view them differently. Poets must be politicized because the masses love and identify with them and want their politicians to have similar ideals and wisdom. Thus in a nation like India, Pakistan, or Bangladesh, poets are crucial to politics.

By the 1960s in East Bengal, the works of Tagore, Nazrul, and a balladeer named Jasmiuddin, who reached out to villagers, comprised the literary foundations of the liberation movement. Tagore, whose centenary was celebrated in the 1960s, undoubtedly appealed to the best educated, to those of Brahmo sensibilities, and to progressives. Nazrul was favored by students, young rebels, teachers, and the near-educated. Jasmiuddin spoke for the peasants. Meanwhile, in the villages, countless unheralded local bards wrote poems of love, nature, and revolt. Together, all these verses voiced the aspirations, the yearnings, and the beliefs of what was to become a new nation. For, as Rafiuddin Ahmed, a Bangladeshi historian, explains, Bangladesh never believes anything until there is a poet to articulate it.

Thus it was this cultural war of Bengali versus Pakistani poets that both elevated the freedom struggle and was a handy tool as Sheikh Mujib led the liberation movement. For the Sheikh had an ear for the war of the poets, an empathetic sense of its rhythm and meaning.

Let us return now to the Sheikh, who was destined to suffer, as do all leaders of such movements. Through the 1960s he was jailed repeatedly by the Pakistanis because, clearly, he was subversive and spoke for the masses in a way Suhrawardy and Huq had not. Mujib voiced the grievances of the people, especially the urbanized and semiurbanized middle and lower middle classes that were the backbone of the Awami League. Educated in modern not Mussalmani Bangla and scornful of the peasants' Mussalmani linguistics, this emerging middle class embraced the totality of the Bengali renewal on the very terms the Calcutta Hindu elite had used against the British in 1905–12, something their grandparents had refused to do. In fact, this generation was to choose as Bangladesh's national anthem Tagore's 1908 poem written to protest Bengal's division.

Herein lies the nub of the liberation struggle. For the Muslim intellectuals of the 1960s grasped the threads and embroidered upon what the Hindu intellectuals had begun six decades earlier. And ironically, when Bengali nationalism finally flowered, it did so in Muslim, not Hindu, Bengal. For Hindu Bengal had become a small Indian state, while Bangladesh was poised to emerge as an independent Bengali nation—*the* Bengali nation.

Meanwhile the Sheikh, who had grown to political maturity in the age of Bose, unconsciously preached the doctrine of that great Bengali's nationalism. The two differed only in that Bose always was an aristocrat, whereas Mujib spoke the language of the people. Still, both appealed to the deeper wells of Bengali nationalism that go beyond communalism to a sense of brotherhood in race, tribe, and language. Thus it was that Hindus and Muslims worked together in the Awami League under the guise of secularism and socialism, but more deeply as blood brothers.

Mujib's Awami League differed from the Congress Party model Suhrawardy had created. For the Sheikh the party became more like the Bengal party under Bose's leadership, whereas under Suhrawardy it had imitated the more open, generous party of Nehru. Thus Nehru and Bose represented two strands in the Bengal politics of the 1930s, while Surhawardy and Mujib represented those same strains in the 1950s and 1960s in East Pakistan.

What is remarkable about the rise of Bengali nationalism is that Muslim feeling declined and Islam ultimately was put on the defensive. This change had been implicit in the founding of the Awami League, a party that, while never anti-Muslim, had not countenanced communalism. However, after the much-agitated Prophet's hair riots of 1964, the Muslim leadership lost its ability to generate mass support. For the upper-class ashraf had lost touch with the masses. Worse, the ashraf also had lost touch with the mosques. For the Pakistani Muslim League was communal only in a political sense, not in a religious one. The major Pakistani leaders, Jinnah, Hassan Ispahani, Ayub Khan, and Yaha Khan, while personally religious in their own way, were humanistic aristocrats. Like Suhrawardy, they saw nothing wrong with having a drink, missing prayers, or living the most modern of lives. Consequently, when the secular challenge emerged, more so under Mujib, the successors of the first generation of Muslim Leaguers were willing to secretly subsidize Maulana Bhasani or leaders of other leftist splinter groups in an attempt to undermine the opposition's political unity. Seldom did they dream of offering leadership to the peasant believer or of exerting themselves to save Islam. Indeed, because he remained loyal to Pakistan, the only Muslim Leaguer to keep his links to the masses, Fazlul Qader Chowdhury, was to die miserably in an Awami League jail, where the Brahmo mind never seemed to find abuses. Indeed, the old Muslim Leaguers feared the Jamaat-e-Islam more than they feared the secular parties, for the Jamaat is a puritanical party. And thanks to their own cynical uses of religion, they could not hope to have the mass base that Mujib worked so hard to generate. The Muslim Leaguers, Anglified and Westernized, felt more at home in London than in Dhaka or Chittagong, in airplanes than in country boats. Likewise, they never tried to work for votes; they only bought them.

As for the Sheikh, hard work shaped his style. Indefatigable, he visited district and subdistrict towns, walked across fields from village to village, and mingled with the people, sharing their tea, rice, dhal, and salt, remembering names, praying at mosques, sweating in fields, visiting flood sites, weeping at funerals and *milads*, services for the dead. Intellectually lazy, he empathized mightily, intuited sympathetically, and reached out and touched—not golf clubs and club chairs but the people's sweaty and grimy hands. By ever returning to the hustings, he imbibed the people's feelings and aspirations, so that when away from them he could gauge with superhuman accuracy their reactions to events. He knew what they believed because he could explain things not only in terms they could understand but in ones they respected. Knowing that, they believed he did not need to lie. They spoke to him honestly, as he spoke to them.

Mujib also brought an immediacy to the political environment. He never tired the people with sophisticated ploys or half-measures. He had no love of office, even though he had held provincial portfolios under Suhrawardy. While he never said so on the record, from the time he emerged until the Pakistanis arrested him on the day the Liberation War began, everyone knew he spoke for independence. Unlike Suhrawardy, who wanted reform within Pakistan, the Sheikh sought independence; and, though he never voiced his desire, this gave his movement more than a hint of danger and excitement, an aura of greatness. By not proclaiming his end, he scared the Pakistanis, without giving them cause to remove or jail him. Never was the government able to gain the moral upper hand. And all the while, Mujib could wink and smile and speak of Bengal, and of Bangladesh, as though it were free to rejoice in green-and-red flags fluttering on rooftops.

Lastly, Sheikh Mujib was able to organize or to get others to do so for him. Neither a manager nor an administrator, he motivated students to stage plays in villages in order to carry the Awami League message. He got economists to study Pakistani policy, seeking evidence of hypocrisy or outright prejudice against the East. He convinced lawyers to find grievances or ways to embarrass the government. He motivated women to demand modern rights that orthodox West Pakistanis found offensive. He motivated dancers to find old folk dances and perform them to the accompaniment of flute and drum. He had poets declaim in pure Bangla and farmers sing songs they never had sung. He promised workers the "glories" of socialism and enlisted them in his cause. To the Brahmo-minded, he crooned the nicey-nice patter of Tagorean humanism and won their salons to his side. Achieving this burst of enthusiasm in the British sense that refers to mass movements, the Sheikh seemed to be a model of moderation, despite the somewhat hysterical background sounds his movement emitted.

Obviously, such a movement was destined to grow. And once it did, the act had to be carried to a conclusion. The more the movement caught on, the more the government sought to repress it. Yet with each round of repression, usually heavy-handed rather than violent, the movement grew stronger. Even when Mujib was arrested for allegedly conspiring with India, something everyone feared he might have done, and the country held its collective breath, even when the moment passed safely, the movement gained momentum. No compromise the Pakistanis offered, no reform, no packages of mutual concessions, could appease such a movement. Recognizing this, the government did not try very hard.

But the movement needed a conclusion, and the government provided it. In 1970 it called an election. The Awami League won, emerging as the largest party in all Pakistan. Now the Sheikh could be prime minister. Instead, he remained adamant, maintaining that the six points he had presented had to be honored. As a whole, these six points amounted to autonomy, to independence. The government then made a drastic blunder. It both refused to grant these six points and delayed calling Parliament into session. Had at least the latter occurred, Mujib might have compromised, for then he would have become prime minister of a united Pakistan, and who can tell how he would have acted in office. Instead, in March 1971 the climax came. On March 8 the Sheikh all but called for independence at a speech at the racetrack in Dhaka. The result was a vast outpouring of enthusiasm which, among other things, saw students begin to fashion both weapons and a green-and-red national flag that soon fluttered on rooftoops throughout East

Pakistan. In this atmosphere of enthusiasm, much hostility erupted: Pakistani soldiers were scorned or beaten, angry words were exchanged, tempers flared. Finally, at midnight on March 26, the dam broke. The Sheikh was arrested, just after telling reporters that an agreement was near.

Almost simultaneously, tanks appeared at Dhaka University and fired into the halls, killing students, mostly Hindu; for Hindus were blamed for the rebellion. Then the Pakistanis started shelling Hindu neighborhoods; thousands died. Throughout that night (and over ensuing months), the Pakistanis searched for intellectuals, business leaders, and others thought to be subversive. One by one they were arrested, packed off to a killing field near Savar outside Dhaka, and there were shot dead, in cold blood. (Years later, General Tikka Khan, who initially had been in command, admitted to murdering "only" thirty-five-thousand people.) The next night, March 27, in Chittagong, a young Bangladeshi Army major, Zia Rahman, rallied his troops and seized the radio station to proclaim, in Sheikh Mujib's name, the independence that all along had been the movement's goal.

From March to December 1971, life in East Pakistan virtually halted. The mere appearance of a Jeep or any other modern vehicle in the countryside sent people into hiding. The Pakistanis took their search for subversives to every village, murdering, nearly on sight, all Hindus. Any man captured was forced to lift his lungi or dhoti so the soldiers could see if he was circumsised; if not, he was dead. In the villages, soldiers also shot anyone even suspected of supporting the Awami League or the Freedom Fighters, as well as anyone the local loyalists accused of helping Pakistan's enemies. Thus many died simply because they were the personal enemies of these local loyalists—pro-Pakistanis who, after liberation, were called by the derogatory term *razakar*, after the armed force the Pakistan Army created to do its policing during the war.

In all, ten million of East Bengal's seventy million people fled to India. Most were Hindus or professionals associated with the Awami League. Most never returned, thus permanently and appreciably reducing the ranks of the Hindu minority.

Meanwhile, a government-in-exile was formed in India, led by Tajuddin Ahmed, Mujib's chief party assistant who served in his stead, while Mujib lived in fear in a Pakistani prison. As for Tajuddin, he did much to cement ties with and to enlist India's help, and to organize the Freedom Fighters, including the Z Force under Major Zia Rahman. Hesitantly at first, but later more confidently, the Freedom Fighters began attacking Pakistani forces. And while they failed even to shake their enemy's hold on East Bengal, they undermined Pakistani rule and gave courage to their compatriots, who had been left behind and who began destroying bridges and roads that were essential to the Pakistanis.

It is worth noting here that the complete story of the Liberation War has not been told. It never was a single war controlled by one command. Instead it was fought, often ineffectively, by small groups that merely harassed the Pakistanis and, heroically and more effectively, by anonymous groups that blasted bridges or cut power supplies, as when Dhaka's electricity went out. As is typical in such situations, only a small number fought. But many were active, and most Bangladeshis supported the rebels despite their ties with India. The connection between the rebels and the Indian government and the Hindus' role in the Awami League always detracted from the rebels' appeal. However, in the heat of war the deep feeling of the tribe prevailed, while appeals to secularism and socialism were less effective.

Finally, in December 1971, the Indian Army entered Bangladesh. After a few firefights, including one major battle at Jessore, the Indians quickly subdued the Pakistanis, who had become dissolute as they murdered scores of innocent people and raped local women. Indeed, the Pakistanis' behavior forever will be an infamous example of an army that bullied, raped, and murdered—then broke, ran, and surrendered in the face of the first organized resitance it faced. Thus ended East Pakistan. Thus was born Bangladesh.

No one knows how many died; the estimates have varied from 300,000 to three million, though the true number is now believed to be less than a million. Such a number, in the context of twentieth-century horrors, is not massive. But when one recalls that many were executed solely as suspected subversives, many for being Hindus, students, or intellectuals, and others for resisting rape, the extent of the slaughter is sickening. Think of it: most victims died seeing their murderers face to face, watching the lust and hate in the eyes of the man with the gun, a man who, though in uniform, no longer was a soldier but a madman. In this sense the slaughter has an incredibly ugly aspect, especially since the murderers never were punished. Today they live in West Pakistan—as heroes. For instance, General Tikka Khan, who was responsible for the arrest and murder of the thirty-five thousand intellectuals, lived in comfort as the "grand old man" of the Pakistan Army and governor general of Punjab Province in 1989–90.

The story of the Independence War came full circle in January 1972 when the Sheikh returned to Dhaka from harrowing captivity in Pakistan, where at any moment he had expected to be executed, to the delirious cheers of his countrymen. On January 10 he proclaimed Sonar Bangla, Golden Bengal, to be free. And linking his own movement to one that had begun sixty years earlier, he quoted Tagore's poem of 1911. That was Mujib's greatest day, the culmination of a life dedicated to independence, the day when the events of 1905–12 became true for Muslim Bengal. As the Sheikh quoted Tagore's Golden Bengal, the crowd sang.

> My Bengal of gold, I love you
> Forever your skies, your air set my heart in tune

As if it were a flute.
In spring, oh mother mine, the fragrance from
Your mango groves makes me wild with joy—
Ah what thrill.
In autumn, oh mother mine
In the full-blossomed paddy fields,
I have seen spread all over—sweet smiles!
Ah, What a beauty, what shades, what an affection
And what a tenderness.
What a quilt you have spread at the feet of
Banyan trees and along the banks of rivers!
Oh mother mine, words from your lips are like
Nectar to my ears!
Ah, what a thrill
If sadness, oh mother mine, cast a gloom on your face,
My eyes well up with tears. . . .

(Theme from Lalan Shah; words by Tagore; source: Bangladesh Embassy, Washington, D.C.)

After that victorious moment, the hysteria that always had surrounded Mujib and had led him to succeed soon changed, and a mere forty months later resulted in his murder. For when he assumed power, the intellectual laziness that had characterized his life became his Achilles' heel. He was unable to govern; he was not a statesman; he did not understand finance, aid, trade, foreign relations, law, ideology, or history, particularly history in the twentieth century, and especially in the USSR and China. He did not understand the U.N., the IMF, the World Bank, or GATT. Nor had he lived in Bangladesh throughout the war, a war that had changed his country, while he had not changed. No longer did he understand his people; no longer did they comprehend him. The toughs he had used to run demonstrations and *hartals* (strikes) no longer needed him and did not obey. They had become a law unto themselves, often only masquerading as Freedom Fighters. They had found the Intercontinental Hotel's Saqi Bar and the corruption of aid sent from around the world. All his charisma could not help Mujib. Hubris had struck, although he did not understand the meaning of the word.

The Sheikh's administration made every possible mistake. Thanks to his ideologically incompetent advisers, he nearly bankrupted the nation. Still worse, he almost permitted a famine that rivaled that of 1943. He antagonized the army by hiring a private army of his own and the civil service by bypassing it; he allowed some of the insiders of the Awami Party to divvy up the aid sent by a generous world and even permitted the donated goods to be sold to India—goods this author and many others saw for sale in Calcutta's wholesale markets—so that his cronies could benefit, cronies who included Mustafa, head of the Red Cross; his own son, Kamal; and Kamal's friend Manju. Even provincial and subdistrict party officers stole large quantities of the aid.

Worse, the Sheikh surrounded himself with incompetents who, while better educated, were just as intellectually lazy. The socialist theories of the Planning Commission economists dissipated the country's foreign exchange, because they pursued policies that led to a massive flight of capital and scared off foreign investment. The Planning Commission and the Foreign Ministry forged links with the bankrupt economies of the Soviet Union, China, and Eastern Europe while shunning World Bank aid. Indeed, the Planning Commission deliberately urged that the World Bank president be snubbed when he visited, thereby keeping Western aid to a minimum. There were nationalizations, which led to huge inefficiencies and destroyed the nation's industrial base, and a grandiose national trading corporation and a huge tool factory that has not yet earned the first payment on its debt. Moreover, there were political leaders who gave the Sheikh bad advice in foreign relations or in law, who, for instance, allowed him to impose arrest and detention laws that were stiffer than those the Pakistanis had used and to promulgate decrees that were more Draconian. And there were Mujib's links to the underground as well as to a new atmosphere of violence he did not understand, one which made murders of his enemies commonplace. He even helped precipitate his own death by plotting with assassins, for one of them, a man named Dalal, later helped kill him. He came to be seen as a puppet of India, thereby arousing old fears of caste Hinduism. And lastly, an air of anarchy hung about the country throughout his years in office.

Given such a political, economic, and social climate, by the time he died Sheikh Mujib, quite unintentionally and ironically, had made Islam respectable again, because the secularists, today called *cha-chas*, gave secularism an awful name. As a result, people began forgetting that the Muslim League and Jamaat-e-Islam had helped the Pakistanis when the situation had deteriorated around them. Instead, the people started longing for change. The Sheikh's raj, or kingdom, had proved to be a bitter disappointment, even to many who had fought for freedom under his leadership. By 1974 famine stalked the land, bringing with it all the primordial fears of 1943, the reality of Zainul Abedin.

Worse still, after his party had won nearly all parliamentary seats, the Sheikh wanted more and more power until, in 1975, he not only assumed full dictatorial powers but also made the country a one-party state under the now hated word *Baksal*, an acronym of the Bangladesh Workers and Farmers party, the same name as Fazlul Huq's party of the 1930s. But there was a major difference. Not only were there internal Marxists; there also were external alliances with the Soviet Union. In his wildest dreams Huq had not wanted a one-party state. Ironically, the goals of Mujib's Baksal were not so much communist as corporatist, nearly fascist. In this his views of government more nearly approximated those of Bose than the ideals of the Congress Party under Gandhi and Nehru.

Ultimately, two incidents led to Mujib's death. The first was when one of his corrupt gomasta friends insulted an army officer's wife; the second was when a rapist and murderer, who had influence with the Sheikh, was freed. As the direct result of these incidents, two army officers determined to assassinate him. In August 1975 the Sheikh, his entire family, and several close associates, more than twenty people, were brutally murdered in the Sheikh's home. The lone survivor was his daughter, Sheikh Hasina, who was in London. As for the murderers, all army officers, they remain alive and well today and generally respected in Bangladesh society—a fact that continues to haunt the country's politics and, in 1992, resulted in an attempt to legally exonerate them without benefit of trial.

It is worth analyzing the years of the Sheikh's rule. Not only is he not considered a saint or martyr; he is not respected as much as he should be. From his start in politics until the end, he found it too easy to mix with the lower elements of politics, with the crooks and the gomastas, with the hoodlums who enforced rent collections from the peasants under the zamindars. His massive hartals often only succeeded under threat of violence from stone-throwers and paid *goondas* who would bust car windows and burn buses. And everyone knows that Mujib took money from many foreign sources, especially from India and the USSR, as well as from businesses, often for "settling" strikes. He did not take money for himself. He took money for his movement.

Moreover, like the secret society members of the 1930s, he vowed loyalty to his friends—loyalty when they insulted an army officer's wife, loyalty when they raped a bride and killed the groom. Loyalty—rather than truth, honest disagreement, or even the shrewd Machiavellianism that governing requires—became the key to his thinking. He was not shrewd, but blunt. He required loyalty. And once in power, he came to doubt people's sincerity and to be paranoid about their loyalty. That he himself was honorable for the most part did not seem to matter. Loyalty mattered.

Finally, like all such intellectually limited men, he demanded both increasing power and more and more trust and loyalty—until he became the single leader of the nation's single party, until he passed laws that exceeded those of the Pakistanis, in press censorship, in preventive arrest and jail without trial, in freedom for his private armies and for the police to torture and kill. The further he retreated into such precautions, the further he moved away from his people. When he no longer went among his people and ceased being able to guess their needs, his intuition, empathy, and sympathy failed him.

The man who faced his killers on the stairway of his home, after his wife and children already had died, no longer resembled the man he had been.

When he said, "Stop, I am your father!" his killers did not stop. They cut him down with AK-47s as he descended, pipe in hand. Power and the ill advice of far brighter but intellectually lazy advisers had so corrupted him that the bullets that entered his body killed a man no one knew. "I am the cyclone; I am destruction!" The words of antinomian values haunted the nation. The destruction had caught up with Mujib.

Few wept at his death. No demonstrations broke out. The countryside remained quiet in the days that followed. Only those who remembered him at his best, including this author, wept.

He is a man to whom history cannot be kind. Someone who knew him called him a freak of history. But an old farmer acquaintance of mine once said it better: "He was not satisfied with being great. He seemed to want to be a god." Alas, that is the ailment of the twentieth century, and Sheikh Mujib was a great man who suffered from that disease. His monument is the Fourth Amendment to the nation's Constitution. It created a totalitarian dictatorship along national and socialist Baksal lines. He believed that if one changed the structures of government, a New Man would arise. The new man did not come, only the old Adam.

In truth, the Bangladesh Museum exhibit never will be complete until the story of Sheikh Mujib's reign and death are included. For in this revolution, the Sheikh becomes his own Lafayette and Robespierre; and just as the French Revolution did not end until Waterloo, so, too, did the Bangladesh revolution not end until the Sheikh's death. For Mujib was both a victim of the revolution as well as its perpetrator. Just as Robespierre betrayed France's revolution and Lenin was a traitor to Russia's liberal revolution, the Sheikh, at the behest of his milieu of well-educated advisers, left the liberal path and opted for a Bangladesh version of a national socialist state internally partly allied to the international socialist movement externally.

Yet, for all that, the Sheikh alone cannot be held responsible. Yes, he had the power. But everyone knows how his advisers offered policy after policy that resulted in one catastrophe after another for poor Bangladesh. The Sheikh never understood that by taking dictatorial powers at the behest of his advisers he seemed to betray his promise of democracy. He was like a man riding a tiger. Mujib was unable to control where it would go next.

For this reason, the Sheikh is not a martyr but a victim—a victim of the restlessness and greed of the gomastas, a victim of the intellectual arrogance of his well-educated advisers. Viewed this way, he cannot be written out of history. After all, more than anyone, he made Bangladesh.

To commemorate this, the Liberation War exhibit at the National Museum needs to be expanded to include the stairway of the Sheikh's house, where Sheikh Hasina, his daughter and only surviving child, has memorialized her father with a picture, bloodstains, and bullet holes. This old man, who meant to do so much, died a horrid death—precipitated by the fact that he was so frail and so susceptible to the disease of our century that says that man is like a god.

He died because his professors, his mentors, his ideologist, Tagore, believed in a New Man, a perfectible man, a man who would replace the old man, the old Adam of the past, as soon as the oppressive structures of society would be changed. This New Man would believe in social utility, socialism, and the remaking of society, so that each man could blossom as a new person, a new type of human being. Unfortunately, while the structures of Bangladesh society changed because of Sheikh Mujibur Rahman's charisma, mankind did not improve. So, the Sheikh died in a pool of blood, his pipe clutched in his hand, his benign face still benign in death, a victim of his own beliefs, his own megalomania, the twentieth-century disease. He began by talking democracy but died advocating a one-party state, like the one Bose dreamed of, and Mujib came of age while Bose was reaching his apex of romantic influence. Any pious farmer in his mosque could have told Mujib that we are born men and die men, and that this is the way it always will be. Man does not change when societal structures do. Man remains man. None of us is without sin, *nafs*, none of us.

Nevertheless, we mourn Mujib personally. He was a simple man with a simple set of beliefs in his nation and people. He tried to do things he did not understand. He failed. Yet he is *Banga Bandhu*, Father of the Nation—not as a perfect statesman but as a man who felt deeply about his people, each and every one of them, people he knew by name, individually. Somehow, he deserved a retirement, his family around him, as he sat, pipe in hand. Somehow, he deserved better than the epitaph "I am the cyclone; I am destruction."

When you visit the Bangladesh Museum exhibit remember the Sheikh at his best, and pay respects at his memorial at his home, a short cab ride away. He was a man who flew as high as an average man can fly. How many of us would have done better?

It is said that history is a mass of facts and that art is a picture of only one person. Why is this so? It is so for the reason that Zainul Abedin so poignantly captured mankind's spirit during the 1943 famine, while the museum exhibit of the Liberation War is so prosaic, so journalistic. The picture of the Sheikh, dead on the stairs, pipe in hand, is the art of the Liberation War. For there is something wonderful about his spirit when it is at his best. The picture tells of the greatness of political man in our century, and of the folly of political hopes and the belief that politics and not society is the center of man's life.

The art of the revolution is seen best in a picture the author bought in 1973 from a young artist. It shows a beautiful milk and strawberry sky with vultures circling. The swirl of the birds forces the eye downwards to a decaying corpse on the street below. That single corpse, those vultures, tell the whole story of the Sheikh. Like Zainul Abedin, Samad, the artist, captured the tragedy and horror of twentieth-century revolution. Never can one look at that picture without thinking of the Sheikh. For one corpse on the *maidan* near the Intercontinental Hotel summarizes the hopes and folly of revolution.

As even his slayers admit, Sheikh Mujib died not because he created a nation (his greatest legacy), but because he tried to "complete a revolution" by fashioning a one-party state intimately tied to totalitarian countries. He was murdered because he had lost touch with his people.

Remember him kindly. He deserves to be honored, as he only knew what his mentors taught him and he only did what his still-living, well-educated advisers recommended. For they, not he, are the authors of Baksal and of the Fourth Amendment. And the Sheikh, who probably never read all the Constitution's 110 articles, trusted them so much. Ultimately, they betrayed him with an empty ideology and separated him from his people, the latter of whom never betrayed him and only brought out the best in him. . . .

6

Further Tales of Murder
and Politics

AND SO, HAVING BEEN SEPARATED from the people in whose name he had inspired and led the independence revolution, Sheikh Mujibur Rahman passed forever from the scene—in the flesh, but not in the spirit.

Remembering what he had been, not what he had become, the nation grieved, deeply but quietly. Surprisingly, there were no demonstrations, no riots. Meanwhile, the Sheikh's so-called loyal supporters remained passive, out of sight. Overnight an uneasy calm settled over the land, as the cabinet minister who had joined the plotters, Khondakar Moustaque Ahmed, aided by Mujib's murderers, army majors Rashid and Farook, tried to form an effective government. Khondakar failed. Given his role in the assassination, neither the civil service nor the army supported him. Besides, Khondakar lacked widespread political appeal. As for the Sheikh's followers, they too were weak and divided, obviously for different reasons. In the ensuing years, none gained real credibility, although the Awami League remained the largest party until 1991, when the Bangladesh Nationalist Party (BNP) came to prominence. Still, for sixteen years the Awami League maintained control, thanks less to its own leadership than to the lingering memory of the Sheikh.

For despite the corruption that had swirled around the regime and Mujib's own megalomania and distance from his people, his leadership also had left a positive legacy. After all, under him Bengal's Muslims had achieved a centuries-old dream. And unlike the subservient Hindu province of Indian West Bengal, East Bengal had become the repository of Bengali nationalism, home to the world's largest number of Bengali people, again in control of its own destiny. More important, Bangladesh was not based on Muslim extremism but was a truly national state founded on language and culture. Indeed, in many ways it is today more liberal in outlook than West Bengal, where caste and communalism still influence politics. Finally, Bangladesh emerged with a constitution, written by the Awami League, that remains the basis of the nation's law—a constitution still revered after more than two decades.

Thus, the Sheikh's political legacy has been a secular nation whose framework is grounded both in its constitution and in its people's hearts and minds. Today no Asian nation is more Muslim yet less likely to persecute religious minorities. For despite the presence of Muslim political parties, Bangladeshi nationalism both recognizes the role that minorities, including secular ones, played in achieving independence and contains a large cultural component that embraces all Bengalis. Finally, there is a strong desire for electoral politics. All this heritage owes much to Mujib. For though, toward the end, his advisers recommended Baksal, his original legacy kept the nation on the constitutional path he had set out upon, rather than allowing it to drift into the totalitarian temptation he succumbed to. Thus, unlike Savonarola, Lenin, Hitler, or Stalin, the charismatic Sheikh left a legacy deserving of respect. Of the four principles of government, he chose socialism and nationalism, while eschewing democracy. Some of his successors were to choose secularism and democracy.

While the Sheikh set Bangladesh on its postindependence political course, the man who preserved that legacy and kept the revolution on its intended path was the one who actually had declared the nation to be free: Zia Rahman, who had seized the Chittagong radio station the night Mujib was arrested and had announced independence in the Sheikh's name. After Mujib's murder and after the failure of two ensuing coups—first by Khondakar, then by a Bangladesh Army general in cahoots with India—Zia, the symbol of the freedom movement's nizamat and the army's chief-of-staff, declared martial law and assumed power. Ending three months of chaos, he immediately restored the military chain of command and returned Bangladesh to its democratic course. Just as he had emerged as the Freedom Fighters' unquestioned leader upon Mujib's arrest, so too did Zia take control when the Sheikh died. In many ways, Zia and Mujib were paired in Bangladesh's early days, as Zia implemented all that was practicable in the Sheikh's program.

The pivotal events in Bangladeshi history impacted upon by Major, then General, then President Zia Rahman are portrayed graphically along a single road that traverses Chittagong. For there are found four historical reminders of Zia's greatness. The first is the place where, when he was a major, Zia and his troops gathered, in March 1971, to rebel against Pakistan. Marking the spot is a park where on late afternoons neighbors gather to walk children or to relax in the sea breeze. Further along is the famous radio tower and concrete block transmitter building where Zia, the rebel with a price on his head, declared the nation to be free. That announcement shocked the East Pakistanis themselves and the world. For not only was it the first sign of an organized resistance, but it helped galvanize further resistance because it gave the impression, at home and abroad, that Pakistan was lying: that Mujib still was leading the fight. Along that road are the two other milestones in Zia's life: the now-infamous Circuit House and Zia Nagar. Of them, more will be said later.

Let us return now to that fateful March of two decades ago when Zia set the nation on its irrevocable course. For it was in the wake of his magnificent, courageous ploy that the rebels continuously gained strength and that, over the next nine months, first rebel transmitters in India, then the BBC, and finally rebel transmitters in the war zone itself began broadcasting information from the newly formed Bangladesh government, brilliantly led by a civilian aide to Mujib, Tajuddin Ahmed, as well as reports of battles being fought by Zia's Z Force, the largest, best-organized, most active of the resistance groups. For Zia brought to it the skills of a well-trained soldier rather than the rag-tag, and not as deadly, guerrilla warfare of self-appointed Freedom Fighter leaders. Having begun his campaign in the Chittagong Hill Tracts, he quickly began moving northward around Comilla and Syhlet, where he played the major role in the Liberation War.

This turned out to be fortunate in another way. For this hero's role enabled him to be a pivotal force in the nation's subsequent politics: to lead the organized, postindependence army. However, his path was not destined to be easy, and his fate probably was predictable. For as a professional soldier and Freedom Fighter, he posed a threat to the rebel Awami League governing class that had spent the war in India talking rather than fighting. Likewise, as a member of the nizamat, he threatened the civil rule and credibility of the diwani. Worse, after the war, Zia, more than anyone in the government, represented the Freedom Fighters, both the minority of Pakistan-trained soldiers who had joined the rebels and the irregular guerrillas who had harassed the Pakistanis. The clash between Zia and other postwar pretenders to power had been inherent in the days of Mujib Nagar, the camp of Taher's army, and at the Z Force's headquarters.

In contrast, Tajuddin, who had become prime minister in Mujib's absence during the war, inadvertently and tragically, as it turned out, had allowed himself to be viewed as the Indian government's man. Moreover, in a broader sense, the educated, polished Tajuddin represented the Brahmo mind of secularism and socialism. In contrast, Zia and his Z Force represented the truly indigenous nationalist movement, as well as Islam, not as a communal force but as a symbol of the overwhelming majority of the people. Personally, Zia was renowned for his iron will and respected as a man. At war's end, on the strength of having led the Freedom Fighters, he chose to return to the army to try to shape it for the future as a force that would serve a democratic state. In this sense, while Mujib is the father of Bangladesh, Zia is the father of its army.

Zia found an army divided. Various Freedom Fighter factions claimed a place in it, as did the Bangladeshi officers who had returned from internment in Pakistan. Chaos reigned, but the Sheikh's regime did not care. In fact, Mujib was forming an independent militia to compete with the army, an ideologically oriented party army that undermined the role of a national one. During this period, Zia met those plotting the Sheikh's assassination. And while he did not join them, neither did he report them. When Mujib was murdered, Zia sat back and waited to be called. Given the chaos and anarchy of the Sheikh's reign, he could not have done otherwise.

The Sheikh's last two summers, in 1974 and 1975, proved to be the worst in recent Bengal history. A food shortage had developed due to late rains in 1974 and flooding in 1975 and to the late arrival of emergency food shipments from the United States. And, as starving poor started streaming into Dhaka and other cities, the government seemed to be paralyzed. Ration shops had long lines; pitiful people, old and young, wandered the streets, while those who had food hoarded it, in the face of a quiet, but palpable terror that 1943 was about to be repeated. The specter of the nightmare portrayed by Zainul Abedin haunted the land. It was this barely suppressed hysteria that fed the sense of urgency of those who plotted to kill the Sheikh. Zia, unable to help Mujib, chose not to stop the assassins. He could only permit the tragedy of the Sheikh and his advisers to play itself out.

Within days of the murder, while Khondakar controlled the government, Army General Khalid Musharaf, in league with Tajuddin and supported by Indian government intelligence services, plotted another coup. But as Awami League supporters danced in the streets, Zia had to decide whether to allow Tajuddin and the Awami League to rule. After being freed from detention by Major Taher, he chose to crush the revolt. Meanwhile, faced by Musharaf's imminent coup, Khondakar helped Mujib's murderers leave the country, issued a decree absolving them of a crime, then resigned. Almost immediately the army moved against Tajuddin and Musharaf, who, with some of their colleagues, were swiftly killed, some say in the Dhaka jail, while others say at the government quarters of Banga Bhavan.

During this period, Lt. Colonel Taher led a sepoy or *jawan's* (soldier's) revolt that expressed a populist revulsion against the corruption and profiteering of Mujib's Awami Leaguers, and the accumulation of Western gadgets and googaws by people close to the party who shut their eyes and hearts to the fact that thousands were starving and dying due to floods, drought, and the sheer incompetence of the Sheikh's advisers. (Today, Major Taher's revolt is recalled each year—as are the deaths of the Sheikh, Tajuddin, and Musharaf, just as Liberty Day is celebrated by the followers of Mujib's assassins, Rashid and Farook.)

In the last analysis, many believe that Taher, who burned the symbols of the Sheikh's corrupt entourage, came closest to portraying the people's real feelings: they did not want Mujib dead; they wanted him and his cronies out of power and corruption to end.

To see why the Sheikh had to be forced from power, violently or otherwise, one must understand three factors that usually are not discussed frankly, even now: ideology, secularism, and *razakars*. These three are intertwined and are problems Zia faced when he took control.

Let us begin with the razakars, armed cadres organized by the Pakistani Army using recruits from the Muslim League and Jamaat supporters. All those who supported Pakistan's unity during the war and who collaborated with the Yaha Khan regime in Islamabad are widely referred to as razakars, even if they did not belong to the armed volunteer corps. Religious and secular, urban and rural, from all classes, they believed in 1971 that the Pakistani state they had sworn allegiance to in 1947 when Britain divided India had been doing a good enough job. While they had diverse political, economic, and religious reasons for remaining loyal to Pakistan, they had one thing in common: opposition to India, out of fear of the caste system and the Hindu zamindars.

From the perspective of an independent Bangladesh, the problem was that many of them had collaborated with the Pakistan Army invaders. Some had identified Freedom Fighters or their supporters, who then were jailed or, more likely, murdered. Some had done killings themselves. Others had joined in volunteer efforts to aid the Pakistan Army, had done propaganda for it, or had loyally stayed at their posts and supported the army. These were the active razakars, whose numbers were so huge that after the war the Mujib government declined to prosecute them because the process of identifying, trying, and jailing them would have overwhelmed the legal system and turned a high percentage of the populace against the government.

There also were many who had collaborated unwillingly, out of fear. While the results often were the same, this sizable group, whose members were found especially in the police and civil service, cannot be ranked with active razakars. Moreover, many of them tried to help the Freedom Fighters.

Lastly, there was the Sixteenth Division, so named because its members remained neutral until, on December 16, 1971, the Pakistanis surrendered to the Indian Army and these "heroes" declared themselves to be Freedom Fighters. Some were civil servants and judges who had stayed at their posts out of loyalty to duty and public order; some were opportunists; some simply lacked the courage to declare loyalty until presented with a *force majeure.*

Today it is not hard to spot the razakars, keeping in mind that there are still Tories in America who remain loyal to Britain or Anglophiles, like Nirad Chaudhuri in England. In private conversations one hears them refer almost longingly to those bygone days of their youth. Moreover, their spirit lives on at public occasions. For instance, at Dhaka Stadium during cricket or football matches between India and Pakistan, an astute observer will note the over-whelming cheers for the Pakistani team—as though at least 300,000 Ban-gladeshis were not murdered by Pakistanis in 1971 and despite the fact that the Indian Army not only helped Bangladesh become free but also withdrew instead of staying on as conquerors.

Complicating the problem of the razakars and constituting a serious issue on its own was ideology. A hard taskmaster, ideology has presided over the most violent revolutions in history. Furthermore, in its name in this century alone, over thirty million people—more than died in all the religious wars in history—were murdered in the camps of Nazi Germany and the Soviet Union, more in Lenin's and Stalin's camps than in Hitler's. Ideology is cru-cial to the story of the razakars. For there were profound ideological factors that kept many people from supporting the Awami Leaguers who controlled the postwar government. For instance, many razakars refused to join the so-called freedom movement because they disagreed with its ideology, which was far more radical than the democratic-socialist rhetoric of today's strongly leftist Awami League. Indeed, the movement's goals were frighten-ing, even by 1960s standards when leftism had been popular worldwide. For those goals, expressed as Baksal and in harsh, radical terms, were to regi-ment the society, to create a near, if not an outright, communist state. Such radicalism scared people, especially the 60 percent of Bangladeshis who own farms of fewer than ten acres, which constitute their livelihood. That land is their capital; any attempt to label these farmers as large landholders was a threat they could not ignore.

The Awami League's ideology also was threatening in another way. By professing secularism, the government came to be seen as an enemy of Is-lam. Reinforcing this was the fact that many Hindu Awami Leaguers preached secularism because, as with all religious minorities, it was advanta-geous to do so.

Finally, given the Awami League's secular ideology and its Hindu mem-bers' attempts to strengthen secularism, it almost seemed as though India had taken over the country. The rhetoric sounded remarkably like that of India, the India of the socialist Indira Gandhi, who was to become a dictator in June 1975, just five months after the Sheikh became one in Bangladesh under Baksal. Indeed, from the people's perspective, Pakistani warnings about an Indian takeover of Bangladesh appeared to have been prophetic, and to threaten them with a Hindu caste society.

Lest the importance of the backlash against the Awami League's secularist campaign be overlooked, one should recall that when Mujib's disgruntled former cabinet minister, Khondakar, announced the Sheikh's death on the radio and proclaimed himself to be in charge, he signed off with the traditional Muslim greeting, *Salaam alaikum*, peace be with you. At that, villagers throughout the land wept. For at last there was a sign that the government was neither "Indian" nor secular and that, after all, the people had not been betrayed. For initially the people had believed that *secular* meant that the government would be neutral among religions; they never dreamt it would be openly hostile. On this, the Sheikh, influenced by his advisers, had let them down.

Undoubtedly, Mujib would not have understood any of the above, for he never thought about ideas in the extreme, never distinguished between substance and style, and personally was a moderate. Unfortunately, instead of following his heart, he listened to his advisers, whose ideology was anathema to Bangladeshi masses.

Therefore, Zia Rahman, after putting down Musharaf and Major Taher in the wake of Mujib's death, had to turn the freedom movement back toward a moderate, centrist stance. He chose to evoke a higher nationalism, one that embraced all parts of the society, tribal peoples as well as religious minorities, and to move the country toward free elections, economic development, and, ultimately, democracy and the original constitution.

His first problem arose in the army, where radical mutinies against authority had shattered the chain of command. Whole units, regiments (including the famed Bengal Lancers), even cantonments revolted at one time or another. The ostensible battle was between the Freedom Fighters who had fought the Pakistanis and those soldiers who had been captive in Pakistan throughout the war. The real issue was discipline and command. The problem was that the army reflected the total anarchy that had been spawned by the Sheikh's Awami League government, wherein many factions were fighting for their points of view. There existed no single set of beliefs around which the army could rally. Every unit became politicized, often with civilian input. The challenge was this: either the army would decide to unify itself in order to serve the nation or it would be forced to unify. In the Zia years, unity was imposed by wholesale executions of officers and men who refused to obey orders, who refused to quit using force to attain power. For until this issue was settled, until the mutinies were quelled, until the army had but one set of orders from constitutionally appointed leaders, Zia could barely turn to civilian political concerns. Unfortunately, the need for a unified army chain of command preoccupied Zia throughout his six years in office and led to his death.

At the same time, he was forced to deal with other concerns. Chief among these was the need to calm the civil service and to provide this diwani branch with sufficient pay, security, training, and goals. He accomplished this in part by obtaining more foreign aid and loans from an international community that was willing to help a stable government. For example, building on the start Mujib had made in repairing this damage, Zia provided foreign aid-givers with proposals designed to spur growth: better roads and communications systems, increased irrigation, electrification of the entire countryside, and industrial growth. In this way he both directly spurred the country's development and gave the civil service the wherewithal to oversee real progress.

On the international level, he also sought to improve Bangladesh's relations with other nations, especially to alleviate the fears of India, Pakistan, and Middle Eastern countries that the People's Republic of Bangladesh was too communist leaning.

Finally, he turned to politics and, in 1978, under the mantle of the Bangladesh Nationalist Party (BNP), was elected president, to work with a functioning parliament. Zia became relatively popular, for he was a vigorous, good, and brave man known for his personal integrity, one who represented that son-of-the-soil hardiness of the Bangladeshi small landowner and the tenaciousness of the peasant farmer, combined with the flare of an officer.

Yet he had enemies. Some believed that he had connived in Mujib's death and, worse, had crushed the coup when Tajuddin and Musharaf tried to seize power. Resentment also existed among those who had profited during the Sheikh's rule and among army officers; both groups wanted a piece of the foreign aid wealth and more power than Zia was willing to grant. In fact, as president Zia relegated the army to a far less powerful position, making it subject to civilian rule. For though as a soldier he had achieved power through martial law, he was not a militarist; he did not believe the army should rule. And that is what distinguished him from those who came after. He never wavered in his belief that the army should serve the government, not vice versa. He himself had used his military role to seize power only because of the Sheikh's flirtation with the idea of a private army, itself a militarist move. He had not acted out of belief that the army should have a corporate role in politics. That was a disease he had seen in the Pakistan Army; he hoped Bangladesh would avoid it.

What ultimately killed Zia was the burning ambition of General Manzur, a Pakistani-trained officer who had escaped detention and had returned to Bangladesh to fight. Several months before his own death, Zia refused to appoint Manzur as the army's chief-of-staff because Manzur had political ambitions and a fiery temper. Instead, Zia chose General Hossain Mohammad Ershad and gave Manzur the important post of commander in Chittagong, where a guerrilla war against Chakma tribals, supported by India, was under way. Manzur fumed and waited his chance. In May 1981 he sought a meeting with Zia in Chittagong to discuss his grievances.

Thus did Zia return to Chittagong to meet his fate, along the road where, precisely a decade earlier, he had ignited a revolution by announcing it on the radio and by taking his soldiers into revolt. According to two men who accompanied Zia that night, he thought that the meeting with Manzur had gone well, that he had calmed his mercurial former colleague without the threat of force. Leaving Manzur, he went to the Circuit House, a residence the British had built for visiting dignitaries that is down the hill from the Chittagong Club, which perches on a small nob and has a luxurious, shaded garden from which one can survey the port below. Bedding down for the night on his pillow, Zia is said to have felt secure. Picking up where Mujib had left off, Zia, during almost seven years as leader, had healed most of the nation's divisions.

Between November 1974 and May 1981, Bangladesh had begun recovering from the Liberation War. Roads gradually opened, shipping started up, industry began, electric power became more readily available, international trade got under way, and Western aid began in earnest. Zia made a habit of visiting villages by car and helicopter and kept in touch with grass-roots movements that sought to organize village centers, called *gram sarkars*, and to implement agricultural and family planning programs. During this era Bangladesh entered the family of nations and worked wholeheartedly with the IMF and the World Bank and in the United Nations. For instance, Zia took the lead in calling for a regional bloc of nations comprised of Pakistan, India, Nepal, and Sri Lanka; and he reestablished Bangladesh's ties with the Muslim world while loosening its attachments to the Eastern Bloc. By all accounts, he had accomplished much. He had brought back democracy and constitutional rule and, in place of the ersatz theories and practices of Mujib's advisers, had begun implementing real economic development. Equally important, he had sought to make the army serve a civilian government. He had cut the army out of policy decisions that did not directly concern it and had abolished many privileges that dated from Pakistani days. As for his one-time compatriots, he had reason to believe that Manzur and Ershad agreed with his ideas, at least in principle. Thus, as he lay his head on that Circuit House pillow, he had reason to feel secure. He failed to recognize that he had given in to one, fateful illusion.

Not that his policy had been wrong. In fact, it had been crucial to Bangladesh's future. For by depriving the army of a power-sharing role he had emphasized a point too often overlooked by Bangladeshi intellectuals and foreign observers alike: that political development along democratic lines is as important as economic development.

Unfortunately, though he thus had made a vast contribution to the nation's future, there were some who felt the pace to be too slow and others who favored a different course or believed that they should rule. On every side there were critics and enemies. Recognizing this, Zia honestly sought to convince them of his point of view. At the same time, according to some who knew him well, toward the end Zia had grown weary of trying to keep discipline, weary of the endless problems, weary of ruling. It was, they say, in a state of emotional exhaustion that Zia went to Chittagong.

The Circuit House is a Tudor-style structure of plaster and exposed beams that sits in a hollow of land high enough up the hill to catch the early evening sea breezes and from which can be seen the red-and-gold glow of the sunset over the Bay of Bengal. The interior is paneled with dark-jungle mahogany. Up a broad stair slept the President of Bangladesh. Under his head was a pillow. Under the pillow lay a pistol.

Just as he was drifting off, shots rang out. He waited. Over the roar of a violent thunderstorm, a dry-season storm of nearly cyclonic strength, he heard a door bang open downstairs. He went to the top of the stairs, holding his gun like a soldier. He never had a chance. Volleys of shots rang out. He was pummeled as if a madman wanted to tear his body apart. He was shot over, and over, and over again, with 7.62-mm bullets from an AK-47.

His remains, for that is all that was left, remains, were taken by truck along that Chittagong road: out of the Circuit House; past the corner lot outside the cantonment where he had rallied his troops in revolt, not mutiny, against the Pakistanis; down the road a few miles, past the radio station, its single tower and concrete block building surrounded by a high fence, where he alone had declared his country's independence; more miles, past the Gomai fields, where there exists one of the most fertile rice cultures in all of Southeast Asia; along the banks of a feeder stream to the Karnaphuli River, and finally up a narrow draw in the hillside. There, in a hollow of the hill, the soldiers dug a shallow grave and threw in his bloody remains. The place is called Zia Nagar. It is the first memorial to his murder, still marked in 1991 by a faded sign under a tattered lean-to. At last he had reached the end of the road—the four stations on the cross of Zia Rahman—murdered as brutally as had been the Sheikh, Tajuddin, Musharaf, and Major Taher. Like each of them, he deserved better than the end he faced.

But such is the fate of political men who live in harsh times. Whilst the Sheikh ruled, Fazlul Qader Chowdhury died in a Dhaka prison cell. He had been speaker of the House of Pakistan and a razakar, not out of opportunism but out of principle. The Sheikh had connived at his death. And the Sheikh, in turn, had faced the machine guns of troops led by Majors Farook and Rashid. Tajuddin and Musharaf also had played the game of coups. They had kept quiet during the Sheikh's reign of terror. They too were to know power and to die brutally at the wrong end of an AK-47. Likewise, Taher had led his mutiny and had died at the hands of a firing squad approved by Zia Rahman. Now had come Zia's turn—he who had put down army mutinies by killing thousands of officers, often without trial, who had known of but had not warned Mujib of the murderous plot. His turn had come, along a road where his greatest, most courageous acts had been memorialized, but where his final memorial was to be what now is called Zia Nagar: a decrepit lean-to, on which hang some rags and under which he first was buried. Fate both made him and broke him on that road. He deserved better. At his death, many wept. For he was a man of real vision.

Unfortunately, there is something in most of us civilians that does not grieve for a soldier like Zia who entered politics and died violently. Most civilians have scant ability to understand that soldiers are men like us, that they have hopes and fears, much like our own. They also often have ideals of democracy and social justice; but only few of them, like Zia, can articulate such ideals. Dealing with the murderous world of a mutinous army, Zia tried to impose such ideals. And he strove to see that the ideals of the Liberation War were restored to where the Sheikh had left them before he went astray. In this sense, Zia is a great man. Rising above the circumstances that brought him to power, he rescued the nation's democratic constitution. He sought neither grandeur nor to make the nizamat the center of power. Like Cincinnatus in ancient Rome, like George Washington and Britain's Wellington, Zia sought to continue the constitution of his nation as a civilian-run affair. By so doing, he established a democratic tradition in the Bangladesh army, one that his successors have yet to grasp.

Within a few days of Zia's murder, the officers involved were tried and hanged. Manzur was shot to death as he tried to escape from Chittagong. But those events need not detain us. Of concern is the fact that we still do not know if others were involved. There are several suspicious unknowns. Why did Zia go to the Circuit House without his bodyguard? Why did army intelligence not know of the plans in advance, especially as the general involved clearly had grievances and had let them be known? Was the army chief-of-staff, General Ershad, among the plotters? Did he let his rival act first, using the president as a pawn, or did he first encourage and then betray the plotters, wiping out his enemies in the army? Were any civilians involved who promised to support Manzur if he could "sort out"—that horrible euphemism left over from British days and used all over the subcontinent—first Zia and then the army? Did any foreign governments play a part—particularly India, which disliked Zia's BNP? As often occurs, the known facts are unsatisfactory, while the possible scenarios are endless. There are those (including this author) who believe that the army command under Ershad and a group of civilians they were close to conspired to murder Zia. This is based on several pieces of circumstantial evidence, on the admission of a longtime university and army friend of Ershad's, and on the comments of others close to Ershad, to the effect that Ershad knew of the plot in advance but, as Zia had done with Mujib, did not warn him. Moreover, while Zia may have suspected danger, others were sure. Certain newspapers definitely knew in advance. So did certain Bangladeshi, and some foreign, diplomats.

Zia's death was a tragedy in the Greek sense of the word. For his own beliefs—in particular that the army should serve the constitution, not the reverse—led inexorably to his death. As with the Sheikh, when Zia died some people wept; but this time, no one danced in the streets. While Mujib had been loved by many, Zia was respected by many. The people did not want Zia's blood, any more than they had wanted Mujib's. Ironically, however, the Bangladeshis, who had never assassinated their ruler during the twenty-four years of Pakistani rule, ended up killing, within the first decade of independence, their only two longtime leaders—both heroes of the freedom movement, both popularly elected presidents. The Sheikh died in his beloved home in Dhanmondi, while Zia met his fate on the *via gloriosa* and *dolorosa* that so attracted him.

General Hossain Mohammad Ershad did not seize power when President Zia died in May 1981. Instead, the constitution was followed and the vice-president, a frail old man named Sattar, assumed power and ninety days later called for elections. In the ensuing political campaign, Kamal Hossain, a chief architect of the constitution, Mujib's foreign minister, an Awami League cha-cha, and one of his nation's most brilliant barristers, represented the opposition. Old President Sattar won by a three-to-one majority. The people thereby knowingly and openly endorsed Zia's democratic path while rejecting the ideals of those who had supported Baksal and Mujib's one-party state.

Affectionately dubbed the "old man" by his supporters, Sattar, in his eighties, set about building his cabinet and organizing Parliament. In the process, which took from November to January, he handed a great many portfolios to BNP people who had served Zia, but in a corrupt way. The venerable, honest Sattar was naïve about who was and was not really important in his party. These mistakes began hurting him.

Actually, the main threat was not political but military. In the ensuing months, this threat became increasingly apparent, although Manzur was gone. Indeed, it could be argued that perhaps Manzur had tried to warn the nation. Whatever the truth, during Sattar's short reign military agents whispered everywhere about "political corruption." Rumors of a need for "national discipline" were described in the local and foreign press. Various embassies took "soundings" of high-ranking officers and established links with all political parties. Editorials in the nation's largest, most influential newspaper by far, *Ittefaq*, praised an ideological campaign for freer trade and commerce, destruction of the socialist shackles of the Mujib era, and Zia's attempts at liberalization. By January 1982 no one doubted that the army, led by Ershad, was poised to act. Indeed, some Awami League cha-chas welcomed the coming coup, as it would represent revenge against the government they had lost to at the polls. That the cha-chas were gleeful and welcomed the imminent coup this writer can personally attest to. Eventually, the only question was not whether, but when.

When the coup came, at the end of March, it was bloodless. President Sattar was confronted by the presence of officers and the overwhelming military might of the nizamat.

The rise to power of the military, for the second time in Bangladesh's brief history, was very important. For once again, while politicians talked and intellectuals dithered, the army acted. Only this time it came to power not as Zia had done, when chaos existed, but at the start of an administration—a democratic one elected by an overwhelming majority—that had not had a chance to make its mark. Moreover, there had been no political restlessness to encourage the coup. Simply put, the sole justification was that Ershad wanted it. And for the first time, a man who did not represent the Brahmos, the religious parties, or the West but who represented the new class came to power.

The coming of martial law was welcomed by the BNP's many enemies. These included Awami Leaguers who, as we have seen, had their personal reasons; army officers, who were glad Zia was gone and hoped that Ershad would restore their many privileges; older businessmen, who felt that liberalization had not gone fast enough under Zia and hoped to get back property that had been nationalized by the Sheikh's Awami League; and, crucially, younger businessmen, part of the new class, who wanted their turn at power. (Indeed, many of this group grew rich in the Ershad era, thanks to new laws, such as one on pharmaceuticals that drove out foreign investment. Fueled by a "new morality," this university miseducated class had no scruples about paying off corrupt parliamentarians or a handful of army officers.) Lastly, there were members of the civil service, the diwani, who collaborated with the army, thus increasing their power relative to that of elected leaders and placing themselves in the line of corruption. (Many former top civil servants collaborated with the army takeover and later joined Ershad's cabinet when, after running unopposed, he became president—though some did so with high ideals and resigned when faced with the corruption that followed on a Hollywood scale.)

As for Ershad, unlike Zia he came to power unknown by the people. Interned by Pakistan, he had not been a Freedom Fighter. Furthermore, in the war's aftermath he had not played politics directly but had worked behind the scenes. A man of considerable charm to ladies and most men, he had a quiet, shy manner, was a listener not a talker, and allowed very few people to really know him. Yet he had the army's support and enjoyed complete control of its chain of command. One reason was his habit of meeting with army representatives frequently, both officers and enlisted men, to explain and justify his policies and actions and to at least listen to their viewpoints. During the initial martial-law phase of his rule, Ershad took over the old Parliament Building, and there his "military parliament" met to discuss its role. First and foremost they wanted a bigger voice in power than Zia had left them. Ultimately Ershad was to publish a piece in the English-language newspaper *New Nation* calling for a return to constitutional rule with some mechanism that gave the military direct input into policy. This was in direct conflict with Zia's position on the supremacy of pure civilian rule.

While many politicians were tried and jailed by military tribunals on a host of charges, legitimate and otherwise, and though some businessmen were imprisoned to force them to bribe the military, for the most part Ershad's eight-year rule was mild. Army murders ceased; a decade-long curfew was lifted; the jails were emptied of thousands who had been held without trial since the Zia or even the Mujib era; businesses were returned to their owners; investment in a new garment industry was encouraged, resulting in vast job growth nationwide; much-needed infrastructure was completed and more was started, including bridges over rivers that never had been spanned; electric power increased and spread to many villages; export zones were founded; and import duties were lifted from tubewell engines, helping nearly all farmers, and the nation, become self-sufficient in fertilizer made from Bangladeshi natural gas.

Economically, the nation raised its per capita income from $130 to more than $170. Moreover, during the Ershad era there were no famines, no excessive loss of life from floods, and fast, efficient aid to those caught in natural disasters. Also, of utmost importance, the government implemented a plan, that had been conceived by the Sheikh, to create new "county seats" at the six hundred *thanahs*, or police stations, thus placing representatives of all relevant ministries near the village level. Among other things, these new governing units, or *upazillas*, would store food surpluses for use in difficult times. This program proved to be more immediately practical than did Zia's gram sarkar program, which would have been too costly at the time.

In summary, as all national and international sources confirm, the Ershad years proved to be good ones for Bangladesh in terms of economic development. This was not true politically speaking. For Ershad and many of his foreign supporters did not have a real sense that political development in democratic terms is more important than economic development, because, over time, a sense of freedom encourages innovation, intellectually, scientifically, politically—and thus economically. Ershad had not a clue as to political development: that freedom is a kind of wealth that creates more wealth and all the other higher values a good society reveres. Under Ershad, political development took a step backward. For unlike Mujib and Zia, Ershad was not a natural politician with a common touch or appeal. He did not have the warmth to attract crowds or to reach the average farmer. On television he appeared stiff and on radio, stilted. In person, tall and well dressed, he seemed aloof. Though he did not mean to come across that way, his shy manner was off-putting. He liked a slow golf game, good food, nice clothes, and fast women. Such was not the makeup of a man of the people; it reflected the values of the miseducated new class, at odds with the poverty and rusticity of the villagers.

When Ershad revived the constitution, he had little interest in it or in legal theory, or in upholding it as a matter of principle. He did not share Zia's love of the constitution. He did not care about it one way or another. He only cared if it helped or hurt him. Thus, though he kept the constitution alive, he did not really live by it, in fact or in spirit. Not that he scorned it. Rather, he failed to spend the intellectual hard work necessary to understand it. He certainly never thought about dying for it. Like many in this materialistic age, Ershad felt that if economic development occurred, political development was unimportant. Indeed, who at the British or U.S. embassies cared about political development in Bangladesh? Nearly everyone in those last years of the Cold War had accepted that economic development preceded political development.

Consequently, while contested parliamentary elections were held in 1986 and the constitution again was in force, Ershad himself never fought a contested election, partly because he would not permit neutral observers but mostly because he was not courageous enough to take a chance. More than once he was quite relieved that he faced no opposition, as the opposition parties refused to grant him the dignity of running anyone against him. And this uncovered one of his weaknesses.

For President Ershad, who was elected unopposed, never really had a vision of what he wanted to do. Throughout his rule, each crisis roiled and boiled while he consulted as many people as possible. At the critical juncture he finally would make a decision, based on whatever power he felt he had or needed to share. Often he retreated in the face of power, dropping advisers, acquiring new ones, then dumping those to suit his needs. He did not like confrontation—which is what an election is—even with his own staff. As a result he made decisions ad hoc when backed into a corner, which meant that as long as luck was on his side, he did all right. And for eight years he avoided any fundamental political decisions.

But he failed to realize that the opposition had taken his measure and had seen that he had no principles. Ultimately they stood up to him in the Bangladeshi way: through student unrest and hartals that shut down the cities and universities for days on end. In the latter years of his rule, there was no end to hartals, which, despite generous wage agreements and other devices, he was unable to stop. What kept him going was his ability to split the opposition. But by 1989 the writing was on the wall. After he had dismissed three ministers who refused to go along with his tactics and in the face of growing consensus among the opposition parties that he had neither principles nor spine, his fatal flaw revealed itself.

First, his expensive tastes were causing an outcry, as he lived too well due to his insatiable appetite for money and women. Second, his weakness in the face of opposition signaled that he would not fight if challenged. Indeed, he kept a plane ready at the airport, just in case.

In October 1990 the end came. His opposition—political parties and students—united and began mass hartals in which the general populace participated. Then the army deserted him because it had seen him retreat too often, so often that civilians were laughing. Also, widespread corruption within the army had further weakened its resolve, and its leaders began thinking they could get a better deal by deserting Ershad. Meanwhile, as the hartals grew larger and more frequent, the troops refused to fire on what had become a mass uprising, and Ershad's own security detail refused to help him. Ignoring his advisers' advice to flee, Ershad thought he could outlast the threat and that, as always, something would come up to save the day. This time he was wrong. His luck had run out. His lack of conviction and principles had caught up. He found himself first under house arrest, then in Dhaka jail, where he remains at this writing, having spent two years there. No golf, no women, no nice clothes. Only bad food . . . of which he has complained.

However, it is a measure of the country's and his opposition's maturity that unlike his predecessors Ershad fell without being assassinated. Shortly after he took power, he had told this writer that the trouble with ruling Bangladesh is that "you know how it will end; you just never know when." He was standing in a foyer of the army chief-of-staff's home in the cantonment, gazing at a picture of President Zia. From the outset he had been prepared for assassination but not for jail, although years earlier he had told one of his ministers that he had dreamed of being tried and sentenced.

As for those of us interested observers of the Bangladesh political scene, let us hope that Ershad finishes his jail sentence or that, if his appeals succeed, he retires—thus ending a tradition of murder in Bangladesh politics, thereby putting to rest, once and for all, the cycle of cyclone and destruction.

Remarkably, the Sheikh's killers, Majors Rashid and Farook, remain at large, as do some of those who planned Zia's murder. In light of this, it is astounding to realize that though he has not been accused of killing anyone or of using terror, and though his regime is infamous for widespread corruption, Ershad was first convicted and jailed for possessing an unlicensed shotgun, a gift from a foreign chief of state, rather than for his and the army's true crime: overthrowing the constitutionally elected government.

Still, what is important is that, at last, a Bangladeshi ruler ended his career in the only fair way: he was prosecuted in a court of law and convicted by a jury; he accepted his sentence and now is going through an appeal process. In the last analysis, Ershad has been protected by the constitution he so carelessly overturned and so weakly defended.

As for his tenure in office, let it be said that he has yet to be accused of murder, wanton shooting of prisoners, or use of terror. His rule proved to be mild, even sensitive, open and relatively free. His government's economic policies resulted in a booming economy, mostly in Dhaka, but elsewhere as well. He visited villages. He made sure that in times of flood and disaster, relief supplies reached the people quickly and effectively. And he brought order to the civil service.

Had he been satisfied with his regime's legitimate accomplishments, Ershad now would be considered Bangladesh's greatest leader. Had he been committed to democracy, he would have been elected on his own merit. Those who knew his personal and tragic flaws feel a sadness that he ended up in jail, widely considered to be a playboy and a selfish leader. However, those who saw his vacillation, his backing and filling, his retreats in the face of opposition, believe that the end he achieved is better than might have been the case had the interim government that took power immediately after his fall not been staffed by some who wrote the constitution and knew its principles. In other words, his prosecutors upheld the rule of law. Ershad could have done likewise, had he tried to understand what that rule meant.

After Ershad's arrest, a temporary government, led by Supreme Court Chief Justice Shahabuddin, took power. Four months later, elections were held and a new parliament came into being under the leadership of President Zia's widow, Khaleda Zia, now leader of the BNP. Almost immediately the new Parliament changed the constitution from a presidential to a parliamentary system and the Baksal amendment was overthrown. Several months later this change was ratified by a referendum. Today, once again, the civilians are in control. However, rumors still fly that the "army will return." Hopefully, this will not occur. Hopefully, the army will give democratic institutions time to develop, for the first time in the nation's brief history. In the meantime, in the army the question is whose tradition will endure: the values of Ershad or those of the first commander and Freedom Fighter, President Zia, who believed that the army should serve the constitution, rather than the constitution serving the army.

On a broader scale, Bangladeshi politics still wanders from the military to the Brahmo mind, from the Muslim to the secular one, from the new class to the rustic, from the Anglophilic mind in all its sophistication to that of the real Bangladesh, the mind of Lalan Shah, of country boats, and of villagers. Bangladesh is a nation that needs a new poet to help it in democratic times and in times when development creates a new class—a class sometimes marvelously productive and creative but often a class that is corrupt. Bangladesh is a country with a constitution that has endured for the two decades of its existence, a constitution that many believe will continue to light the way as the pole star of the nation.

Finally, it is worthwhile noting two aspects of Bangladeshi political life that often are overlooked. The first is that in times of crisis Bangladesh often turns to High Court justices to lead it. For example, Justice Sayem became president—in name only, but president—after Sheikh Mujib died and when Zia became martial law administrator; Justice Sattar was elevated from the vice-presidency when Zia died, then was elected on his own; and in 1991, when President Ershad's government imploded, Justice Shahabuddin emerged as interim president.

This respect for law and justice appears to be a characteristic unique to Bangladesh. There is a symbolism to such recourse that says a great deal about the makeup of the country. The courts are trusted more than they are anywhere else in Asia, despite their failings, because there is a sense of legal justice.

Another aspect of the fall of Ershad's government is that at the end all political parties agreed that the government had to go. This consensus, which overcame party differences, could not possibly have benefited any one party. For the consensus called for free, open, and monitored elections, elections that neither of the two major parties could be confident of winning, followed by a constitutional change implemented by the winning party, then by a referendum on that change, which provided for a parliamentary system. Fortunately for the nation's future, this consensus resulted in all the steps being followed—a major undertaking for which all parties deserve credit, especially the two largest parties: the BNP, led by Begum (Mrs.) Zia Rahman, widow of the former military man who had favored a strong presidential system of government; and the Awami League, led by Sheikh Hasina, daughter of Sheikh Mujib, who thus agreed to removal of the constitution's fourth (Baksal) amendment, which had been one of the worst legacies of her father's rule. Accepted by parties that were out of power and, thus, uncertain of the outcome, this consensus is a sign of a new political awareness among civilians that they cannot allow their differences to become the basis for military rule. Perhaps they have learned that, like the army, they must decide that there are certain principles they believe in and will adhere to, so that they can enjoy the freedom to compete and debate without undermining democratic institutions.

Lastly, the consensus upheld the validity of the constitution and, most importantly, of constitutional procedure, by asserting that the constitution is supreme over both the army and the political parties—thereby negating the

Sheikh's attempt to use the constitution for his own ends and the Ershad regime's attempt to make the government serve the military. This victory by both parties should establish a precedent that will benefit future generations as the nation's political development continues. And as political development is as important as economic development, this is no mean accomplishment. This is no small result for all the agony that Bangladesh has endured in its first two decades.

7

Bangladesh and the
United States

B ANGLADESH AND AMERICA: HOW DO THEY RELATE TO EACH OTHER?
Despite the United States' ongoing huge aid contribution to Bangladesh
since the latter's independence and its own superpower role during the Cold
War, neither most Americans nor Bangladeshis understand the nature of this
relationship. This is unfortunate, since the answer is quite interesting.

Practically speaking, the relationship is a relatively old, if not quite
straightforward, one. It harks back nearly two-and-a-half centuries, to 1757,
when Great Britain captured Bengal. For the next twenty-six years, until
1783, when the British colonies in America won their independence, the
nations that now are the United States and Bangladesh shared a common
British government. Ever since, this tenuous link has been perpetuated in a
number of ways that mostly have been forgotten or ignored, sometimes
deliberately, by both sides. For since 1757, the two nations have shared a
certain ambiguous relationship, one that is sometimes frustrating and contrary.

To begin to understand this relationship, one must recall the outcome, in
1763, of the major conflict that U.S. historians refer to as the French and
Indian War and those in India call the Seven Years' War. For one consequence was that Britain defeated France in Canada, the Caribbean, Bengal,
and the thirteen American colonies. The colonies then found themselves part
of an enlarged British Empire that included, as its richest possession, Bengal,
ruled by the British-run East India Company. After that first "world war,"
the American colonists noted a distinct change in their relationship with

London. No longer were they, along with Jamaica and the West Indies, the darlings of the British Parliament's eye. Instead they found themselves competing with the new wealth of the East India Company, as personified by its leaders, or *nabobs*, who returned home and bought country houses and seats in Parliament. For the new wealth from India far outweighed that emanating from trade with the American colonies—some four million pounds sterling, about forty billion dollars at today's prices. This wealth resulted from the looting of Bengal by Colonel Clive, when he won the Battle of Plassey in 1757, at a time when it cost Britain more to fight the French and Indian War than Britain obtained from its thirteen American colonies. For even in the best of times, as in the period of the Townshend duties in the 1770s, revenue from the colonies amounted to a mere 400,000 pounds sterling.

In the period immediately after the war, especially from 1765 to 1783, Bengal was the subject of the most hotly debated issue in Britain. For instance, Cobbett, the great journalist, wrote that India occupied as much of Parliament's time as did the nation's budget; sometimes nine parliamentary papers a year were devoted to it. For India offered unparalleled wealth, wealth that had eluded the British in North America.

It is well known that the American Revolution was ignited by the Townshend duties, which were designed to help the East India Company sell surplus tea by permitting it to bypass sending tea to England, where tax would be paid, and to sell it directly to the colonists, who would pay the tax. Though the tax would have raised a mere forty thousand pounds sterling for England and the colonists would have paid 30 percent less for tea, this tax precipitated the revolution. The well-known motive behind the revolution was the taxation-without-representation issue. The other factor, which largely has been forgotten, was the colonies' fear of the East India Company, whose ravages in Bengal were well known.

However, whatever the Americans thought, the only opinions of consequence were those of England's imperial thinkers. Lords Townshend, North, and Fox argued that the colonies ought to pay their own way and to be more carefully governed. Based on this policy, the Americans were challenged to war—a challenge impossible to ignore. The ministry in London, thinking it would be a short war, dispatched troops.

In the midst of the war, with Spain, France, the colonies, and Holland lined up against Britain, Lord Chatham (the former Prime Minister William Pitt), at the advice of Lord Beckford, who had close links to City of London financiers, advised the king to overthrow Lord North, which is what transpired. That allowed Chatham to increase his efforts to preserve Bengal, even at the cost of losing the colonies. For the finances of the realm depended, then and for years to come, on Bengal, not on America, even though Bengal then was suffering from British depredations, massive floods, and maladministration. Thus Chatham and the City of London saw that

Bengal promised an enormous monetary return and that Britain could spend
its money much more wisely by saving the East India Company's investment
in Bengal than by fighting the colonies.

Helping Chatham argue his case was his friend Shelburne, who contended that trade with the colonies would continue if they became independent and that London would be little less well-off without them. As for
Bengal and India, well, that was different. Ultimately, then, it was Chatham
and his followers who saw the importance of Bengal relative to the colonies
and who argued, successfully, for ending the war in America and granting
independence.

Chatham died in 1778, and it was five years before first Shelburne and
then Chatham's son, William Pitt the Younger, became prime minister, supported by the City of London and the East India Company. Ultimately, with
the backing of Beckford, Shelburne, and the younger Pitt, peace was con-
cluded with the thirteen colonies, France, Holland, and Spain, and the first
steps were taken to reform the administration of Bengal in order to increase
East India Company revenues. Thus were the colonies sacrificed in order to
keep Bengal in the British Empire. For unquestionably Bengal was the sole
source which could provide sufficient needed revenues, with lower taxes at
home. As for Lord Chatham, who made his fortune in India, he is memorialized in the United States in the naming of Pittsburgh, Pennsylvania.

Thus, owing in large part to Bengal's wealth, the American colonies
gained their freedom—indirectly at the price of Bengal's and, ultimately, of
India's. Such indirectness can be said to characterize all subsequent U.S.-
Bengali relations. One reason is that Bengal is one of the farthest places on
earth from the United States, some 180 degrees longitude from its center.
Moreover, from the perspective of neither security nor trade has Bengal ever
been central to U.S. interests. So the relationship always has been indirect,
oblique, ambiguous; some other party, some other goal has interfered with
direct relations. Let us look at some diverse examples.

Jute bags do not mean much to most people in the United States today.
But there was a time, in the ports of the southern states and the grain areas
of the North, when they were very important. It was a condition of sale to
the London grain and cotton markets that all shipments be made in jute
baling, which provided both an orderly measure of the crop and a manage-
able, sturdy container for the transshipment by rail, wagon, or ship. Thus for
years, at Savannah, New Orleans, or Chicago, cotton and grain crops were
bagged in uniform-sized jute packages. Similarly, until synthetics pulled the
rug out from under the jute market in the 1970s, all American-made carpets
had jute backings. Thus, mostly via the London market, there existed between the two nations an indirect trade link. Even today, to some extent, the
ties thus forged endure, as a few old Chittagong families maintain links to
families in Savannah, Pennsylvania, and elsewhere.

Another link harks back to America's early trading days, when merchants who sold furs to China were paid in silver, which British tea buyers borrowed from America in exchange for notes to be honored in London. Also, many American ships, having emptied their cargo in China, journeyed to Calcutta in West Bengal (where they often outnumbered British ships) to pick up freight bound for London, New York, or Boston. In London, the ships loaded jute or cotton goods for the return trip home.

Another indirect link dates to 1784, when the United States exported its first bales of cotton to England and created a fuss, because customs believed the cotton to have originated in the West Indies, hitherto Britain's largest cotton supplier. Within three decades the long-fibered U.S. cotton had become the favorite of Manchester's and Lancashire's textile business, Whitney had invented the cotton gin, and slavery, which had been disappearing, had been revitalized in the United States, as slaves were bought initially from British slavers. Cotton became king in the South, with slavery being little more than the means of getting cotton to Manchester's liberals.

Where does Bengal fit in this tale? The answer is related to the rise of cotton goods manufacture in England. After establishing Calcutta in 1690 as a major trading city and implementing a significant trading relationship with Bengal over the ensuing decade, in 1700, to encourage growth of its own manufacturing industry, Britain did two things. It banned many classes of cotton textile imports and established a cotton-growing culture in its West Indies colonies to compete with that of Bengal and India. Henceforth, as its own cotton textiles and garment industries prospered, Britain increasingly sought to decrease Bengal's production.

Meanwhile, however, as British exports grew, the West Indies was unable to produce enough cotton to keep up with increasing British needs. The answer, of course was the United States, where cotton was flourishing. Before long, U.S. cotton began replacing that of the West Indies. And while both Britain and its former colonies thus benefited, Bengal increasingly lost out—especially when British-made textiles and garments, which used U.S.-grown cotton, began selling in Bengal and India. By the 1830s the United States had become England's premier cotton supplier, while, as we have seen, Bengal's textile industry had been shattered. That is how, in the nineteenth and twentieth centuries, the United States indirectly benefited from the decline of Bengal's cotton industry, which had accounted for so much of its wealth in the seventeenth and eighteenth centuries.

An interesting footnote to this twisted tale of king cotton involves slavery. In the mid–seventeenth century Britain had obtained the *asciento*, or slave trade monopoly, from Portugal as part of a royal marriage contract. Later, when slaves were needed to provide the cotton that Britain no longer wanted to obtain from Bengal, U.S. traders bought slaves from British companies in Africa. Ironically, in 1808, not long after the U.S. cotton industry had become reliant on slavery, England banned slavery, while British nationals continued supplying slaves for the South's expanding cotton fields.

Still another indirect trade link between the United States and Bengal involves the origin of the heroin trade. This story begins in the late eighteenth and early nineteenth centuries when Britain, no longer exporting Bengali textiles to China to help pay for tea, had to find alternatives to balance its China trade. Unlike the U.S. furriers, British manufacturers had few markets in China. By chance, Britain began exporting Indian-grown opium to China. Managed by John Stuart Mill, the great liberal thinker who served as an executive of the East India Company (as had his father), this trade grew enormously in the first half of the nineteenth century. Ultimately it led Britain to fight two opium wars with China. China wanted to end the "trade," which was greatly increasing British wealth and power in Asia without enriching India, from whence the opium came. As for the United States, the money thus generated helped the capital markets in London, which no longer had to ship coin to China and thus could make credit available to America.

Turning to "official," though still indirect, links, a major one occurred during World War II, when the United States sent a large force to help Britain defend India after Japan attacked Assam and Burma. Led by General Stillwell, the chief commander in China, U.S. forces, at Calcutta, Chittagong, and Dhaka, helped oust the Japanese and ultimately liberate Burma. At that time, too, large numbers of U.S. pilots flew freight over the "hump" of the Himalayas in a successful attempt to relieve beleaguered China and keep it in the war against Japan. Indirectly, these U.S. endeavors helped Bengal by repelling the Japanese and making supplies available to that famine-wracked province of British India.

At war's end, as the price of Lend-Lease during the conflict and of a postwar loan, the United States pushed Britain into opening its empire to free trade, reversing its imperial tariff preferences of 1933 and enabling U.S. goods to compete in India and all other British colonies. This indirect factor, supported by intensive U.S. diplomatic pressure for India-Pakistan independence (a self-serving position, wrapped in idealist rhetoric and moral superiority over Britain), helped precipitate the partition of India in 1947.

From the standpoint of the circuitous U.S.-Bengali relationship, that year is important. It marked the end of an era that had lasted 164 years—the period that had begun with U.S independence in 1783. For until Britain relinquished control, the United States (and all other countries) had to view and deal with India, including Bengal, solely through British eyes. Still, this is not to imply that, where Bengal is concerned, much has changed, practically speaking. From a U.S. perspective, Bengal simply does not merit much priority. In fact, the exact opposite was true two decades ago, at one of the most crucial junctures in Bengal's history.

The incident occurred in 1971 when, at the height of the Vietnam War, the United States planned to reopen links with Communist China in a ploy designed to precipitate an end to the Cold War. The means lay in Islamabad, Pakistan's capital, where Foreign Minister (later President) Bhutto had been acting as a go-between, negotiating with U.S. presidential adviser Henry Kissinger. At the very tensest moments of this diplomatic démarche, civil war erupted between Pakistan's two wings. But unlike Lord Chatham, who had chosen Bengal, Kissinger chose West Pakistan, despite the pleas of the U.S. consul general in Dhaka that the United States should side with East Pakistan. Thus occurred what some people still consider the infamous "tilt" toward Pakistan—a choice that soured U.S.-Bangladesh relations for years and left an anti-U.S. legacy that occasionally flares, as during the 1991 Gulf War, when rioters heavily damaged the American Club in Dhaka and many Bangladeshis demanded that troops sent by their government to support the U.S.-led effort not be used in combat. Indeed, until perhaps 1976, Bangladesh-U.S. relations did not recover from Kissinger's choice—which proved to be correct, as it led in 1972 to President Richard Nixon's historic visit to China. In the heat of the moment, however, U.S. support for West Pakistan was incomprehensible to many Americans and to most Bangladeshis, who only learned of the China mission much later.

In a similar vein, the indirection that has characterized U.S.-Bengal relations endures today. For instance, in 1979 the United States, under President Jimmy Carter, proclaimed India to be the paramount power in South Asia, the regional superpower which, within the limits of good sense and international law, was responsible for maintaining the region's stability. In fact, India already had played this role in 1971–72, when it helped liberate Bangladesh, and it did so again in the late 1980s, when it helped quell a separatist revolt by Sri Lankan Tamils. Therefore, relying on India to maintain the region's stability, Washington understandably views Bangladesh through an Indian prism, especially as it considers Bangladesh's poverty and growing population to be a possible source of instability in South Asia and, possibly, in Southeast Asia and northern Burma.

For example, while applauding Bangladeshi efforts to modernize its economy within the international context, to reduce population growth (population policy being a major USAID project), and to keep the country stable and democratic, the United States has little interest in military cooperation beyond officer training. In fact, with the end of the Cold War, only its presumed nuclear capability keeps Pakistan important to U.S. foreign policy. If possible, the United States would rather deal with Pakistan, too, through India.

Turning to Bangladesh's perspective, its view of the United States is colored by a number of folk myths about U.S. intentions, myths partly planted first by Britain and then by British-influenced Bangladeshi communists to stoke anti-U.S. sentiments. For instance, during World War II, resenting U.S. pressures in favor of independence, the British suggested, by innuendo and rumor, that if England left India, the United States would take over. Furbished with standard British dislike of U.S. crassness and wealth, this claim helped fuel a standard image of Americans as ill-educated, generous but stupid, lazy, impatient, and, at worst, very treacherous.

Such anti-Americanism was further inflamed at the war's end when the homegrown communists, who had betrayed England by backing uprisings against it during the war and were now in ill repute, sought to curry popular favor by condemning the United States as neoimperialist. Harping on such claims throughout the Cold War, these communists and certain other Bangladeshi leaders presented the United States as a threat to Bengal, Bangladesh, and all of India—even though U.S. trade, investment, and strategic interests in Bangladesh were minimal, compared with those in East Asia or the Middle East.

At the same time, such negative images of the United States were perpetuated into the Pakistan era, when U.S. aid went mostly to West Pakistan, which, given its proximity to Afghanistan and the Soviet Union, was seen as strategically far more important than poverty-stricken, resource-poor, overpopulated East Pakistan. Moreover, influenced by a worldwide leftist resurgence that occurred in the 1960s, by radical Naxalite movements in India's West Bengal State, and by Soviet friendship with India and enmity for Pakistan, the Bangladeshi image of the United States suffered severe damage in the 1947–71 era—damage greatly exacerbated in 1972 by Kissinger's "tilt" toward Pakistan.

Finally, and again indirectly, more damage was done to U.S.-Bangladeshi relations by another aspect of the infamous "tilt." At the heart of the issue lies the fact that Bangladesh borders on Southeast Asia and has a tribal people who are ethnically Southeast Asian. The Chittagong District and some of central Bangladesh once belonged to the Arakan Empire, ruled by the Maghs, from today's Burma. Because of this, pre-Bangladesh Pakistan joined SEATO, the Southeast Asia Treaty Organization, Asia's version of NATO, which was a crucial force in maintaining regional stability and supporting the U.S.-led democracy effort both before and during the Vietnam War. However, after West Pakistan lost its civil war, it dropped out of SEATO. About this time, the United States "tilted" toward Pakistan, and Bangladesh never joined. Thus did the United States betray and lose during its crucial Vietnam period.

Related to this has been another aspect of tensions in U.S.-Bangladeshi relations, one that still lingers. For during the Vietnam era, many high-placed Bangladeshis and others believed that the United States wanted to build a military base in the Bay of Bengal to "control" the area's seaways. Many still believe that the United States is eyeing Saint Martin's Island south of Chittagong. Thus in 1991, when U.S. troops were sent to help Bangladesh in the aftermath of a devastating hurricane near Chittagong, many were the knowing Bangladeshi grins that this operation foreshadowed the longtime U.S. goal—especially as this rescue operation paralleled a U.S. decision to move its naval base from Cavite in the Philippines to Singapore at the eastern entrance of the Bay of Bengal.

Such a view is buttressed by some facts of geography. Northern Southeast Asia and southwest China, a region rich in oil, minerals, and forest products, is one of the earth's least settled areas. It lies just north of Burma, Laos, Vietnam, India, and Bangladesh and borders huge population centers in India, China, and parts of Southeast Asia. Given China's interest in the area, especially in North Burma, and India's traditional interest in Burma (once part of Britain's Indian Empire), there is genuine risk of a conflict, one the United States would not ignore if it threatened the region. Though it is a long-term concern, it surely plays a role, admittedly a marginal one, in U.S-Bangladeshi relations, not due to direct U.S. interest in Bangladesh but because of Bangladesh's adjacent areas where China and India compete.

Having dwelt at some length on tensions, real and imaginable, it behooves us now to examine positive aspects of the relationship. First and foremost has been U.S. aid to Bangladesh since 1975, which has been masterful in helping precipitate the progress the nation has made. Overall, the United States has been the biggest donor, providing critical food aid to prevent famine and fears of famine and aid for family planning, rural electrification, building of roads, bridges, and other infrastructures, and aid for oil and natural gas exploration, the latter of which was found in large supply. That discovery led the United States, the Soviets, and the Japanese to finance construction of power plants and factories that convert gas to nitrogenous fertilizers. And thanks in large part to a U.S. open-market policy, Bangladesh has developed a thriving garment industry. Also greatly helping improve Bangladeshi-U.S. relations have been a succession of first-rate U.S. ambassadors and their staffs, people who have been interested in the country and its problems and prospects and who, by and large, have been caring, compassionate, and well liked.

In return, Bangladesh has played a responsible role in international forums and has been a friend to the United States on most key issues of war and peace. Though officially nonaligned in the Cold War, Bangladesh has not been a radical nation, even under Sheikh Mujib. Relative to the Middle East, this Muslim nation unsurprisingly sympathizes with the Palestinians but has never engaged in radical Muslim behavior. Indeed, if anything its stance has been leftist rather than religiously oriented, even though its ties to Muslim holy places in Saudi Arabia and Jerusalem cannot be underestimated.

Likewise, within the Islamic Bloc, that United Nations group of forty-six nations, Bangladesh, which has 10 percent of the world's Muslims, has played a forceful role; yet it has been a constructive player, concerned mainly with economic aid to Muslim nations and with peace among the Muslim Umah, or Brotherhood. Still, within this matrix, it often votes with its Middle East Muslim friends—who provide increasing aid.

As for the future, with passing time Bangladesh is likely to move closer to Japan and China as protection against India and, to a lesser degree, to depend on European support, especially that of Britain and Germany, which have taken a deep interest in it, as have France, Belgium, Denmark, and Holland. At the same time, as the United States becomes less concerned with foreign affairs in the wake of the Cold War's demise, its relations with Bangladesh most likely will move increasingly to international forums, where the two nations often find reason to side with each other. In such a milieu, U.S.-Bangladesh relations increasingly will be filtered through regional and supraregional groupings, as these groups contribute to Bangladesh's economic progress and place in the developing world.

Finally, no portrait of Bangladeshi-U.S. relations would be complete without some description of the critical roles that have been played by unofficial U.S. ambassadors of good will: members of diverse Protestant and Catholic missionary groups and of such voluntary agencies as Planned Parenthood, CARE, Save the Children USA, the Ford Foundation, the Asia Foundation, and Catholic Relief. Their work, dedication, and accomplishments over the years have been invaluable to the strengthening of informal though critical ties, often despite U.S. government policy.

In fact, the oldest and in many ways the most enduring of U.S. ties was forged by missionaries at the start of the nineteenth century. Then, after years of being prevented by the East India Company from entering Bengal, a group of Baptists established an outpost at Serampore near Calcutta, where they set up a Christian printing press. Ultimately this press helped rejuvenate modern Bangla and began spreading Christian teachings through Bengal. Controversies surrounding the written word, especially polemical exchanges over religion, not only helped rejuvenate the Bangla language but also helped spark the Bengali enlightenment. It was in the midst of this rhetorical battle that the Brahmo religion, the reformed Hinduism described earlier, was created. The legacy of the early U.S. Baptists endures, because those missionaries supported the British-backed Brahmo movement. They also built schools and hospitals that either have survived or at least have provided models upon which to build. Indeed, the work of these missionaries in education and medicine receives too little attention in the histories of Bengal.

Likewise, major contributions have been made by two branches of the Catholic Church's Holy Cross order. Thus, in the mid–nineteenth century, when French Jesuits abandoned their mission in Dhaka, the Pope called upon France's Holy Cross order to take up the burden. As it turned out, the main burden fell to the U.S. and Canadian branches. Several colleges, including Notre Dame and Holy Cross, named for the schools in South Bend, Indiana, were created in Dhaka. Still considered the best schools for preuniversity training, they are run now mostly by aging Holy Cross priests, whose Bangla is tinged with a distinctly Midwestern twang.

Today these priests, who have devoted their lives to East Bengal/Bangladesh, some having lived there more than thirty years, continue to uphold the highest standards of quality and incorruptibility—standards which make their schools the most desirous and thus the hardest to enter. Sponsoring or running schools, hospitals, health clinics, and orphanages, these religious operate throughout the country, sometimes alone, offering not only an education but often food and other forms of aid. Their enduring legacy is evident everywhere, as their graduates often are the most likely to succeed in the endeavor of their choice. Many, albeit those from relatively wealthy families, go to universities overseas. And while, like their parents, many gravitate to England, increasing numbers are choosing the United States, where they can be found around the country, at such prominent schools as Harvard, Princeton, Williams, and Boston University, as well as at such lesser lights as Indiana University of Pennsylvania, to name a popular one. Since most eventually return home, often to become leaders in diverse fields, Bangladesh's relations with the United States thus have been growing warmer with time.

8

Will Bangladesh Survive?

W HEN, IN 1971, BANGLADESH GAINED INDEPENDENCE from Pakistan and was recognized by the whole world, the first question asked was: could it survive?

For the nation that emerged not only had been the poorest place on earth in per capita income before the Liberation War, but after the war was even more devastated. Roads were closed due to the bombing of bridges; electric power had been interrupted; most industry had been nationalized, as it had belonged either to foreigners or Pakistanis; foreign exchange shortages made scarce not only imports but many critical medicines and other vital goods; and Bangladesh did not even have its own currency, but instead stamped the word *taka* over the face of Pakistani rupees. Moreover, millions of villagers had been displaced by the war and large numbers of refugees, especially Hindus, had fled to India, never to return, or to the cities, where they dwelt in abject squalor (and were to remain that way for many years); minorities that had prospered under the Pakistanis filled refugee camps, waiting to be sent to Pakistan; bus, rail, and air travel were problematic; smuggling to and from India and Burma and the nations along the Bay of Bengal flourished, along with black markets in currencies and most manufactured goods.

Furthermore, at independence Dhaka appeared to be an overgrown county seat, not even in the same league as Pakistan's Rawalpindi, Karachi, and Lahore and certainly not comparable to Calcutta. Dhaka then stretched from the river only about two miles out to the Farmgate area near today's Sonargaon Hotel, where most visitors now stay. The Parliament Building, then being built, lay on the edge of town, with cows wandering its grounds. Massive old trees graced center islands along the main roads, and there were only two tall buildings, the Intercontinental Hotel and the Central Bank. Most foreigners lived in Dhanmondi, while Gulshan and Banani, where most foreigners reside today, were just being built, in the far suburbs. In toto, the Dhaka of two decades ago occupied only about half its current size.

Politically speaking, while the nation unified itself magnificently, there existed an air of unreality based on socialist hopes, an air of rugged self-reliance and xenophobia, and one of growing intimacy with allies of Eastern Bloc communist countries. Ties to the West, while not unimportant, were not strong initially; and indeed, much bitterness, not unfairly, was directed against the West, especially the United States. Unquestionably, at liberation India, the USSR, China, and Vietnam held pride of place, not only as allies and aid-givers, but, as is often forgotten now that the Cold War is over, as providers of intellectual and moral leadership. This latter fact today is not too proudly remembered, in the face of mounting revelations about East Bloc abuses.

Not that the Western world ignored the new nation. On the contrary, from the beginning of Bangladesh's agony in late 1970, due to the aftermath of a massive typhoon, to the refusal of the Pakistanis to recognize the election results in 1971, to the murderous persecution of the East Bengalis and their rebellion against their Pakistani rulers, there had been a building wave of sympathy in the West for Bangladesh's independence struggle. For instance, rallies in London, New York, and Washington demonstrated that popular sentiment supported liberation, even though the United States government withheld support for fledgling Bangladesh and actually "tilted" toward Pakistan.

However, in January 1972, as soon as a free Bangladesh emerged and airports and ports were open, an outpouring of aid streamed in, first from India and then from Western governments and private agencies. Included were food, medicine, blankets, clothing, construction materials for housing, roads, and utilities, and equipment of all sorts. Also arriving in significant numbers were doctors, nurses, engineers, and development experts, many from aid agencies worldwide. The influx was evident everywhere. For instance, massive supplies of heavy equipment, awaiting spare parts, were stored in parking lots near what is now the Government Tourist Office near the old airport. In development circles, nay in multinational circles, to have been to Bangladesh during that period had a certain dash about it, when one mentioned it casually but knowingly at cocktail parties. In 1972 Bangladesh represented the most politically correct place to be in sympathy with and to visit, second only to China after President Nixon's visit later that year.

Nevertheless, the atmosphere surrounding the country remained doubtful as more facts came to light. Thus it became an "international basket case," in the U.S. State Department's unhopeful phrase, and a "bottomless basket case" among the Bangladeshi cognoscenti who shared the gloom. To this day the "basket case" aura endures.

And for good reason. Bangladesh emerged with some seventy-five million people in a land with only fifty-five thousand square miles, more densely populated than any nation except Taiwan. Its people had an annual per capita income of less than $100, in a land where one-third of the surface area is water during the good times of the year and up to 70 percent is submerged for at least two months annually, a land bereft of major resources and fuels. Moreover, the country had no stone or gravel for roads (all roads had to be built high above the flood level), and major bridges appeared to be unknown. In 1972 the main port remained blocked, and freight arrived after arduous transshipment by lighters. Literacy rates ranked among the world's lowest.

This writer recalls earnest and dire predictions made about the nation. For example, while holding forth at the Intercontinental Hotel poolside, a venerable older man who had spent much time in Bangladesh's development community told anyone from the foreign community who would listen that the best business brains of the country, Bihari and Hindu, had fled and that the Muslims remaining were, for the most part, benighted medieval fanatics, socialist or Muslim fanatics, and that the country ought to be given to India. Not only would the benighted Bangladeshis never do well in business, he contended, but the ignorant Muslim farmer would never innovate and use new fertilizers and tubewells.

At the same time, population experts, on more solid ground, predicted that if the economic situation did not improve dramatically, population growth rates could lead to destabilization and, possibly, to mass deaths, at least by the 1980s. Likewise, agricultural experts, noting that the world jute market was being displaced by synthetic fibers, agonized at the "cash squeeze" faced by the farmers. Other agriculturalists pointed out that while the country had adequate water in the rainy season, if it wanted to expand production it would need more irrigation for the dry seasons. Still others noted that the country's drier northern part needed even more aid in the form of irrigation equipment. Expanded irrigation, others said, would spark a need for electric power or investment in canals and water storage facilities. Also, new fast-growing and more-productive seed varieties were needed. And fertilizers. And insect sprays.

The needs seemed to multiply, while the resources remained static. The helpless feeling, this writer recalls, reached its apogee in 1974, when a combination of drought in one part of the country and floods elsewhere, plus massive mismanagement of food reserves, led to a great hunger that caused many deaths and massive suffering. Every "basket case" and Malthusian "population bomb" theory seemed to be coming true. Despite aid, despite the opening of roads and the building of better utilities, the country appeared to many observers to be on the brink of greater poverty than it had faced in 1943. So hopeless did the situation seem that a sympathetic but pessimistic senior manager of a U.S. pharmaceutical company approved shipment of more equipment, maintaining that it could be construed as a charitable donation, as he did not believe that Bangladesh would overcome its problems without hunger, war, and, perhaps, economic collapse and revolution.

Thus to this day visitors almost automatically and immediately ask about birth rates, what family planning projects are in place, per capita income, malnutrition, disease, and rural development. Thoughts of prosperity, or even of hope, inevitably seem to have been discounted in advance. Such views are not without merit. For as Bangladesh remains one of the poorest nations, such concerns are likely to be timely and sensitive for another decade at least.

Nevertheless, the basic question has been answered: barring unmitigated disaster of a scale yet unimagined, Bangladesh will survive and prosper in the years to come.

There are good reasons for optimism. Rice production has more than doubled, growing faster than population, due to the spread of irrigation, new seeds, fertilizer, better roads, storage facilities, and marketing procedures. There has not been widespread hunger since 1974, and food reserves have been located in warehouses all over the country, including in cool and refrigerated ones. Electric power, once erratic even in the capital cities, now is stable in larger district towns and is spreading to the villages. In fact, the power grid now embraces the entire country, if not every village within the system, and all villages now are capable of being connected. Nitrogenous fertilizers are widely available and used, thanks to large and expanding supplies of indigenous natural gas. Tubewells dot the green countryside with silvery reflections from the water flow. New strains of seeds and crop varieties have proliferated among farmers, who are more ready to change than many expected. New industries, such as garment making, textiles, leather goods, electronic assembly, shoemaking, and machine tool trades, have expanded. Cities are able to absorb some parts of the surplus rural population, because employment is growing, except in periods of political change. Literacy is growing, despite major problems in the educational system due to excessive politicization. And Dhaka has expanded about ten miles to the north of the Parliament Building, which itself was on the fringe of town two decades ago. This growth, in part due to misguided use of funds spent in Dhaka to the exclusion of the regional cities, had a purpose, because there are jobs in the capital. People do not migrate to places devoid of work. They migrate toward prosperity.

As for population growth, it has been a benefit as well as a detriment, although so far it has been more of the latter. For Bangladesh is a reservoir of labor, labor that is helping the nation compete in two ways. First, hundreds of thousands of Bangladeshis have migrated to temporary jobs in the Middle East and other places where labor is short. In the aftermath of the Iraqi invasion, many refugees from Kuwait were Bangladeshi. These workers and their compatriots elsewhere send home huge amounts of foreign earnings that are crucial to the nation's per capita income and provide foreign exchange to help buy needed investment goods. Moreover, this labor force learns new trades, and often returning workers start businesses or bring home new technologies and skills. Many of these skills are immediately turned into innovations in the workers' home villages, where often the returnee is the first to organize cooperatives for bringing in electricity—a resource that the returned worker has learned is essential to development.

In addition, the surplus work force that remains home attracts investment in those industries searching for hard-working labor at low prices. In recent years, increasing amounts of such investment have been entering the country, especially in export zones established to emulate ones in South Korea and Taiwan, countries which, in the 1950s, used these industries to successfully launch economic development. That Bangladesh labor is being employed this way is a sign that the future bodes well, as other developing countries have used this as a starting point in the process of transition from a rural-based to a balanced rural-urban economy. Still, in Bangladesh this process has not yet absorbed the excess labor leaving agriculture and seeking industrial employment.

It is worthwhile to pause here and note that the trend of migration from agriculture to industry is one of the first signs that development is under way. Indeed, before 1971 the trend had begun but had not been a major part of the nation's development process. Since 1972 and especially in the past few years, the process has become more insistent, more pronounced, forcing the country's planners to widen their interests from integrated agricultural development to more intensive and, hopefully, environmentally safe means of urbanization and industrialization. This transition is normal, a sign of change and progress. Yet the process is painful, as it forces families to leave the land where their ancestors have lived for millennia and to change their whole life-style, not via education and acculturation but through impoverished migration from farm to nearby larger village and thence to subdistrict towns, district towns, provincial capitals, and, finally, Dhaka. Those dispossessed by this painful but crucial transition are all too obvious throughout the country. They comprise a river of people wending their way from rural to industrial settings. The most heart-rending among them are visible in the landfill areas around Dhaka and Chittagong, where mostly women and children live in garbage heaps, searching for food or scraps that they can sell for food. Only the healthy survive the process. Who knows what happens to the old and the weak along the path of relocation?

Still, the migration itself is a sign of prosperity, as no country yet has developed until the balance between industry and agriculture tips toward the former. At independence, Bangladeshi agriculture accounted for 77.5 percent of all employment. By 1986 this figure had dropped to 57.2 percent. Nevertheless, while the nation thus is in the throes of major economic transition, more than 80 percent of its people still live in villages and urban life, Dhaka excepted, has yet to flower. However, in the past ten years district towns, called upazillas, 460 of them, have grown rapidly and represent a new tier of urban growth almost unimaginable in 1971, as government money, offices, and courts have been placed there to bring government closer to the people. If these towns can develop small industries, they will help absorb the continued migration of people from the countryside looking for work. Still, since industry depends on communication, transport, fuel, and electricity and as these essentials, especially telephones and good roads, have not yet been well developed in the upazillas, movement of industry to these district towns has not been as fast as had been hoped. Yet in some areas this process has proceeded fairly rapidly, especially along the rivers where transport is fast and cheap.

Also encouraging is the fact that not only has Bangladesh been able to increase grain production faster than population, but the population growth rate has declined to less than 2.5 percent a year, from far higher rates in the 1960s. In addition, agriculturally speaking, dramatic trends are under way in terms of diversification of crops and use of low-cost labor, which makes possible exports of fruits and vegetables to the Middle East and East Asia. Thus air freighters already carry such vegetables as asparagus and cauliflower to Saudi Arabia, while watermelons, cantaloupes, mangoes, and chilies are being exported to a wide range of countries.

On the health front, smallpox and leprosy, major problems two decades ago, virtually have been eliminated, thanks in part to grass-roots efforts to vaccinate against the former and to provide early care for the latter, a treatable disease. Likewise, malaria is much more under control.

Diarrheal diseases, especially cholera, remain the second largest killers after tuberculosis and other upper respiratory infections. Still, they are far less devastating, thanks to the discovery, in the midst of the Liberation War, of the correct formula for an oral rehydration solution (ORS) that swiftly replenishes bodily fluids whose loss is debilitating or life-threatening. Credit for this discovery goes to the International Centre of Diarrhoeal Diseases Research, Bangladesh, a two-thousand-employee internationally sponsored-and-run hospital-cum-research center headquartered in Dhaka. And credit for massive dissemination of ORS's use in the countryside goes to a Bangladeshi voluntary agency, BRAC, which, using USAID funds, has dramatically spurred spread of this therapy from village to village by training women to use it and teach its use. As a result, cholera deaths have been reduced by more than 80 percent since 1972.

At the same time, however, malnutrition remains a major problem among the population migrating to cities, and slums continue growing around urban areas. Yet despite improving but by no means adequate health care, population growth rates are down, owing to the widespread availability of contraceptive devices. Some sources estimate that up to 45 percent of Bangladeshi women use some form of contraceptive. This is due to the work of outstanding local women's organizations, supported by The Asia Foundation, the Ford Foundation, USAID, and the United Nations' FPA.

The foregoing successes by no means imply that Bangladesh will not continue needing aid, investment, and expertise for some years to come. Nor do they mean that anyone can relax. But if further success can continue building upon past achievements and there are no major setbacks, the country's first twenty years have seen significant health, population, infrastructure, agricultural, and industrial advancements—ones that even the most optimistic observers would not have predicted in 1972. Realistically, however, Bangladesh today is a nation in the first phases of developmental transition—one which continues to face a long haul, under conditions as challenging as exist anywhere on earth, before anyone will be able to say that the country has achieved "takeoff," that is, self-generating growth.

Therefore the greatest uncertainty, about the nation's viability, has been answered. Bangladesh is not a "bottomless basket case." Though still very poor, it is not static. It is a thriving, growing, dynamic country that will survive the first phases of development. No longer is there any economic reason to doubt that development will continue, as long as peace prevails and world markets remain open. In the last analysis, the nation's very poverty drives it to compete, and to work more for less, in order to prosper.

Yet the nagging question about population persists. At its current 2.4 percent growth rate, Bangladesh's population will double in 29.5 years—to about 220 million people by the year 2022, a total of more than five thousand people per square mile. Thus a fundamental question remains: is such a population sustainable?

At present it is impossible to imagine a scenario wherein Bangladesh would be able to support that many people, if all of them remained home. Where would the funds come from for investment in infrastructure, industry, and agriculture? The only current conceivable answer is that if anything near such population growth rates are sustained, massive emigration would have to occur, first to the Middle East or to labor-starved areas such as Australia and Canada and then across Bangladesh's borders to India and Burma, with all the political destabilization this could imply. Already tensions are high between Bangladesh and India due to a westward migration into Assam. Meanwhile, on Bangladesh's eastern border, the Burmese government in 1992 was trying to force out an ethnic minority, Muslim Bengalis called Rohingas, generations-long residents of Burma's relatively unpopulated Arakan region. In the coming two decades, as population pressures mount in Bangladesh, it is quite possible that ethnic Bangladeshis related to the Rohingas increasingly might migrate eastward. In other words, just as Mexican and Caribbean peoples today are emigrating to the United States, Bangladeshis could start overflowing their borders into India and Burma.

Thus, the crucial population issue darkens every optimistic projection for Bangladesh. And that is why the "basket case" image never quite disappears. Moreover, given the lack of urgency about this problem that characterizes most Bangladeshi government agencies and political parties despite universal lip service, even this author, among the most optimistic of Bangladesh's friends, finds it hard not to be pessimistic.

To deal with this issue the nation's planners need to confront the three major factors that help determine population growth. The first, of course, is the need for an effective family planning campaign, one that would ensure every mother and each new child sufficient nutrition, pre- and post-natal care, and much-increased access to proper family planning advice and procedures, as well as to overall health care.

The second factor is social. Later marriages, coupled with increased education of both boys and girls, should be encouraged. This not only will reduce women's fertility spans and begin lifting the populace to another economic level but will lead to better treatment of women and, ultimately, to fewer children. For in all societies it is well known that economically better-off families not only exhibit greater respect for women but begin having fewer children. The reason is simple. As people get richer, their health improves and more children survive to adulthood and thus are available to care for their parents later on. Also, as the benefits of education multiply, families realize that fewer children can be better educated, resulting in more comfortable lives.

The third crucial factor is industrialization, which brings a shift to urbanization and, eventually, to lower birth rates. For the expenses of urban life themselves are natural checks on population. Thus a population that is receiving increased health care and education and is being urbanized and becoming more affluent goes through a "demographic transition," wherein population growth rates decline rapidly. Most of the developed world today is at or near negative population growth, while many newly industrialized nations are on the verge of achieving very low or zero population growth rates. Unfortunately, Bangladesh has a long, long way to go in this regard.

Still, progress is being made. The first part of population planning gradually is being accomplished, so that most people have access to family planning services. Likewise, more health services, though only marginally better, are in place. Still lacking are significantly increased educational opportunities and the conditions for a demographic transition, although some movement toward urbanization is under way. The problem is that to achieve this growth phase the nation needs to attract investment and aid on a far larger scale. Sufficient efforts in this direction still are lacking, as is a sense of urgency great enough to precipitate the political transition that will result in solicitation of private investment to supplement aid. This last point is the real crisis facing Bangladesh.

This author believes that if the population bomb that is ticking is not to destroy the nation's fabric, Bangladesh's leaders must take drastic action to achieve the social changes associated with a demographic transition. That such action will be taken this author has no doubt. For despite the utopian socialist concepts that the nation was born with, the progress made thus far in disregarding those over-optimistic hopes has proved the ultimate practicality of Bangladeshi society.

The best bet is that Bangladesh will make the necessary changes and survive, even if the pace, in the eyes of foreigners, is too slow. Certainly in its first twenty years it has confounded most of the pessimistic reports that greeted its birth. Compared with many other nations only two decades after independence, Bangladesh has done well—not as well as Taiwan and South Korea but better than Indonesia and the Philippines at the same twenty-year marker. The situation in Bangladesh remains precarious, however, and the dangers of failure are still very real.

To survive, Bangladesh needs friends. It is surrounded on three sides, west, north, and east, by India, and to the south, the Indian Navy controls the Bay of Bengal. Relations, then, with India are the essential ingredient in the long-run survival of Bangladesh as an independent nation. India is a much larger country, far more industrialized, with a huge industrial infrastructure to support its 1.2-million-man military establishment. At any time India can militarily conquer and rule Bangladesh. There simply is no outside power at present that has an economic interest in Bangladesh sufficient to justify intervention on behalf of Bangladesh. China has enough power on the Burmese border to put pressure on India, but it is highly unlikely that China would come to Bangladesh's aid should India decide to invade. China's interest in Bangladesh would be important only in the event of a war between Beijing and New Delhi. Short of that, China's interests in Bangladesh are not decisive.

But are India and Bangladesh friends or enemies?

Bangladesh exists, as has been stated above, because most Indian Muslims at the time Britain left India did not want to live in a country dominated by caste Hindus. Partition of the Indian subcontinent was based on this premise. And the enmity between Pakistan and India to this day, including the troubles in the Muslim majority state of Kashmir, are rooted in that enmity.

Hindus felt a similar sense of estrangement, nay, a fear and hatred of Islam. The founders of modern India did not want a large Muslim minority within its borders—a minority that, under the Moghuls, once had ruled most of the subcontinent and had made major contributions to India's culture, economy, and political and legal life. Given a united India with an initial Muslim prime minister versus a divided India with an independent Pakistan, the Hindus opted for partition. Of all the leaders, including Nehru and Vilabhai Patel, only Gandhi saw this as tragic. Ultimately, however, leaders on both sides chose separation based on the concept of "good fences make good neighbors," as Robert Frost phrased it.

To this day, Bangladesh's two giant neighbors, India and Pakistan, never have gotten on well. For in the nearly half-century since partition, more often than not, relations between them have been characterized by large troop concentrations, air forces on alert, sealed borders, even skirmishes. Significantly, the same has not been true for India and Bangladesh. Indeed, even when Pakistan ruled East Bengal, there were virtually no defenses on either side of the East Pakistan–Indian border. In fact, during the 1965 Pakistan-India war, what now is Bangladesh simply had no credible defending force. Today the same could be said. The Bangladesh army, only one-eighth the size of India's, is not on alert; nor does either nation have a rational war plan that would even suggest a possible war in any foreseeable future. As Indian General B. K. Nehru told this writer more than two decades ago on a flight from London to Delhi, "The worst result anyone could predict for a war between India and [then] East Pakistan would be that India would win and have to absorb the territory."

His statement, made before December 1971, when Bangladeshi Freedom Fighters and the Indian Army invaded East Pakistan and succeeded in liberating Bangladesh, proved prophetic. More to the point is the fact that India then controlled Bangladesh and probably could have cut off the Freedom Fighters' supplies and defeated them. Instead, India turned over the government to the Bangladesh liberation movement and withdrew its forces rapidly, taking along about 100,000 Pakistani prisoners. On one hand, poor India did not want to absorb into its social matrix poor, and what would have been sullen, Muslim Bangladesh. On the other hand, India exhibited wisdom and generosity by withdrawing quickly without making impossible demands on the new country—an act that Indian statesmanship and Indira Gandhi deserve much more praise for than they currently receive in Bangladesh and elsewhere.

Since then, only over a single, crucial issue have India-Bangladesh relations become distant, correct, and tense. The issue concerns a barrage that, to meet its own water needs, India built at Farraka on the Padma (Ganges) River right across the Bangladesh border. Changing the course of the Ganges, the barrage siphons off two-thirds of the mighty river's water that used to enter western Bangladesh from that source. Despite more than two decades of endless negotiations, India has basically ignored Bangladeshi objections to the barrage and/or suggestions for alternate water-usage schemes. However, greater than the problems that this has caused, what really frightens Bangladesh is that India has a similar plan to siphon off water from the Jamuna, or Brahmaputra, River. Although this plan has been discussed with the World Bank and possibly could benefit both India and Bangladesh, given the Farraka experience Bangladesh fears the implications such action could have for its delta ecology. For Bangladesh is situated on an active delta that provides the world's greatest flow of fresh water to the ocean, and is the reason that Bangladesh is such a rich alluvial plain. Bangladesh rightly fears that any major diminution of fresh water flow could disrupt its entire ecological balance. In an age of environmental concerns, such a risk cannot be taken lightly.

Beyond these serious water disputes, other disagreements, as on trade, smuggling, and border rectification, are minor. The only other possibly critical problem looming on the horizon emerged a few years ago when India threatened to fence off its border with Bangladesh to stop migration of Muslim Bengalis into less densely populated eastern and northern areas of India. For India's Assam State in particular has seen large migrations, mostly because Assam and Bangladesh's Sylhet District share a common mountain and riverine area and economy. Thus, in the future, if Bangladeshi population problems and hence migration are not controlled, this issue could erupt into a major diplomatic crisis. Even so, over the long run not even this problem would be likely to disrupt the longstanding friendly premises of India-Bangladesh relations. It is in the interests of both sides to maintain cordiality. For instance, as a former Bangladesh foreign minister, Minhu Doha, told this author, "As long as Delhi is stable, our affairs will be stable."

Finally, there is another aspect of relations between Dhaka and Delhi that lingers in the background, occasionally resurfaces, and remains just beyond anyone's control but never quite emerges as a problem: a movement to reunify Bangladesh (East Bengal) with India's West Bengal State, to form a new nation. Thus, even if the voice is weak and remote, the cry of "united Bengal," which dates back to the first, short-lived partition of 1905, still has resonance. Not that anyone truly believes such an event to be remotely politically possible. Indeed, many around whom such a movement might have coalesced were among the thirty-five thousand intellectuals the Pakistanis murdered in 1971. Nevertheless, given the common language and culture, dreams of reunification endure in some circles; and if the right air of crisis were to exist, a movement for unification conceivably could become a factor in relations, especially as population growth in both Bengals and increasing trade between them encourages closer relations. Such an eventuality would greatly upset both Delhi and Dhaka, for it could destabilize both governments as they now exist.

Preventing this is the fact that the two Bengals have grown apart over the years, with West Bengal's young looking toward Delhi and Bangladesh's enjoying the rights of independent nationhood. Moreover, this new generation lacks its parents' and grandparents' emotional and other prepartition ties. Another factor that militates against any successful appeal to a united Bengal is the rise of a new fundamentalist Hindu movement in India led by the Bharat Janata Party, which wants to establish the Hindu identity of India over the secular identity that Nehru wanted. The BJP has made strong inroads in West Bengal, where the communists have ruled for nearly fifteen years and where there are strong fears of Muslim penetration due to ongoing immigration and possible border rectifications. The border issue involves returning various enclaves of Hindus and Muslims to places where they more naturally fit. The problem dates to partition, when the British, in dividing the subcontinent, carelessly put many villages and enclaves on the wrong side of the border. One such enclave is at Tin Bigha, where a Muslim settlement lies about two hundred yards outside Bangladesh. India has agreed to a corridor between the village and Bangladesh, but Hindus complain that this corridor cuts off some Hindu villages from one another. The BJP has been able to use this issue to good effect among Hindus in West Bengal. This issue could become increasingly divisive were emigration of Muslim Bangladeshis to grow significantly. That would create a large Muslim minority in West Bengal whose presence could spark a political crisis, which the BJP could use to great effect. In the last analysis, then, dreams of a united Bengal live on in the hearts and minds of some people on both sides of the border, as the spirit of Sarat Bose, who led a united Bengal movement in 1945, continues to haunt the land.

At the same time, a more positive side of India-Bangladeshi relations dates to 1978, when Bangladesh's president Zia Rahman called for the formation of a South Asian Regional Cooperation movement, much like the EEC in Europe or ASEAN in Southeast Asia. Each year since, SARC, consisting of India, Pakistan, Bangladesh, Nepal, and Sri Lanka, has met at various diplomatic levels and has made progress in some areas of trade and business relations, as evidenced by the fact that airline flights among these nations catering to businessmen are fully booked and trade is growing. Unfortunately, still greater cooperation has been stymied by tense relations between Pakistan and India and by the fact that the economies of the three subcontinent nations have grown apart in the nearly half-century since partition. For instance, while in recent years India's economy has liberalized rapidly from its socialist and autarchic path, it has not been as open to the world as have the economies of Pakistan and Bangladesh. Indeed, many Western goods are smuggled into India from Bangladesh. Still, in the last analysis, SARC is beginning to take shape, and it represents the best single chance for solidifying the subcontinent into a single economic bloc.

Also of consequence is the fact that in order to offset dependence on India, over the past two decades Bangladesh gradually has strengthened ties to the East Asian nations of Japan, China, South Korea, Malaysia, and Indonesia. Similarly, it has repaired its relationship with Pakistan and has forged more intensive ties with its South Asian neighbors Nepal, Burma, and Sri Lanka. Consequently, Bangladesh does not feel as exposed to "raw," and the term is well chosen, Indian power plays. RAW, by the way, is the acronym of India's version of the Central Intelligence Agency, the Research and Analysis Wing. RAW is a powerful presence in Bangladesh because of the country's significant Hindu minority, the sympathies of certain groups of secular and Muslim Bangladeshis for rapprochement with India, the occasional infiltration of West Bengali spies who speak the same language and are ethnically identical to Bangladeshi Muslims, and the resources that the Indian government devotes to this crucial neighbor. For Delhi can never forget that the British conquered all of India via Bengal. As for the rest of Asia, though India remains the dominant regional power, other states have an interest in seeing that Bangladesh remains free, as a counterbalance to India.

INVESTING AND VISITING

Is foreign investment welcome?

The answer is "Yes, but. . . . "

Bangladesh has a large but very poor population compared to other countries, with a new infrastructure of roads, electricity, and fuels, as yet underutilized. As a market, it needs everything but has relatively little means of payment. Thus it has not attracted much investment by companies that manufacture industrial or consumer goods. Indeed, because of unfavorable regulations or other actions concerning intellectual property or trademarks, the government has driven investment out, partly to protect local manufacturers but also as a result of simple bureaucratic xenophobia or ideology.

Bangladesh is interested in attracting investors who want cheap labor. A "one stop" office has been set up to process applications, and major, partially successful, campaigns are under way. However, wise investors have chosen to work with local partners who can help them both with the problems of establishing a business and with the myriad regulations and crises related to taxes, electric hookups, land use, and so forth. Bangladesh is not an easy place to operate. For example, though hungry for jobs, Bangladeshis are quick to form unions and to make demands and are skilled at getting politicians to back their wishes, as when, in 1984, President Ershad demanded that all private firms raise wages by 10 percent without individual company negotiations. Likewise, there is a widespread assumption that the foreigner is rich and able to pay more than he is offering, and great imaginings of outside-the-country profits spin through everyone's head. Consequently, while they want investment, few Bangladeshis understand what investors are looking for or what terms and conditions neighboring countries are offering.

Worse, while the government will agree to all broad conditions demanded at the time of initial investment, government ministers and other high officials no longer are interested in the investor when he is tormented by critical day-to-day details. Indeed, once the money is in, the government feels that it has done everything necessary and turns to its favorite role of demanding things from the investors.

Thus, Bangladesh wants and needs investment. Some has come and done well; some has come and left; and some has sensed that the environment is unhealthy. There is an air of suspense, a palpable feeling that even one's local partners, like vultures, are waiting to pounce if an investor loses his nerve. Therefore this is not yet a good place to invest, because Bangladesh does not understand that investment requires reciprocity. Moreover, the government is no guarantee of anything unless the minister will see the investor in the first place. And that is not always guaranteed.

Part of the problem is that Bangladesh has a hangover of anticolonial and antiforeign ideas, some socialist-tinged but most based on a long memory of East India Company depredations and a fear that because a foreign company once conquered the country, it could happen again, despite vastly changed conditions. India, especially West Bengal, is filled with this syndrome, as are Burma, China, Vietnam, and Laos. Bangladesh is not unusual in this; it is only more timid, perhaps less understanding of the situation. Consequently, an investor should be careful, should set limited objectives, should commit further funds only after each objective has been met, and should get his money out fast, until Bangladesh really decides it wants to join the international economic community. Unfortunately, for the moment xenophobia, the language fascism described earlier, is part of the nation's psyche, and a liberal outlook has yet to emerge. That is not unusual in a nation twenty years after independence, as has been seen all over the Third World. Such a view after thirty years would be disastrous.

Is Bangladesh safe to visit?

The answer is "Yes." No buts.

Bangladesh is a peaceful country, with a homogeneous population that precludes much ethnic or religious strife, the kind of strife that is most dangerous. Middle East-style terrorism never has occurred.

That does not mean there cannot be danger; it means that most of the time foreigners are safer in Dhaka than they would be, say, in New York or Washington, D.C.

Still, there are frequent tensions, especially those occasioned by general strikes, or hartals, which are announced well in advance and close down major cities and country roads alike. At such times, one definitely does not drive a car; it is likely to be met with brickbats. And while prudent foreigners tend to remain indoors during the appointed hours, many an old Dhaka hand has been known to wander the streets, to be rewarded by interesting discussions with Bangladeshis similarly restless.

Once in a great while there are anti-U.S. riots, such as the attack on the American Club during the Gulf War. Such demonstrations probably are not locally inspired but are instigated and supported by foreign intelligence agencies stirring up sympathizers of whichever dictator, such as Gaddafi or Saddam Hussein, will pay to rent a crowd. Such riots never occur without plenty of warning.

Perhaps the most dangerous place for foreigners is at the universities, where, as we have seen, the nation's political parties subsidize students and faculty alike to demonstrate or otherwise show their power. Such violence can be sudden, unplanned, and dangerous. But because Dhaka University, for example, tends to be closed down for many months at a time, even this threat is not great. Besides, foreigners usually do not visit the universities, which are the nation's greatest disgrace.

Crime is rarely a problem in Dhaka before midnight; and while hartals can seem threatening, they usually represent an extra holiday for almost everyone. In the countryside, provincial towns are safe, regional hotels usually are both clean and safe, and travel on roads and the railway is as safe as one will find in most places. River travel, however, can be dangerous in times of flood or storm, as most boats are old and not always well maintained. Rail travel is often late and uncomfortable, but there is privacy in first-class cars, at low rates. Air travel can be dangerous during severe storms in the dry season, when the region's air patterns tend to be unstable.

Why would anyone want to visit Bangladesh?

For the intelligent traveler, that is, the tourist who is not looking for good food or luxury hotels, trips to countries such as Bangladesh, India, Pakistan, Afghanistan, and now those in Central Asia can be challenging and mentally stimulating. Excluding the "tourists of poverty," who are happy only when they can sympathize with the poor and bash the rich, the intelligent traveler (who may also bash the rich and love the poor) visits a place like Bangladesh to learn. He or she may be interested not only in politics and economics (subjects our century has made boring, due to endless discussion in various media) but also in philosophy, art, music, history, spiritual quests, and old-fashioned adventure. The intelligent traveler neither patronizes the poor nor assumes that only the rich and well-educated are wise. Rather, like Socrates, he or she wants to question, listen, and learn; this traveler is seeking a well-ordered life and wants to meet others of similar persuasion.

Wisdom, of course, can be found just walking down the street where you live. But for those who have decided, deliberately or accidentally, to learn about and from other cultures, Bangladesh is as good a place to visit as any. And for those interested specifically in South and Central Asia, Bangladesh is an excellent starting point. By following the old Grand Trunk Road across northern India—a road that begins at the first-class Sonargaon Hotel in the heart of Dhaka—it is possible to trace the history of one of the oldest known civilizations, one rich in wisdom, philosophical, religious, and spiritual. By making this journey one will be rewarded by some of the most stupendous sights and insights: the Brahmaputra River at full flood; the humble peasant near his hut, with wife, children, cow, and goat nearby; Siberian ducks flying southward over the rivers in October; the unbelievable courage of poor slum dwellers; ancient Buddhist ruins, massive and peaceful, surrounded by verdant farms; historic cities that date in millennia; thousands praying at the Central Mosque; the incredible beauty of the land in the rain or the more splendid period when the rains stop and flowers are reborn; reflections of white cranes on water; the sight of a new city, such as Dhaka, shimmering in the river, as seen from a ferry floating on the Burriganga; a boat ride down narrow jungle streams amid chattering birds and past tiny villages with flickering fires; an auto ride from Bogra to Rajshahi along the Varendra plain, verdant as far as the eye can see; the Tipperah plain near Comilla, the earth's richest, most intensely farmed land; the languid, breathtaking Gomai plain in Chittagong District.

Amid such sights are to be found some of the warmest, most argumentative people on earth, people who want to know you, and to discuss, endlessly. Bangladeshis are opinionated and love to talk. Smiling, bright-eyed, interested, and open, they certainly are finalists in any contest for the world's most charming people—though one should not admit that to them, rascals that they can be. Their scholars are serious and often wise, their artists often sage. Old men can be amusing, with twinkling, teasing eyes, as well as especially thoughtful and surprisingly helpful with advice.

As for the women, one needs to travel far to find women, taken in their state of grace and given their economic pressures, as solidly intelligent and beautiful as those in Bangladesh. Moreover, contrary to gossip among foreign females, Bangladeshi women not only enjoy more freedom and power than do their sisters elsewhere in the Muslim, or even the Hindu, world, but their power within family and clan is greater than is apparent. No man traveling in Bangladesh would ever get the bottom of things if he ignored the women and their opinions.

For example, as chief of a U.S. funding agency, this writer was intimately involved with development projects, including ones established by *samities*, *sangsthas*, or other local voluntary groups. It was his perception that groups formed by women or in which women played a key role were, on average, the best run and most likely to succeed. Why? Because Bangladeshi women tend to work together very well compared to the men. Why? Because the women are not shy and weak; rather, they are confident that they can accomplish things. Such confidence is born not of oppression but of a culture that understands voluntary cooperation. This writer doubts if there is a culture anywhere that forms as many voluntary groups.

Finally, Bangladeshi women doctors, scholars, writers, entrepreneurs, and professionals of all kinds are as dynamic a group as will be found anywhere in the world.

Thus Bangladesh offers the traveler fantastic scenery, warm, friendly, intelligent people, and an ancient history that blends with the modern. But Bangladesh is not an easy country for travel. Except for Dhaka, there are no first-class hotels. The quality of food is erratic. Stomach upsets, due to water or food, are common and often are quite debilitating for a few days. The weather can be hot, rainy, or both; it can be dusty, humid, or both. Traveling to the provinces, it is best to have a guide and, if you wish to meet interesting, well-educated people, letters of introduction. In the last analysis, if your goal is to learn, the hardships are worth it. However, if you are a typical tourist, you would be better off going elsewhere, such as resorts in Thailand or Malaysia.

Finally, if you can master Bangladesh, you will be undaunted by anywhere else in South Asia. That's why, as a popular local poster proclaims, "Visit Bangladesh . . . before tourists come."

BIBLIOGRAPHICAL ESSAY

This list of sources is only partial, but it does include those to which I am most heavily indebted. Many studies and monographs done by aid agencies, consultants, or others with an interest in the country, including numerous pamphlets and articles in such newspapers as the *New Nation, Observer, Holiday,* and the *Bangladesh Times,* are not noted, yet their influence was strong. Conversations and other such inputs are listed last.

General

The essential story of India and Bengal is told by W. W. Hunter in *The Indian Empire* (London: Oriental Publishers, 1973 reprint), especially chapter 1 on the rivers and land. See also H. G. Rawlinson, *India* (London: Crescent Press, 1965); Romesh Dutt, *Economic History of India under Early British Rule* (London: Kegan Paul, 1902; reprint Augustus Kelley, 1969); Ainslee Embree, ed., *Alberuni's India* (New York: Norton, 1971); Jansen, Dolman, Jerve, and Nazibor Rahman, *The Country Boats of Bangladesh* (Dhaka: University Press, 1989); Kazi S. Ahmad, *A Geography of Pakistan* (Karachi: Oxford University Press, 1969); Richard M. Eaton, *Islamic History as Global History* (Washington, D.C.: American Historical Association, 1990); Bhabani Sen Gupta, *The Fulcrum of Asia* (New York: Pegasus, 1970); Nirad C. Chaudhuri, *Continent of Circe* (Bombay: Jaico, 1965); Elie Kedourie, *Islam in World History* (New York: Holt, Rinehart and Winston, 1980); Wilifred Cantwell Smith, *Islam in the Modern World* (New York: New American Library, Mentor Book, 1957); Swami Prabhavananda, *Spiritual Heritage of India* (New York: Doubleday, 1963); Ira M. Lapidus, *Histories of Islamic Societies* (Cambridge: Cambridge University Press, 1990); Dilip Chakrabarti, *The External Trade of Indus Civilization* (New Delhi: Munshiram Manoharlal, 1990); Dietmar Rothermund, *Economic History of India* (London: Croom Helm, 1987); Haroun Er Rashid, *An Economic Geography of Bengal* (Dhaka: University Press, 1981); R. C. Zaehner, *Hinduism* (Oxford: Oxford University Press, 1969); Fazlul Rahman, *Islam* (2nd ed. Chicago: University of Chicago Press, 1979).

On the British role in India aside from Dutt listed above are: Michael Edwardes, *The Last Days of British India* (London: New English Library, 1967); P. Mason, *The Men Who Ruled India,* abridged (London: Pan and Cape, 1985); Reginald Reynolds, *White Sahibs in India* (Westport, Conn.: Greenwood Press, 1970; reprint of 1937 edition); Jawaharlal Nehru,

Glimpses of World History (New York: John Day, 1942); K. K. Aziz, *The British in India* (Islamabad: National Commission on Historical Research, 1976); Ramkrishna Mukerjee, *The Rise and Fall of the East India Company* (New York: Monthly Review Press, 1974); Lance E. Davis and Robert A. Huttenback, *Mammon and the Pursuit of Empire* (Cambridge: Cambridge University Press, 1986); Edward Ingram, ed., *Two Views of British India* (Bath: Adams and Dart, 1962); James Morris, *Pax Britannica*, 3 volumes (New York: Harcourt Brace, 1968); William Tayler, *Thirty-Eight Years in India* (Calcutta: Bibhash Gupta; reprint of 1861 book, 1987); Brian Gardner, *The East Indian Company* (New York: Dorset Press, 1971); Jack Russel, *Clive of India* (New York: Putnam, 1965); Noel Barber, *Black Hole of Calcutta* (New York: Dorset Press, 1989); Geoffrey Moorhouse, *Calcutta, the City Revealed* (London: Penguin Travel Library, 1988); Michael Greenberg, *British Trade and the Opening of China* (New York: Monthly Review Press, 1979); H. S. Bhatia, *Political, Legal and Military History of India*, 5 volumes (New Delhi: Deep and Deep Publications, 1984); Maurice Collis, *Foreign Mud* (London: Faber, 1969); M. Prabhakaran, *Historical Origins of Indian Underdevelopment* (New York: University Press of America, 1990); Suhash Chakravarty, *The Raj Syndrome* (India: Penguin, 1991); for a word on the relation between the American Revolution and Bengal within the British Empire, see Ian R. Christie and Benjamin W. Labaree, *Empire or Independence* (Oxford: Phaidon Press, 1976); M. A. Laird, *Missionaries and Education in Bengal, 1793–1837* (Oxford: Oxford University Press, 1972); Nani Gopal Chaudhuri, *Cartier, Governor of Bengal, 1769–1772* (Calcutta: Firma K. L. Mukhupadahyay, 1970); Mohiuddin Alamgir, *Famine in South Asia* (Cambridge, Mass.: Gunn and Hain, 1980); Charles Ritcheson, *British Politics and the American Revolution* (Norman: University of Oklahoma Press, 1964); Andrew Valentine, *Lord North* (Norman: University of Oklahoma Press, 1967); Vincent T. Harlow, *The Founding of the Second British Empire* (London: Longmans, 1964); Eric Hobsbawm, *Industry and Empire* (London: Pelican Economic History of Britain, Volume 3, 1979); John Campbell, *F. E. Smith, The First Earl of Birkenhead* (London: Jonathan Cape, 1983).

I was greatly assisted by R. C. Majumdar's magisterial *History of Bengal* (Calcutta: Asiatic Society, 1943) and by the *Cambridge History of India* and the *New Cambridge History of India*, especially volumes II-1 and II-2. Syed Mahmudul Hasan, *Gaud and Hazrat Pandua* (Dhaka: Islamic Foundation, 1987); *Buchanan's Journey through Chittagong and Tipperah*, handwritten copy, Dhaka University Library, 1798; J. J. A. Campos, *History of the Portuguese in Bengal* (Calcutta: Butterworth, 1919). The best book on the Muslim conquest and rule in Bengal is Charles Stewart, *History of Bengal* (London: Black, Parry, 1847); others are Subhas Chandra Mukhopadhyay, *Diwani in Bengal, 1765* (Vishwaridyakya Prakashan, 1980); Sarat Chandra Mitra, *The Cult of the Sun God in Medieval Eastern Bengal* (New Delhi: Northern Book

Centre, 1986); *Folk Poems from Bangladesh*, translated by Kabir Chowdhury, Serajul Islam Chowdhury, Khondakar Ashraf Hossain (Dhaka: Bangla Academy, 1985); P. C. Roy Chaudhury, *Folk Tales of Bangladesh* (New Delhi: Sterling, 1982); Muhammad Shahidullah and Muhammad Abdul Hai, *Traditional Culture in East Pakistan* (Dacca: University of Dacca, 1963); Kabir Chowdhury, *Folktales of Bangladesh* (Dhaka: Bangla Academy, 1972).

On the evolution of Bangladesh, the following were major influences on my thought: Latifa Akanda, *Social History of Muslim Bengal* (Lahore: ICCD Publications, 1955); Sufia Ahmed, *The Muslim Community in Bengal* (Dhaka: Oxford University Press, 1974); Rafiuddin Ahmed, *The Bengal Muslims* (New York: Oxford University Press, 1981); Rafiuddin Ahmed, *Religion and Politics in Bangladesh* (New Delhi: South Asian Publishers, 1990); Kamruddin Ahmed, *A Socio-Political History of Bengal and the Birth of Bangladesh* (Dhaka: Inside Library, revised 1975); Kamrunessa Islam, *Aspects of Economic History of Bengal* (Dhaka: Asiatic Society of Bangladesh, 1984); F. B. Bradley-Birt, *The Romance of an Eastern Capital* (Delhi: Metropolitan Book Company, 1975 reprint); Fazlul Rahman, *Culture Conflicts in East Pakistan* (Dhaka: Nazneen Sejuty Prokhashani, 1990); A. M. A. Muhith, *Emergence of a Nation* (Dhaka: University Press, 1978); Shyamala Ghosh, *The Awami League* (Dhaka: Academic Publishers, 1990); Abu Jaffar, *Muslim Festivals in Bangladesh* (Dhaka: Islamic Foundation, 1980); Mohammed Enamul Huq, *History of Sufism in Bengal* (Dhaka: Asiatic Society of Bangladesh, 1975); Asim Roy, *Islamic Syncretism in Bengal* (Princeton: Princeton University Press, 1988); Ajit K. Neogy, *Partitions of Bengal* (Calcutta: A. Mukerjee, 1987); Newmai Sadhan Bose, *The Indian Awakening of Bengal* (Calcutta: Firma K. L. Mukhopadhyay, 3d edition, 1976); David Kopf, *The Brahmo Samaj and the Shaping of the Modern Indian Mind* (Princeton: Princeton University Press, 1979); Razia Ahmed, *Financing the Rural Poor* (Dhaka: University Press, 1983); Hameeda Hossain, *The Company of Weavers of Bengal* (Oxford: Oxford University Press, 1988); Rehman Sobhan, *The Crisis of External Dependence* (Dhaka: University Press, 1982); Rehman Sobhan and Muzaffer Ahmed, *Public Enterprise in an Intermediate Regime* (Dhaka: Bangladesh Institute of Development Studies, 1978); Mohammad H. R. Talukdar, editor, *Memoirs of Hossain Shaheed Suhrawardy*, foreword by Kamal Hossain (Dhaka: University Press, 1987); Kirsten Westergard, *State and Rural Society in Bangladesh* (London: Curzon Press, 1985); Kamal Siddiqui, *The Political Economy of Rural Poverty in Bangladesh* (Dhaka: National Institute of Local Government, 1982); Leonard A. Gordon, *Bengal, the Nationalist Movement, 1876–1940* (New York: Columbia University Press, 1974); Marcus F. Franda, *Radical Politics in West Bengal* (Cambridge: M.I.T. Press, 1981); *Current Issues in the Bangladesh Economy* (Dhaka: Bangladesh International Ltd., 1978); Blair B. Kling, *Partner in Empire: Dwarkanath Tagore and the Age of Enterprise in Eastern India* (Berkeley: University of California Press, 1976); *Calcutta Illustrated* (Calcutta: Central

Press, 1945); A. Farouk, *Changes in the Economy of Bangladesh* (Dhaka: University Press, 1982); Leonard A. Gordon, *Brothers against the Raj* (New York: Columbia University Press, 1990); B. L. C. Johnson, *Bangladesh* (London: Heinemann Educational Books, 1975); Tapan Raychaudhuri, *Europe Reconsidered* (Oxford: Oxford University Press, 1988); Suniti Bhushan Qanungo, *A History of Chittagong*, volume 1 (Chittagong: Dipanko Qanaungo, 1988); M. Atiqullah and F. Karim Khan, *The Growth of Dacca City* (Dacca: Social Science Department, Dacca University, 1975); A. K. Choudhury, *The Independence of East Bengal: A Historical Process* (Jatiya Grantha Kendra, 1984).

On the Bangladesh Liberation War and its aftermath, the following were helpful: Siddiq Salik, *Witness to Surrender* (Karachi: Oxford University Press, 1978); Fazlul Quader Quaderi, editor, *Bangladesh, Genocide and the World Press* (Dhaka: Dilafroz Quaderi, Abco Press, 2d edition, 1972); Anthony Mascarenhas, *The Rape of Bangladesh* (New Delhi: Vikas Publications, 1971); M. D. Husain, *International Press on Bangladesh Liberation War* (Dhaka: Rahfat M. Husain, 1989); Anthony Mascarenhas, *Bangladesh Legacy of Blood* (London: Hodder and Stoughton, 1986); Talukder Maniruzzaman, *Bangladesh Revolution and Its Aftermath* (Dhaka: Bangladesh Books International, 1980); Moudud Ahmed, *Bangladesh Era: Sheikh Mujibur Rahman* (Dhaka: University Press, 1983); G. W. Choudhury, *The Last Days of United Pakistan* (London: Hurst, 1974); Lawrence Ziring, *Pakistan: The Enigma of Political Development* (Boulder: Westview, 1980); Major (Rtd.) S. G. Jilani, *Fifteen Governors I Served With: The Untold Story of East Pakistan* (Lahore: Bookmark: 1979); Betsy Hartmann and James K. Boyce, *A Quiet Violence* (London: Zed Press, 1983); Craig Baxter, *Bangladesh: A New Nation in an Old Setting* (Boulder: Westview Press, 1984); Colonel Farook and Colonel Rashid, *The Road to Freedom* (Dhaka: published by Major [Ret.] Syed Ataur Rahman, 1984); M. Atiqullah and F. Karim Khan, *The Growth of Dacca City* (Dacca: Social Science Research Department, University of Dacca, 1975); Kabir Chowdhury et al., editors, *A Nation Is Born: International Seminar on Bangladesh* (Calcutta: Calcutta University, Bangladesh, Sahayak Samiti, 1974); Akbar Khan, *The Mystery of the Debacle of Pakistan* (Karachi: Islamic Military Science Association, 1972–73); S. M. Ali, *After the Dark Night: Problems of Sheikh Mujibur Rahman* (New Delhi: Thomson Press, 1973); A Mascarenas, *Midnight Massacre in Dacca* (Delhi: Vikas Press, 1978); Richard F. Nyorp et al., *Handbook for Bangladesh* (Washington, D.C.: Government Printing Office, 1975); Marcus Franda, *Bangladesh: The First Decade* (Hanover, N.H.: South Asian Publishers, 1982); *Bangladesh Country Study*, DA 550–175 (Washington, D.C.: Government Printing Office, 1989); *Statistical Pocket Book of Bangladesh–1989* (Dacca: Bangladesh Bureau of Statistics).

Some references to archaeological digs in Bangladesh are A. K. M. Shamsul Alam, *Mainamati* (Dhaka: Department of Archaeology and Museums, Government of Bangladesh, 2nd edition, 1982); *Album of Archaeological*

Relics in Bangladesh, foreword by A. Majeed Khan (Dhaka: Directorate of Archaeology and Museums, 1984); Nazimuddin Ahmed, *Mahasthan* (Dhaka: Department of Archaeology and Museums, 1975); M. A. A. Qadir, *Paharapur* (Dhaka: Department of Archaeology and Museums, 1980 reprint); Syed Mahmudal Hassan, *Dacca City of Mosques* (Islamic Foundation of Bangladesh, 1981); Nazziudin Ahmed, *Buildings of the British Raj* (Dhaka: University Press, 1986); Nazimuddin Ahmed, *Buildings of Khan Jahan in and around Bagerhat* (Dhaka: University Press, 1989); Anwarul Karim, *Myths of Bangladesh* (Kushtia: Folklore Research Institution, 1975); Nazimuddin Ahmed, *Discover the Monuments of Bangladesh* (Dhaka: University Press, 1984); M. Aminul Islam and Maniruzzaman Miah, general editors, *Bangladesh in Maps* (Dhaka: University of Dacca, 1981); *Gaud and Hazrat Pandua*, Syed Mahmudal Hasan, Islamic Foundation of Bangladesh, 1987.

It would be impossible to overestimate the influence on me of the writings of Nirad C. Chaudhuri, given his love of Bengal. Although a Hindu, Brahmo, and Anglophile, his love of the country and its dignity, despite his lesser love for Muslims, is an inspiration for those who want to view people in their state of grace. More than anyone, he helped me understand Tagore, a writer whose works in translation are difficult to grasp, as their English versions seem weak and limp by comparison with the works of other poets. In particular, Chaudhuri's *Autobiography of an Unknown Indian* (Hogarth Press, 1987) and *Thine Hand, Great Anarch!,* the continuation of his autobiography (London: Addison Wesley, 1990), provided insights into what is good and decent in Bengali society. His work stimulated me to empathize and to look for meaning where we Westerners often do not. Chaudhuri was born and raised in East Bengal, in what is now Bangladesh, in the town of Kishorganj, and his memories and descriptions of life at the beginning of the twentieth century are the most readable and reliable sources on the country as seen by a sensitive man.

Some references on the poets are: Brother James, *Songs of Lalon* (Dhaka: University Press, 1987); Brother James, translator, *The Gitmalya of Rabindranath Tagore* (Dhaka: University Press, 1984) (the late Brother James also helped me understand the role of the poets in Bangladesh and their generally uplifting effects on the level of debate and of political discourse); Rabindranath Tagore, *The Religion of Man* (London: Unwin Paperbacks, 1988).

On Kazi Nazrul Islam, the following books proved to be of great influence: Mizanur Rahman Khan, *Nazrul Islam* (Dhaka: Tarun Pakistan Publishers, 1966 3rd edition); Gopal Haldar, *Kazi Nazrul Islam* (New Delhi: Sahitya Akademi, 1973); and Rafiqul Islam, editor, *Kazi Nazrul Islam: A New Anthology* (Dhaka: Bangla Academy, 1990). On Iqbal, the best translations are those of Michael Arberry, *Iqbal, Poet-Philosopher of Pakistan*, edited by Hafeez Malik (New York: Columbia University Press, 1971); and A. R. Tariq, *Speeches and Statements of Iqbal* (Lahore: Sh. Ghulam Ali, 1973). These references are limited only because I have read numerous biographies, pamphlets, and translations of the poets.

It is virtually impossible to list all those who have helped in some way on this book. However, I would be remiss not to mention those who have been especially kind and provided ideas of what to read as well as discussion of those readings: Ahmedul (Monu) Kabir, publisher of *Dainik Sangbad* and Begum Laila Kabir; Anwar Hossain (Manju), publisher of *Ittefaq* and Begum Tasmina (Tip-Tip) Hossain; Enayatullah Khan, publisher of *Holiday;* Md. Ikramullah and Begum Nellie Ikramullah, of Mirpur Agricultural Workshops and Prism; Fazlul Halim Chowdhury, Vice Chancellor, Dhaka University; Boerum De, Calcutta University; Sufia Ahmed, Dhaka University; Rafiuddin Ahmed, Chittagong and Cornell universities; Marcus Franda, American Field Service; Kanta Bhatia, University of Pennsylvania; Major General N. I. Chisti (Ret.), Bangladesh Army and Begum Chisti; the late Jamil ur-Rahman Khan, Jute Board and Begum Sarwar; Moudud Ahmed, former Vice President, Prime Minister and author; and Hasna Moudud, poet; former Chief Justice Kamaluddin Hossain, Supreme Court of Bangladesh; Daud Khan Majlis, former advisor to President Zia Rahman and Begum Kamela; A. M. A. Muhith, former Minister, External Resources and Begum Sabiha Muhith; Qazi Jalaluddin Ahmed, former Defence Secretary; Salauddin Qader Chowdhury, M.P., and Begum Seema Qader Chowdhury; Humayan Kabir, Pfizer Corporation; Richard Baxter Eaton, University of Arizona; Shajehan Kabir and Begum Farah Kabir, Sharif Aftab Uddin, Samsuddin Ahmed, Nargis Jafar, Iman Ali, and Mahmud, The Asia Foundation; Ali Behrouze Ispahani and Begum Amenah Ispahani; Mhuto De, scholar, and Ira De, poet, New Delhi; Anil Palchoudhuri and Ruby Palchoudhuri, Calcutta; Muzzafer Ahmed, Institute of Business Administration, Dhaka; Alim ur-Rahman Khan and Begum Colette Khan, Eden Press; Gulam Azam, President, Jamaat-e-Islam; Hossein Mohammad Ershad, President of Bangladesh; Monirul Islam Chowdhury, press aide to President Ershad; Najmul Huda, Cabinet Minister under President Zia and under Khaleda Zia and founder, Bangladesh Society for Human Rights; Justice Monim, Chief Justice, Supreme Court of Bangladesh; Khondaker Moustaque Ahmed, leader of coup against Sheikh Muibur Rahman; Syed Ishtiaque Hossain, Attorney General under President Mujibur Rahman; Murshed Khan, Eastern Motors; Colonel Farooq and Colonel Rashid, assassins of Sheikh Mujib; Sheikh Hasina, leader, Awami League and daughter of Sheikh Mujib; Major Rasheed, JSD Party founder; Joya Pati, Kumudini Industries; Rehka Kabir, artist; Kabir Chowdhury, professor of literature, Dhaka University; Amirul Islam, former cabinet member, Awami League; Father Richard Timm, CSC, human rights activist; Moinul Hossain, publisher, *New Nation;* Farooq Chowdhury, Foreign Ministry; Brigadier Hafiz and Brigadier Momen, Bangladesh Institute of Strategic Studies; Rehman Sobhan, Bangladesh Institute of Development Studies; Mahbub Matin,

World Bank; Captain Mahzarul Hoq, ADC to President Zia; Shamsud Doha, former Foreign Minister; Justice Syed Mohammad Hossain, deceased Supreme Court Justice who resigned under President Ershad; Major General Amjad Choudhury and Begum Amjad; and Rowshan Ali Hirji, business leader and esteemed leader of the Ismailian Community and Begum Hirji, Dhaka; Dr. Kamal Hossain, Foreign Minister under Sheikh Mujib; Stanley Kochanek and Kum Kum Chatterjee, professors, Pennsylvania State University; Md. Mohiuddin, External Resources Division, Ministry of Finance; Dr. A. M. Malik, Asiatic Society of Bangladesh; Abdus Samad, External Resources Division and Young Economists' Association; Brother James, CSC, scholar, St. Joseph School, Dhaka and pioneering translator of Tagore; Bashirul Huq, architect, scholar, friend; Father Antoine, S.J., Sanskrit scholar, St. Xavier's College, Calcutta; Dr. Jharna Nath, Rajshahi University; Suzanne Wallen and Geof Taylor, The Asia Foundation.

INDEX

JAMES J. NOVAK, a writer, has lived and traveled in Asia for thirty years. Formerly a pharmaceutical corporation executive, he was Resident Representative of The Asia Foundation in Bangladesh in 1982–85. He has been a columnist for the *Asia Mail*, *World View*, and the *Eastern Financial Times* and has written for various magazines and newspapers, including the *Atlantic Monthly, Asian Finance, America Magazine*, the *Times of India*, the *Washington Post, Christian Science Monitor, Los Angeles Times, Newsday*, and the *New York Times*. ◆